Karl Barth and the
Resurrection of the Flesh

Karl Barth and the Resurrection of the Flesh

The Loss of the Body in Participatory Eschatology

Nathan Hitchcock

James Clarke & Co

James Clarke & Co
P.O. Box 60
Cambridge
CB1 2NT
United Kingdom

www.jamesclarke.co
publishing@jamesclarke.co

ISBN: 978 0 227 17410 4

British Library Cataloguing in Publication Data
A record is available from the British Library

First published by James Clarke & Co, 2013

Published by arrangement
with Pickwick Publications

Contents

For Mark Kincaid
(1964–2008)

Foreword

FROM THE MOMENT HE burst onto the European theological scene with his *Romans* commentary, Karl Barth was a thoroughly eschatological thinker. On the main, his early investments in eschatology were largely concentrated on its role as a discourse by means of which Christian faith registers the transcendent freedom, and so utter graciousness, of the sovereign God of the gospel. Eschatology was and remained closely associated in his developing theology with the themes of the eternal deity of God, the resurrection of Christ, and the incontestable finality of the salvation wrought in Jesus Christ. For this reason, eschatology was much more often the discursive medium of Barth's theology than it was a discrete topic within it.

Yet any Christian theology committed to reflecting systematically upon the entire faith of the Church must come to treat of eschatological matters more narrowly, those "last things" concerning the ultimate fate of creatures within the economy of salvation. It is here that theologian comes face to face with the ancient Christian affirmation of the hope for the resurrection of the body. As Nathan Hitchcock demonstrates in the text you have before you, notwithstanding the truncated body of his *Church Dogmatics*, Karl Barth did venture a good deal of commentary on this particular eschatological theme, stressing throughout the importance of both elements, namely, the wondrous mystery of the *resurrection* of the body, as well as the crucial importance for faith of hope in the resurrection *of the body*.

Set against the backdrop of the wider theological tradition of reflection on the resurrection, Hitchcock expounds Barth's efforts to conceive of the resurrection of the body as a threefold hope that our bodily and temporal existence may be rendered at once eternal, manifest, and incorporated into Christ's own body, itself risen and eternal. As the exposition makes clear, Barth is respectively concerned to contemplate how the final resurrection of the body entails the salutary transformation of creaturely *time*, creaturely *self-knowledge*, and creaturely *identity*. Readers will benefit from the clarity that this schematic analysis brings to appreciating the scope and nuances of Barth's varied and somewhat diffuse discussion of the subject.

Hitchcock himself is vitally concerned with the question of the integrity of the human creature in all this, insisting as he says in the preface, upon a "significant, earthly, corporeal, and concrete identity" for the human being raised to new life in the resurrection of the dead. The critical evaluation of Barth's theology with which this study concludes sees the author prosecute a case that Barth's account of resurrection of the body ultimately cannot deliver on such concerns. At root, he contends, to conceive of salvation as in some way creaturely participation in the divine nature is to be forced ultimately to forfeit the human as a distinctive, embodied agent in the *eschaton*. For Hitchcock, adequate defence of the full meaning of a *bodily* resurrection will require some notable revisions of the line of argument Barth (and others like him) pursue in their respective treatments. In light of wide-ranging interest in recovering "participation" as a key category in contemporary soteriology, Hitchcock's criticisms and cautions on this score merit close consideration.

Karl Rahner's classicly suggested that eschatological claims are ever extrapolations of present Christian experience which, as such, always concern the present as much as they do the future.[1] If this is so, then readers may well fruitfully reflect on the features of current Christian faith, life and theology which motivate Hitchcock's study generally and, in particular, animate his vigorous deference of the eternal future of human bodily identity and agency. But however that may be, there is much to be gained from taking Hitchcock's study as an able and provocative guide into the thicket of intricately interlocking questions and arguments into which we are led in any serious effort to plumb the depth of the evangelical faith that, "the dead shall be raised incorruptible, and we shall be changed" (1 Cor 15:52).

Philip G. Ziegler
University of Aberdeen

---

1. See Karl Rahner, "The Hermeneutics of Eschatological Assertions," in *Theological Investigations* IV, trans. by K. Smyth (London: Darton, Longman & Todd, 1966), 337 [323–46].

Preface

IN CONTRAST TO GENERATIONS of western theological thinkers, Karl Barth confessed the resurrection, indeed, the resurrection of the *flesh*, daring to express his belief about eternal life in the sense of the raising of the selfsame physical body. Truly, few theologians of the modern period have proclaimed so stridently as Barth the corporeal nature of the resurrection. Throughout his career he spilled much ink defending the corporeal quality of the resurrection, whether it be the resurrection of Jesus at Easter or His followers at the end of time. Perhaps more impressively, one finds a kind of resurrection-shape throughout Barth's dogmatic projects. As a sort of structural principle, resurrection can be construed as the connective tissue for Barth's entire theological undertaking, something of "axiomatic importance."[2]

A seeming contradiction has limited Barth studies, however. For all his orientation to eschatology, it sometimes appears that Barth is silent when it comes to matters pertaining to eschatology proper. For all his talk of resurrection, he does not elaborate when speaking of the coming resurrection of the dead. Readers of Barth are hard-pressed to find sustained discussion of the end-times events, the return of Christ, the Last Judgment, and activity in the New Jerusalem. It does not help that volume V of his magisterial *Church Dogmatics*, intended to cover "The Doctrine of Redemption," went unwritten. To date no major work has addressed eschatology proper in Barth's voluminous work, in large part because it as such does not appear to be a locus of theological inquiry for Barth.

Barth's silence is misleading, I suggest. One uncovers significant deposits of eschatological content scattered throughout Barth's work, including and especially statements about the resurrection of the flesh. More importantly, an eschatology proper can be compiled by deriving end-time doctrines from other areas of Barth's theology. His doctrine of the Word of God displays a resurrection character. His doctrines of God

---

2. Dawson, *The Resurrection in Karl Barth*, 2.

and creation bear the logic of resurrection. His discussion of the risen Christ lays out the parameters for the general resurrection. His pneumatology too, sparse as it is at times, is intimately related to a doctrine of the resurrection. In this study I unpack a wide range of Barth's writings for the purpose of showing that Barth is always speaking about how humans are "raised to God," a miraculous event which, when extrapolated as an absolute future state, yields the doctrine of the resurrection. And I will show that Barth, though he fails in the long run, always attempts to cast the resurrection as something dynamic, earthly, and specific, always something bodily, always something involving the *flesh*.

The study unfolds as follows. In chapter 1 I rehearse a history of the doctrine of the resurrection of the flesh. The patristic usage of the term "flesh" reflects the early Church's lofty view of the body as the locus of responsibility and redemption. As the doctrine of the resurrection of the flesh developed, two basic trajectories emerged: one understanding the resurrection as the collection of the selfsame particles from the person's earthly life so as to restore their fullness, the other portraying the resurrection as a participation in God in which the fleshly person is taken up into the divine life. The collection view (developed mainly in the west by thinkers such as Jerome, Augustine, and Thomas Aquinas) and the participation view (developed mainly in the east by the likes of Origen, Athanasius, and Maximus) each bore theological fruit—though each trajectory suffered from a Hellenistic tendency to spiritualize, attaching the flesh to the redeemed human person as an auxiliary dimension of human life. Some readers may find this chapter a helpful survey, regardless of their interest in Barth; others familiar with the history of the doctrine may choose to move on to the second chapter.

In chapter 2 I explain the formation of Barth's theology leading up to the start of the *Church Dogmatics* in the early 1930s. Influence from pietism, romantic idealism, and religious socialism gave his theology a distinctive shape, one that was articulated under the rubric of "the resurrection of the dead." During these decades he identified and radicalized a dialectical way of speaking about humanity confronted by God's transcendent immanence. Barth describes the "moment" of encounter between God and the human in terms of a resurrection (viz., that in the moment of revelation we, "the dead," become what we are not, "resurrected"). In fact, Barth equates resurrection with revelation. God's Self-disclosure effects a "raising" of dead humanity into God's life; humans are "dissolved and established" in the presence of God. In this complicated way, Barth sees the resurrection of the dead as a kind of basic methodology for talk about God. While Barth makes the doctrines of the Trinity and Christ take on some of the axiomatic burden along the way, he continues to construct his eschatology in terms of the "lifting of human existence" into God's own presence. Again, Barth's critical reformulation here is the equation of resurrection with revelation. Everything characteristic about the event of God's supernatural taking up of humanity in revelation is characteristic of God taking up of humanity in the ultimate state of risen-ness. As ethereal and abstruse as the young Barth can wax, he is consistent in his profession that the resurrection is the raising of the flesh because revelation happens to us who are now in the flesh.

In chapter 3 I move to Barth's mature dogmatic work pursuing a first aspect, that of the resurrection of the flesh as *eternalization*. He spells out a conception of God's eternity in which God's transcendence of time is also His freedom to lift time into itself. Jesus Christ's own resurrection is the Father's eternalizing verdict which imparts a pan-temporal quality to Jesus' concluded, historical life. Barth's "actualistic" ontology expresses the finite arc of human existence as something complete only through the gift of eternity from God. Human lives are necessarily demarcated by conception and death, but these limitations become good in that they define the terminated life that is "raised" into the simultaneity of times enjoyed by God. I question whether Barth has quarantined temporal process too much here, and whether he is unintentionally paying honor to God's enemy, death.

In chapter 4 I look to another aspect, the idea of the resurrection of the flesh as *manifestation*. Barth describes Jesus Christ's incarnate being as having perfect integrity, characterized by the full fellowship of the human with the divine. Along Alexandrian and Lutheran lines, Barth says the exaltation of the human essence stems from its communication with His divine essence even before the resurrection. To protect the finality of Christ's reconciling work, Barth will go so far as to say that Easter does not add anything to Christ's perfect work and being (which was finished in His incarnate ministry). What is His resurrection, then? Barth says that the resurrection of Christ simply manifests His reconciling life and makes it effective for others. Humans do not have Christ's integrity by nature, muddled as they are by creational ambiguity, the sin of self-reliance, and a dialectical identity in the penultimate age. But Barth explains that our own resurrection will be the disclosure of our hidden glory in Christ. In all this, the concept of "presence" is key. Our life is unveiled with the Son in His three-fold parousia: an identity definitively revealed at Easter, currently being revealed (however ambiguously) in the age of Pentecost, and fully manifested at Christ's return. For all the novelty of Barth's proposals, I question whether his highly noetic conception of the resurrection has not given way to a somewhat spiritualistic concept of the *visio Dei* in heaven, and whether he has not in his Alexandrian discourse perhaps violated some creaturely parameters through the logic of deification.

In chapter 5 I grapple with Barth's relational protocol through a conception of the resurrection of the flesh as *incorporation*. God the Holy Spirit orchestrates the movement of communion, incorporating the expansion of the divine power and the retrieval of others into God. Similarly, in the resurrection Jesus Christ appears as the prophet of incorporation who calls, upbuilds, and sends out the community so that all might gravitate to Him. The human as such suffers from isolation, from the alienation possible in creation and caused by sin. The resurrection of the flesh, however, overcomes this isolation through the incorporation of all history into the capacious body of the living Christ. For all of Barth's care, I suggest that a series of absorptions are at work: the resurrection is conflated into the work of the Spirit, the Holy Spirit is conflated into the ministry of the risen Christ, and, it seems, all human beings (once the outward movement of the resurrection ceases, at least) are absorbed into Christ at His return. That is, human particularity is threatened by the resurrection, for, in Barth's view, it is difficult to see how the coming Day will renew individuated, concrete identities.

To repeat, Barth describes the resurrection of the flesh in three complementary ways. First, resurrection is eternalization, i.e., the Father's "raising up" of a person's temporal history into the eternal contemporaneity of God. Second, resurrection is manifestation, i.e., a "raising to the surface" of a person's true identity in Jesus Christ. Third, resurrection is incorporation, i.e., a "raising into God" through participation in the living Christ by His Holy Spirit. In each of these three aspects one finds Barth working creatively to make room for corporeal affirmations. Eternalization, manifestation, and incorporation each retain a sense of bodily redemption, though I call into question the extent to which they qualify as a genuine resurrection of the flesh.

It may be helpful to the reader to keep in mind that chapters 3, 4, and 5 correspond roughly to the persons of the Trinity. These chapters also interact chiefly with IV/1, IV/2, and IV/3, respectively. Dealing with the philosophical question of perdurance of human selfhood, they also reflect Barth's provision for material, formal, and numerical identity. Most importantly, one should also note that within each chapter I have followed a consistent program of analysis: a) the divine reality, b) Christ's expression of the divine reality in the resurrection, c) our fleshly need, and d) our own divine (yet somehow fleshly) expression in the resurrection.

Though it was not my original intention to do so, my study leads to a rather stern critique. Increasingly with each chapter I take up the mantle of agitator and interlocutor, insisting upon a significant, earthly, corporeal, and concrete identity of the raised human. Barth speaks of eternalization—but does he eradicate temporal process in God's simultaneous Now? Barth speaks of the manifestation of the flesh in its proximity to the divine—but what of our distinct creaturehood when it appears in the divine essence of Christ? Barth speaks of incorporation—but what becomes of fleshly individuality as human lives are knit into Christ fully by the Holy Spirit? For all of his profound affirmations of physicality, Barth's construction of the doctrine comes up wanting. In his presentation of the resurrection body there is a certain changelessness, a certain lightness, and a certain indistinguishability, all of which suggests a fleshless existence. Along the course of the study I argue that Barth eschatological predicament was produced by some theological conflations, each of which must be undone.

In my opinion, all of Barth's missteps are related to his deep-seated commitment to speaking of salvation as participation in the divine nature. Accordingly, *Karl Barth and the Resurrection of the Flesh* can and should be read as a warning toward theologians pursuing a full-fledged doctrine of glorification based on participatory categories. For the sake of directedness I have made only passing reference to those with comparable ideas on "eternal life," whether it be Barth's contemporaries (Gogarten, Tillich, Brunner), his theological offspring (Torrance, Moltmann, Pannenberg, Jüngel), or more recent Barth-influenced scholars (Jenson, Lash, Tanner, McCormack, Neder, Habets). I trust that discerning readers will begin to see just how much each of these thinkers, for all their diversity of opinion, must confront the same theoretical problems when it comes to participatory eschatology. One should not hear my warning as a call to dismiss a theologian's work simply because it banks on participatory dynamics (I am convinced that the concept of participation should have a prominent place in Christian doctrine). Neither am I suggesting that one dismiss participation as a device for eschatology (I suspect a repurposed doctrine of participation may offer new avenues for describing the intermediate state). This study, however, demonstrates that any reconfiguration of the doctrine of the resurrection in terms of a "relational ontology" is a project laden with serious difficulties.

On a final note, I beg the reader to grant me the same patience I have had to afford Barth. The doctrine of the resurrection of the flesh only surfaces after a circuitous journey through dogmatics. Barth unearths theological riches all along the meandering path to an eschatology proper, and verily, something like human flesh is there at the end of that road. But if the reader is ultimately disappointed to discover how static, vaporous, and indistinct that resurrection body seems in the end, my roundabout approach will have made its rather unsettling point.

Acknowledgments

FOR ALL ITS AIRY qualities, research is a concrete activity performed among real humans. Many people sacrificed time, energy, and resources on my behalf during the long arc of this project.

Such a wealth of theological friends here in South Dakota! I offer special thanks to Philip Thompson, whose constant encouragement gave me strength to pursue and enjoy and critique the Barthian corpus. Many others at Sioux Falls Seminary provided support over the years, notably Paul Rainbow, Benjamin Leslie, and Richard Reitsma. I am grateful for the company of Kimlyn Bender and the members of the Sioux Falls chapter of the Karl Barth Society.

In Edinburgh too I was given kind support, welcomed in by the saints at St. Philip's and St. James'. Rectors Kevin Scott and Tembu Rongong proved themselves true ministers. I am especially grateful to Robin and Rachel McLean and family for their unceasing hospitality. The wise Prof. David Fergusson piloted me through many dangers—only he and the Lord know how many. Regarding the eerie providence of God, I am thankful for the body in the ditch; I did not pull him out so much as he pulled me from heaven back to earth.

Others across the globe lent their support as this project unfolded. I am thankful to John C. McDowell, as well as to Salvatore Musumeci, Mark Squire, Travis Winckler, and Travis McMaken. I can hardly imagine an ally better than John Lierman.

Closest to me in this whole project was Dr. Christina Hitchcock, who listened to me and challenged me and endured me and loved me with an unending love. How lonely is research, even research on the flesh. But I deserve little pity, being accompanied at every turn by such a devoted companion.

Abbreviations

1Rö	*Der Römerbrief* (first edition)
2Rö	*Der Römerbrief* (second edition)
AT	*Die Auferstehung der Toten*
CD	*Church Dogmatics*[3]
DO	*Dogmatics in Outline*
ER	*Epistle to the Romans*
GA	*Gesamtausgabe*
GD	*Göttingen Dogmatics*
PTNC	*Protestant Theology in the Nineteenth Century*
KD	*Die kirchliche Dogmatik*
UCR	*Unterricht in der christlichen Religion*
WGWM	*The Word of God and the Word of Man*

3. All freestanding Roman numeral references in parentheses refer to *Church Dogmatics*.

1

Redeeming the Flesh

IN THE END, *FLESH*. That has been the conviction of the Church's best theologians, who in their eschatological imagination have dared to populate the coming world with living humans, that is, bodies fully alive, rejoined and renewed in the coming world. According to this vision, nothing is lost at the resurrection. On the day of Christ's return the saints are made new, yet in this newness everything is strangely familiar: muscle and bones, skin and scars, all beautiful, and altogether the persons who once lived. Bodies which grew and acted and sickened and died are somehow identical with the bodies raised by God on the last day. *Credo in resurrectionem carnis*, says the Apostles Creed, representative of this holy imagination: *I believe in the resurrection of the flesh*.

Before examining Karl Barth's fresh and multifaceted view, one does well to know a bit about the development of the doctrine of the general resurrection through the centuries. This chapter provides part of that history, making two observations. First, every theologian within the bounds of the holy catholic Church felt a common burden to describe the resurrected person in physical, material, earthly terms. The earliest Christians articulated hope in that way, and later thinkers sought to do the same in more sophisticated ways. However—and this is the second point of the chapter—theologians from Origen to Thomas Aquinas came up with rather different descriptions of the future body. Specifically, I detect two basic trajectories of thought regarding the resurrection of the flesh. A sketch of the two paths serves as a valuable historical backdrop as I set up some parameters of conversation about Barth's own view.

THE EARLY CHURCH'S SCANDALOUS DOCTRINE

While Jewish thought had wide precedent for belief in the resurrection of the dead,[1] the uncircumcised were baffled over the idea of bodily resurrection. Mockery and curiosity typified the reception of the gospel in Paul's gentile mission. Various Platonists had immunized themselves against such an idea through their own doctrine of the immortality of the soul; blurry Stoical conceptions of semi-personal soul survival or cosmic reintegration hardly welcomed bodily renewal. Even the more materialistic philosophers of the period would have found the Christian hope inane at worst, curious at best,[2] exemplified by Paul's audience at the Areopagus: "When they heard about the resurrection of the dead some scoffed, but others said, 'We will hear you again on this'" (Acts 17:32). Their grounds for skepticism were quite simple: to the philosophical mind the flesh epitomized change, which in turn suggested the restlessness inherent in imperfection. Flesh is that which morphs, ages, sickens, dies, decays, disintegrates. For the Greco-Roman world which prized immutability so highly, it seemed unthinkable to entertain a gospel that vouchsafed a temporal, concrete, bodily future to humans.

We have no record of anyone in the primitive Church longing for simple resuscitation. The resurrection was newness of life, after all, the entrance into immortality. Yet for the early Christians the resurrection suggested something of a re-surrection, something of a coming back, a return of what was, a newness of the old. Had this not been the double affirmation of their Christ? Jesus "appeared" to the disciples in newness (Luke 24:34; 1 Cor 15:5–8)—yet the old tomb was emphatically empty (Matt 28:6; Mark 16:4–8; Luke 24:3,12; John 20:1–9).[3] In His newness He could circumvent locked doors, arriving and vanishing instantaneously (Luke 24:31, 35; John 20:26)—yet He proved Himself through physical demonstrations to be the same flesh and bone (Matt 28:9; Luke 24:13–31; 24:37–43; John 20:17; 21:12–13). The risen Jesus ascended into heaven

1. Of course, most Jews of the first century were scandalized not so much by the claim of a coming resurrection as with the idea that the eschaton had come in an unlikely messiah, Jesus of Nazareth. For the various views inherited by the first century AD and their political interpretations, see Setzer, "Resurrection of the Dead as Symbol and Strategy," 65–101. For the doctrine's development and its multifaceted significance as a Jewish doctrine, see Levenson, Resurrection and the Restoration of Israel.

2. Cf. Croy, "Hellenistic Philosophies and the Preaching of the Resurrection," 21–39.

3. For a discussion of the language of the resurrection appearances see Harris, From Grave to Glory, 129–46.

to prepare a celestial house (Luke 24:51; Acts 1:9; John 14:1–4; 2 Cor 5:1–10)—yet that house was destined for the terrestrial setting (Matt 5:4; Rev 21:2; cf. Zech 14:6–11).

This fundamental juxtaposition of new and old, of discontinuity and continuity, is nowhere more concentrated than in the *locus classicus* of the resurrection doctrine, 1 Corinthians 15. There Paul entertains the question of the glorified body in images of similitude and dissimilitude.[4] The seed metaphor (vv.36–38, 42–44) depicts a body in radical alteration, passing beyond death to a new form of the person, wholly fructified, yet somehow identical with the original, pre-death seed. The differing fleshes of living organisms (v.39) suggest the possibility of different bodies, as do the disparate glories of heavenly orbs (vv.40–41). But it is really the seed-to-plant-metaphor which best describes the change Paul has in mind: the seed is sown a "natural" body (*sōma psuchikon*) and raised a "spiritual" body (*sōma pneumatikon*). Identity-in-difference itself is governed by Christology in the form of a dialectic between the earthly and heavenly Man (vv.45–50). The first Adam, a "natural soul" (*psuchēn zōsan*), had to become the last Adam, Jesus Christ, a "lifegiving spirit" (*pneuma zōopoioun*). The logic extends to the general resurrection: just as the first Adam became the last Adam, our old body-self will become its new body-self. We will overcome death in this consummate *transformation*, though it will be *we* ourselves who "put on" immortality, imperishability, glory and power (vv.51–57). It is not my purpose to untangle Paul's semiotics, only to appreciate how themes of discontinuity and continuity converge dramatically in talk of eschatological flesh. We will live again—to the life which is and is not the life we had before. Our flesh will be raised—which will and will not be the flesh of our former existence. Both sides of the paradox must be upheld.

It is striking, then, how in the earliest records after the apostles we find defense after defense of the *continuity* of the body. Greek and Latin writers alike prefer to speak of the resurrection of the dead not in terms of the raising of the person (*prosōpon*; *persona*), or even of the body (*sōma*; *corpus*), but of the flesh (*sarx*; *caro*). While they utilize Pauline texts, the early apologists and ecclesiastical writers prefer to dialogue in the Johannine idiom: the Savior came "in the flesh" (John 1:14; 1 John 4:2; 2 John 7), suffered "in the flesh" (1 John 5:6–8) and rose again giving many corporeal

---

4. For the following, see the discussion of Paul's rhetorico-logical flow in the second *refutatio* and *confirmatio* of 1 Cor 15 in Thiselton, *The First Epistle to the Corinthians*, 1176–78, 1257–1306.

proofs (John 20:19–31, 21:9–14; 1 John 1:1?). The early fathers take up residence in this kind of discourse. Better, one might say that in their prose and poetry they choose to abide in the Hebraic mindset: flesh *is* what is means to be human, what it means to be the creature of God, even the covenant-partner of YHWH, showered with all His material blessings. God is pouring out His Spirit upon all flesh—but flesh is flesh.

Since others have supplied exhaustive documentation of writings about the Christian hope in the second and early third centuries,[5] let me touch on some select examples of the robust, gritty sense with which the fathers spoke of the resurrection of the flesh. In a document that may be contemporaneous with the later New Testament writers, Clement of Rome writes that the resurrection of the dead is a concrete and credible future occurrence, as evidenced by the example of the (supposedly real) phoenix, which rises out of the same material in which it died.[6] Ignatius repeats the Johannine language when he says that Jesus after His resurrection "ate and drank as a fleshly one [*hōs sarkikos*], though He was spiritually united to the Father."[7] That kind of earthly continuity matters for the general resurrection too, according to the narrative of the second century *Epistula Apostolorum*, which can be read as a rebuke to spiritualizing eschatology. When the disciples state that it is the flesh that falls in death, Jesus responds, "What is fallen will arise, and what is ill will be sound, that my Father may be praised therein."[8] The site of death and decay will be the site of redemption. In this vein the writer of the pseudepigraphal 2 *Clement* teaches, "If Christ the Lord who saved us, though he was first a Spirit, became flesh and thus called us, so also shall we receive the reward in the same flesh [*en tautē tē sarki*]."[9] Examples like these demonstrate that many in the early Church embraced the resurrection in a straightforward sense, highlighting ontological continuity in the body-material that is raised.

Why did the primitive Church choose to state its position in such an abrasive form? Two functionalist explanations have been suggested. The

---

5. E.g., Wright, *The Resurrection of the Son of God*, 480–552; Lona, *Über die Auferstehung des Fleisches*; Bynum, *The Resurrection of the Body in Western Christianity*, 200–1336, 21–58.

6. 1 *Clement* 24:1—26:3.

7. Ignatius, *Ad Smyrnaos* 3:3. Cf. *Barnabas* 5:6.

8. *Epistula Apostolorum* 25 (Coptic text), cited in Schneemelcher, *New Testament Apocrypha*, 264. The epistle's attention to corporeality affirms the resurrection of the whole person at the very least, and may be quarreling openly with a dualistic anthropology (Lona, *Über die Auferstehung des Fleisches*, 88).

9. 2 *Clement* 9:5.

first draws attention to the clergy's desire to establish a stronger hierarchy by rebuffing the lawlessness entailed in a spiritualized eschatology of Gnostic groups. Gnosticism's claim that each person possesses (and is) a spiritual, divine spark came with an attendant disdain for the body, a belief system which culminated in the rejection of "apparent" earthly order and centralized ecclesiastical government. By rejecting the value of the physical body one also rejects the value of the political body. The eschatology of the second-century catholic writers, by intentional contrast, reinforced the goodness of Christians' present governed, physical lives by speaking of their future governed, physical lives.[10] A second social explanation says that the resurrection of the flesh addressed the problem of martyrdom.[11] Theologians used the doctrine to encourage the saints as they suffered brutal violence and degradation at the hands of their Roman oppressors. If Christians were tortured and slain in the body, God would raise up that selfsame body. Even if Christians were mutilated, devoured by beasts, and given over to defilement and decay, they would rise again utterly victorious in the exact flesh in which they were humiliated. God would triumph in that very place.

As helpful as these explanations are to providing a fuller picture of the early Church, one should not necessarily agree with Caroline Walker Bynum's assessment that the early Church's theological reasoning (the model of Jesus' own resurrection, the impact of millenarianism, refutation of the Gnostic threat, etc.) was mostly tautological.[12] Social factors certainly intensified theologians' witness to corporeality, but in their reductionistic form such explanations skim over the ways in which early Christians understood the integrity of the apostolic message to hang on the doctrine of the resurrection. Why not Docetism? Because if Christ only "appeared" to conquer death, the gospel story would be no more than a ruse. Why not Marcionitism? Because if the divine scorns materiality, then our created lives are worthless, Israel's God is demonic, and salvation itself is an impotent work of an impotent god. Why not the Gnostic option? Because in their account everything about Jesus Christ and His gospel evaporates into vacuous spirit. That is, all of these anti-corporealist options reject the heart of the apostolic message of *Emmanuel*: that God actually lived and actually died and actually lives forevermore with us. He

10. See the hypothesis of John G. Gager in "Body Symbols and Social Reality," 345–64.

11. Cf. Bynum, *The Resurrection of the Body*, 21–58.

12. Ibid., 26.

saves by inhabiting the creation, redeeming it from the inside-out. For the early Church, only an eschatology that affirmed a concrete place for the created body could hope to stand with the gospel against such convenient Christianities.

Stated another way, second-century theologians championed the doctrine of the resurrection of the flesh as a critical strategy to keep creation and re-creation united. Athenagoras in his *De resurrectione* makes pains to forge a bond between the two, doing it so strongly that a good portion of the treatise is necessarily devoted to dealing with the cannibalism objection (viz., If the created body and redeemed body are identical, what of the bits that are assimilated by other humans? To whom will they belong?). God as the Redeemer is no less God the Creator; therefore the redeemed body cannot be less than the created body. In this line of argumentation, a strident Tertullian enjoins his readers to embrace the pure message of Scripture and to scorn the "admixture of heretical subtleties" by affirming that "the flesh will rise again: it wholly [*omnis*], it identically [*ipsa*], it entirely [*integra*]."[13]

The unity of creation and re-creation in God's plans affected orthopraxy too, a point that was not lost on patristic writers. For example, Justin Martyr makes a splendid argument against spiritualizers by making them out to be bad worshipers. Such people believe that their naturally-good souls go on to immortality while their wicked bodies perish; but if this is the case, Justin deduces, they are also averring that nothing of themselves needs to be saved by God, and so they blasphemously assume that they owe Him no thanks and gratitude.[14] To them nature feels more and more like a burden, so much so that, disregarding the value of the body, they abandon themselves to extreme asceticism on one hand or flagrant libertinism on the other. In contrast, God will heal His good creation when "the flesh shall rise perfect and entire."[15] This is the reason why Christians must live holy lives in the present age, Justin teaches, for God will hold us responsible for all the acts done in the body and judge us accordingly.[16]

Faith statements developing in the early centuries of the Church reflect this sentiment. For instance, around 215 Hippolytus of Rome instructed that those being baptized must affirm, among other things, that they believe "in the Holy Spirit and the Holy Church and the resurrection

---

13. Tertullian, *De resurrectione carnis*, lxiii.

14. Justin Martyr, *De resurrectione*, viii.

15. Ibid., iv.

16. Ibid., x; Justin Martyr, *Apologia* viii.18; cf. Tertullian, *De resurrectione carnis*, xiv.

of the flesh."[17] Content and structure dating to the latter half of the second century informs the creed of Marcellus (c.340) when it espouses the "resurrection of the flesh."[18] Marcellus's creed takes on great importance when one considers how close it is to the received form of the Apostles Creed. On the point of eschatology the two documents are identical in their profession of belief in *sarkos anastasin* (equivalent to the Latin *carnis resurrectionem*). As for the Apostles Creed, the "apostolic" title may be misleading on its face, but J. N. D. Kelley concludes that the early version of the Old Roman Symbol represented "a compendium of popular theology," an accurate portrayal of "the faith and hope of the primitive Church."[19] All of this goes to say that the resurrection of the flesh was not some idiosyncratic belief held by a few, or a mere residue from Christianity's Hebraic inheritance. For all its obvious difficulties, the doctrine presented the chief hope of the Church.

To summarize, the early Church fathers were consistent in their teaching of a resurrection of the flesh, that the selfsame body (whatever that might mean) is reconstituted in the eschaton for judgment and salvation. Against those spiritualizers who would abstract or reject the tangible body, the fathers emphasized continuity amidst transformation in the resurrection. They asserted this for reasons of praxis as well as theological integrity. In the earliest Church context, the resurrection of the flesh was one of the best ways to promote the gospel of Jesus Christ in its received form, to link together creation and redemption under one God, and to commend personal, bodily holiness within the tangible, catholic Church. The uniform concern with a strong corporeal eschatology registered a loud testimony in the Apostles Creed: *credo . . . in carnis resurrectionem*. For all their glaring logical, theological and scientific loose ends, the earliest fathers were able to hold onto the physical body as the locus of redemption. They sought it out as the place of human identity, dignity, and responsibility. But many questions remained, leading later theologians to propose quite disparate models of interpretation for Christianity's scandalous tenet.

---

17. Hippolytus, *The Apostolic Tradition*, 21:17. For the absence of the phrase in one branch of its transmission, see Dix and Chadwick, ed., *The Treatise on the Apostolic Tradition of St. Hippolytus of Rome, Bishop and Martyr*, lxix.

18. See Boliek, *The Resurrection of the Flesh*, 13–21.

19. Kelley, *Early Christian Creeds*, 131.

TWO TRAJECTORIES OF THE DOCTRINE

From the third century onward theological accounts of the resurrection of the flesh grew more diverse. Christians in the 200s lightened their grip on the strong view of the corporeality of the resurrection, a trend evident in the forerunning documents of the Apostles Creed. Belief meant belief not only "in the resurrection of the flesh" but also in "life eternal [*vitam aeternum*]."[20] The waning threat from anti-materialistic heresies had something to do with this shift, no doubt. Less probably, the shift also stemmed from a diminished sense of urgency resulting from the delay of the parousia and periods of tolerance from the Roman government. The fourth century signaled a more considerable shift in eschatology. Toleration from Emperor Galerius, then religious privilege from Constantine, then official sanction from Theodosius and others utterly changed the status of Christianity in the Roman Empire. Over the same period, the Arian controversy dominated the theological mindset, so much so that the architects of the Nicene Creed around 381 moved quite naturally from a defense of materiality/humanity to a defense of Jesus Christ's deity. Their eschatological profession? The more generic belief in "the resurrection of the dead [*anastasin nekrōn*]." That phrase, "resurrection of the dead," with its uncontestable biblical pedigree, seemed a suitable statement for the widening catholic communion. Nevertheless, many circles of Christians retained the fleshy language of the earlier creeds; creeds that underscored creaturely dimensions and counterbalanced the realized eschatology of imperial Christendom.[21] It should come as no surprise, then, that from the third and fourth centuries theological explanation of the doctrine of the resurrection diversified.

I have taken the liberty of compiling two general views about the flesh. The two trajectories below represent families of theological thought with regard to what happens to the flesh at the resurrection. The two, which I will call "the collection view" and "the participation view," correspond roughly with the program of Western Christianity and the program of Eastern Christianity. For each trajectory I have diagrammed the thought of three theologians (two patristic and one medieval). While I am forced to paint in broad strokes, I believe the following categories help to

---

20. It may be that some developed the creed so as to preserve continuity through the *carnis resurrectionem* and discontinuity through the *vitam aeternum*, but Kattenbusch is probably right to conclude the latter clause is meant to explicate the resurrection itself (Kattenbusch, *Das apostolische Symbol*, Band II, 952).

21. Cf. Pelikan, *The Emergence of the Catholic Tradition (100–600)*, 127.

set the stage for how Karl Barth, truly an ecumenical theologian, grapples with the corporeal Christian hope.

The Collection of the Flesh

Christians had legitimate reasons to stress the discontinuity of the resurrected body, but they also had good reason to underscore the continuity between that which was and that which is to come. As described earlier in this chapter, the first Christian theologians had defended the identity, dignity, and responsibility of human beings by defending the doctrine of the resurrection of the flesh. Lest Christianity evaporate into spiritualism, salvation had to be spoken of in the most concrete terms possible: the Savior became human flesh; He and many others, martyred in the flesh, had to be raised in the flesh; good and evil deeds alike were committed in the flesh. What better way than to express the concrete parallels between this life and the next than to draw a strict equation between the bodily material of this life and the bodily material of the next?

According to a first theological program, the resurrection of the flesh involves the wholesale collection and reassembly of the bits of one's flesh. The collection view posited a materialistic solution, keeping the matter and adjusting the form. Certain Church fathers found warrant in the Scriptures for this latter view, calling attention to the protection against bodily decay in Psalm 16 and the reanimated bones of Ezekiel 37. And did not Christ promise that "not one hair from your head will perish" (Luke 21:18)? Even without a wooden reading, many Christians in antiquity and the middle ages discerned that the Scriptures identified humans as undeniably physical, not just psychical, and that God intended to restore, judge, and honor the earthly vessel. The materialist sentiment—no doubt helped by the growing need to justify the use of relics[22]—led Christians to posit that continuity resided in the bodily material itself. The resurrection of the flesh, understood as a collection of a person's selfsame matter, was the dominant view in the West until the thirteenth century, though it gained expression in the third and fourth.[23]

---

22. Bynum, *The Resurrection of the Body*, 92–94, 104–14.

23. Or perhaps the third century under Methodius of Olympus and his followers. Bynum's magnificent study recounts dozens of advocates of the collection view, a view which generated increasingly vivid images of regurgitation and reassembly (ibid., 59–225).

Jerome of Stridon (c. 345–420), following in the footsteps of Theophilus, Athenagoras, and Methodius, developed the collection view. In his eschatological vision, the raising of the dead entails the preservation of both the exact material of the present life. He describes the resurrection body in terms of reconstruction: it is a recast clay pot, constructed in such a way that every speck comes back together to form the whole. It is a ship fully mended, and "if you want to restore a ship after shipwreck, do you deny a single part [singula] of which the ship is constituted?"[24]

Going further, Jerome speaks of a continuity of the form of the resurrection body. For all its freedom from wicked desires, that body will be structured in the same way as before. Unlike his forebears, Jerome vociferates an amillennial position, one that moves earth toward heaven even as it lowers heaven toward earth; the Church is raised to God even as God is lowered to the Church. Earth mirrors heaven in such a way that heaven may be understood as a parallel to earth, so much so that when the future arrives, it will bring little that is surprising or new. Elizabeth Clark has explained how Jerome's doctrine of the resurrection buttressed his rigid social structure. That structure posited strict order between male and female, leader and follower, virgins and whores, even ascetic and non-ascetic—a full-scale "hierarchy of bodies."[25] The eschaton would not undo that which had been successfully ordered according to heavenly principles. To this end Jerome depicts the resurrection in terms of material *and* formal continuity, with the supernatural addition being only the "clothing" of immortality.[26]

It is not that Jerome loves creaturely patterns of growth and change. On the contrary. He detests fluctuation in the body. The collection view freezes the flux of this present age in anticipation of the age to come. For our second type, only a permanent collection of bones and breasts, teeth and testicles, all sorted out and permanently assembled as the right individuals, will solve the problem of corruptibility and change. Bodies

---

24. Cited in ibid., 88.

25. Clark, "New Perspectives on the Origenist Controversy," 162. Even before Jerome, Methodius of Olympus celebrated the fact that the chaste flesh could serve as the mediator of heaven and earth, so much so that "the bridge across the chasm between God and man passed through the bodies of his virgin girls" (Brown, *The Body and Society*, 384).

26. "Thus Jerome's stress was not so much on material continuity as on *integrity*," says Bynum, "on the reconstitution and hardening of the bodily vessel so that every organ is intact and eternally protected from amputation" (*The Resurrection of the Body*, 89).

must be gathered and made invincible, much like the hardened flesh of the monastic saints.

Augustine of Hippo (354–430) also promotes the idea of collection— though his theology consistently defaults to something more patently spiritualistic. Since Augustine associates mental properties (memory, intellect, and will) with the image of God, it comes as no surprise that he describes the hereafter in terms of soul-knowledge, of the contemplation of God. Glorification is no less than the *visio Dei,* the soul perfected and standing before the Almighty, beholding Him face to face. For Augustine, paradise will be a place where the enlightened saint perceives the invisible realities and experiences spiritual rest and eternal bliss. He or she has ascended beyond any bodily need. Being "suited for the assembly of the angels," the risen saint has surpassed all physical limitations; even with closed eyelids, the glorious vision stays before the person.[27]

Paradoxically, Augustine adds to this serene soul-future a resurrected body, and in terms every bit as materialistic as Jerome's. The resurrection body is a collection. Like a recast statue, Augustine says, all the fragments of the former body come together into a new one. Each atom is there, but it is now made perfectly beautiful, perfectly symmetrical, without defect.[28] Miscarried children and dead infants will be raised according to their "seminal principle," with God adding (but never subtracting) material from bodies to make them flawless. Does the risen flesh add anything to the glorified soul? Augustine appears to want to say something along this line, but his argument founders as he speculates about the physical body allowing greater perception of God's presence in visible bodies.[29] Despite the fact that the collection of the body is only an addendum to the soul's vision of God, Augustine takes up the refrain that the only true faith is that which preaches *carnis in aeternum resurrectio,*[30] by which he means precise continuity of both body and soul. Everything must be gathered; nothing can be lost.

On its face, the collectionist type takes the flesh most seriously. But Jerome and Augustine demonstrate how continuity of the person through

---

27. For this and the following, see Augustine, *Enchiridion,* 84–95; Augustine, *Civitatis Dei,* xxii.

28. Beauty (not ability) is Augustine's primary concern for eschatological corporeality: bodies molded to ideal proportions, though still marked by religiously significant scars (Upson-Saia, "Scars, Marks, and Deformities in Augustine's Resurrected Bodies").

29. Augustine, *Civitatis Dei,* xxii.29.

30. Ibid., xxii.9.

the flesh can, oddly enough, terminate all of the predicates associated with flesh. In being reconnected to their respective souls, resurrected bodies are sanitized, quarantined, sterilized, made into something auxiliary and aesthetic. Such bodies hardly carry out actual human life in eternity, one might argue. The body, far from being vivified, is sculpted and hardened. The resurrection eternally enshrines the present order, reinstating the panoply of saints and ascetics along with the ecclesiastical principalities and powers, giving them a permanent place before the throne of God. Equally concerning is the collection view's tendency (through Augustine) to speak of a collection of particles as a side-item of the true glorification, the beatific vision. Paradoxically, the materialistic nature of this type is subordinate to, if not subsumed within, the spiritual hope of psychic bliss in heaven.

The collection view as defined by Augustine (that is, a resurrection equally materialistic and spiritualistic) became the dominant perspective in the West through the middle ages and beyond,[31] though a fresh perspective emerged around the turn of the thirteenth century. This late-breaking variant of the collection view affirmed the gathering together of the exact particles of the former body, but with a different mechanism of glorification: the transmission of the soul's dignity to the body. More than just recollection of atoms, resurrection involved overflow, gift, and infusion—the *endowment* of the soul's celestial riches to its body.

Thomas Aquinas (c.1225–74), in the company of Albertus Magnus, Robert Grosseteste, and Bonaventure, exploited the Aristotelian renaissance for new conceptions of soul and body. If form were to be conceived as the pattern within things, inherent within matter, rather than a transcendent archetype, soul could be seen as the underlying grid of the body, the blueprint which impresses and shapes and orders the body—a view known as hylomorphism. Like a painter who expresses his workmanship through his work, the soul produces a body representative of its own virtue.[32] When extended to the doctrine of the resurrection, hylomorphism operates in terms of endowment. Out of the abundance of its own perfection the soul shares glory with the body. As the soul becomes glorious in

---

31. Most of the Reformers perpetuated this line of thought, confessing the resurrection of the "selfsame flesh" even as they longed for disembodied existence in heaven. See the collation of Reformation documents in Darragh, *The Resurrection of the Flesh*, 213ff.

32. Thomas Aquinas, *Summa Theologica*, Supplementum, q.80, a.1 (response).

its communion with God, it bestows its beauty upon the flesh, a transfer of glory. That endowment is resurrection.[33]

Thomas agrees with Augustine regarding the collection of bodily material at the Last Day. In the resurrection God can recall the old particles from the earth or from the stomachs of cannibals. Indeed, even bodily fluids re-gather: according to Thomas, Christ's own blood which was lost at the crucifixion gathered again to His body on Easter morning—"and the same holds good for all the particles which belong to the truth and integrity of human nature."[34] For many of the same reasons as his Western forebears—personal identity, integrity, reward and punishment—Thomas casts the resurrection of the flesh as a reconsolidation of bodily material.

The mechanism of glorification turns on a spiritual transfer, however. What really matters in the resurrection is that a person's collected atoms receive the ethereal qualities of a glorified soul. The postmortem soul, though blissfully beholding God, still desires to have a body with it. It longs to have the body with it in the state of glory, to bestow its endowment, to reconfigure flesh after its redeemed image.[35] In this life the (imperfect) soul blesses and shines through the body in part; in the coming life the (glorious) soul blesses and shines through the body in full.

To what effect? Thomas, speaking after William of Auxerre, describes the endowed resurrection body as possessing impassibility (*impassibilitas*), subtlety (*subtilitas*), agility (*agilitas*), and clarity (*claritas*).[36] One's body will be comprised of the same material as before, though it will have another form (*aliam dispositionem habebunt*).[37] The saints' bodies "are invested with an immortality coming from a divine strength which enables the soul so to dominate the body that corruption cannot enter."[38] More specifically,

> Entirely possessed by soul, the body will then be fine and spirited. Then also will it be endowed with the noble lightsomeness of beauty; it will be invulnerable, and no outside forces can

33. One might conclude that Thomas' conception operates along medieval patriarchal lines: just as a man disseminates wealth to his own household, the soul manages its resources and bestows them upon its body (Howell, *Women, Production and Patriarchy in Late Medieval Cities*, 15).

34. Thomas Aquinas, *Summa Theologica* III, q.54, art.3, reply obj. 3.

35. For the theology of desire as developed in Bonaventure and Thomas, see Bynum, *The Resurrection of the Body*, 247ff.

36. Ibid., qq.82–85.

37. Thomas Aquinas, *Summa contra gentiles*, IV.lxxxv.

38. Quoted in Gilby, *St. Thomas Aquinas*, 408–9.

damage it; it will be lissom and agile, entirely responsive to the soul, like an instrument in the hands of a skilled player.[39]

The flesh, formerly unexpressive and unsubmissive and retarding to the soul,[40] in the eschaton becomes responsive to the kingly psyche, thereby acquiring soul-like properties. The resurrection body, like a fine instrument, vibrates with the soul's qualities: impassibility, subtlety, agility, and clarity. How Thomas defines each quality is not so important as the fact that for him the flesh must be re-predicated with psychic attributes.

The spiritualizing tendency goes further as Thomas admits that the soul does not need the body, technically. The nobility of the soul permits it independence from the body in the instance of one's death. Physical matter relies on the soul's impress, but the soul itself does not rely upon matter for expression, for it of itself has "somatomorphic" qualities, to use Carol Zaleski's term.[41] It is capable of full sensation even apart from the flesh, a kind of proto-bodily mobility. After death souls may long for their bodies, but they are not in any significant way disabled or unhappy without them. Therefore, no hard distinction need be made between an individual's death and the final return of Christ to complete all things. One might very well permit the confusion of the individual eschaton at death and the cosmic consummation at Christ's return.[42]

In its modified form under Thomas, the doctrine of the resurrection of the flesh seems to make a bit of progress. Soul and body are brought a step closer together. The relationship between glorified soul and glorified body is exposited more fully. Yet considerable difficulties exist in Thomas' presentation. Its exact recollection notwithstanding, the flesh's concrete qualities exist to be immobilized and dominated by its nobler counterpart, the soul. One strains to see any way in which the flesh operates as the actual locus of human life in the eschaton. In this respect, Thomas repeats the vexed legacy of the West.

---

39. Ibid., 409.

40. Cf. Bynum, *The Resurrection of the Body*, 266.

41. Zaleski, *Otherworldly Journeys*, 51. For expression of this in the *Divine Comedy*, see Bynum, "Faith Imagining the Self," 83–106.

42. Such confusion is a feature of the thirteenth-century *Stabat Mater*. It also became dogma through Benedict XII's 1336 decree insisting that the soul's bliss is perfect at death, so that the resurrection of the body adds nothing in terms of beatification. For the fascinating papal debate leading to the pronouncement, see especially Douie, "John XXII and the Beatific Vision," 154–74, and Bynum, *The Resurrection of the Body*, 279–85.

In retrospect, three things may be noted about the collection view. First, this view did the best job of preserving the testimony of the earliest fathers, insisting upon nothing less than flesh, the very flesh of its previous earthly existence, for the resurrection of the body. The West continued to answer questions of identity, integrity, and personal responsibility through a strikingly materialistic doctrine. Second, however, theologians of the collection view counteracted their own materialistic explanation through a pronounced body-soul dualism. At the heart of glorification lay the soul's beatification, the vision of God, the heavenly life in the presence of God. The addition of resurrected flesh to the perfected soul appeared to threaten the state of psychic perfection, leading theologians to speak all too often about the collected body as something auxiliary, sanitized, and even immutable to the point of being frozen. Such flesh hardly functions as the center of life! Third, the collection view increasingly drew off of themes of participation. By the time of Thomas Aquinas, the miracle of flesh-collection by God did not stick out so much as the miracle of participation: the soul participates in God's glory and the body participates in the soul's glory. That trend toward participation requires us to back up to the third century and consider the Church's other theological trajectory.

The Participation of the Flesh

Another broad trajectory can be detected in the history of the doctrine of the resurrection of the flesh. Where the Church in the West started from the idea of the collection of the flesh, the Church in the East preferred to think in terms of the *participation* of the flesh. Instead of finding ways to guarantee the material identity between the flesh of this age and that in the age to come, Eastern theologians looked for ways to express a doctrine of glorification in terms of proximity to God. A person received salvation by participation in the divine nature, by communion with God, by intimacy with the Godhead. In this paradigm, the resurrection of the flesh comes to mean that even the flesh, the lowliest part of human existence, is raised up through participation in the divine life.

The development of the participation trajectory received its first real articulation at the hands of the great third-century monastic, Origen of Alexandria (c.185–254).[43] In his writings Origen clearly intends to honor the

---

43. Clement of Alexandria (c.150–c.215), the great Platonist apologist, alludes to a work of his entitled *On the Resurrection*, a piece, sadly, that was never penned or was lost.

gospel tradition even as he sets it in a fresh philosophical-theological matrix. His project revolves around connectivity with the Logos, Jesus Christ, the One who descended to humanity so that others might be participants in His divine rationality. Because of the superiority of the spiritual realm, Origen's cosmology looks like a parabola, wherein pre-existent (though created) souls are cast from heaven into bodies, then reconciled by the Logos so that a return to heaven is possible.[44] While the return of the soul to God is a constant feature of his theology, Origen admits that there will be a resurrection body too.

When Origen speaks of the resurrection, he means the resurrection of *a* body, something with a continuity of *form* though not a continuity of material. This form lies behind the matter and is non-identical with it. In an important fragment, he teaches that "although the form [*eidos*] is saved, we are going to put away nearly [every] earthly quality in the resurrection," meaning that "for the saint there will indeed be [a body] preserved by him who once endued the flesh with form, but [there will] no longer [be] flesh; yet the very thing which was once being characterized in the flesh will be characterized in the spiritual body."[45] Origen will not permit the redemption of the flesh as such, and therefore he separates out a mediating body-form with some of the properties of the soul.[46] This *eidos* is immortal and sacred, yet what it draws to the soul at the resurrection is very different stuff than its previous earthly attachments. In the place of flesh God puts spiritual matter. Why not the same flesh as before? Because that flesh is a river of change, Origen says, a flux of desire and imperfection. The fleshly material of the body must be exchanged for a new attending substance; the *eidos*-body must be raised (i.e., filled out) with something spiritual and tranquil. Elaborating Paul's argument in 1 Corinthians 15, Origen sees the resurrection as the germination of a mediating principle, the spiritual realization of what once was fleshly but is now heavenly.

This substitution of the flesh, Origen's critics over the centuries have pointed out, conveys itself as an attempt to shirk bodiliness altogether.

44. For a summary of the controversial nature of *Peri Archon*, see Trigg, *Origen*, 29–32. Origen's parabola is explained in Pelikan, *The Shape of Death*, 77–97.

45. Origen, *Commentary on Psalm* 1, cited in Dechow, *Dogma and Mysticism in Early Christianity*, 375, bracketed words in original; cf. Methodius's longer quotation in *De resurrectione*, i.22.

46. See the work of Henri Crouzel ("La doctrine origenienne du corps réssuscité," 679–716), who describes the *eidos* as a substratum conceived along Platonic and Stoic lines. Origen can elsewhere refer to this form as a "seminal principle" or "underlying matter" (cf. Boliek, *The Resurrection of the Flesh*, 47–51, though one should bypass Boliek's assessment that the three terms can be distinguished as "elements" of continuity).

Since God swaps out the old for the new, who is to say that this new, upgraded commodity could not also be further upgraded, or disposed with altogether? Yes, Origen asserts that every being (God alone excepted) possesses bodily substance. But his infatuation with the return of the soul to primordial unity, lightness, and spirituality indicates that corporeality is a cumbersome addition to the metaphysical hierarchy. He makes strides towards a philosophically consistent position by developing a conception of participation, though, tellingly, participation applies only to the soul.[47] Lynn Boliek observes how Origen's train of thought seems to lead in the direction of the elimination of the body altogether, something akin to the Neo-Platonic astral body. The outer self is (en)lightened until all traces of corporeality become spiritual and luminous and weightless. Ultimately all remaining corporeality is either shed or converted into one's soul, which in turn is subsumed into God.[48]

To be fair, Origen never spelled out this otherworldly vision so far as to deny the bodily resurrection. His solution accorded with the biblical language of discontinuation: that what is raised is a different, "spiritual body." Yet Origen's creative rethinking of the problem was not enough to protect him from ecclesiastic censure. His ordination was revoked in 231 and his views posthumously condemned by a council in 400, by imperial decree in 543, and a decade thereafter by the fifth ecumenical council. In more recent years it has been suggested that Origen was constructing a far more sophisticated system than is reflected in the glossed manuscripts passed down to us. It is probably the case that his lost treatise on the resurrection was more in line with orthodoxy than the teachings of his disciples, who were not nearly so careful in safeguarding continuity in the resurrection.[49] Just as probable is the case that Origen, being aware of the ideological difficulties involved with marrying the doctrinal tradition with the philosophical currency of his day, sought out a fine line of congruence.

47. Though it seems that the soul has already positioned the glorified body under or within itself (Russell, *The Doctrine of Deification in the Greek Patristic Tradition*, 147–48). The lower parts of the human must be subsumed by the higher, soul, in order to make progress into deification, to become spiritual through the Holy Spirit, at which point one's spiritual soul may acquire the attributes of Logos by itself becoming logical (p.154).

48. Boliek, *The Resurrection of the Flesh*, 59–67. In our present (and likely corrupted) manuscripts, Origen is at odds with himself, foreseeing an end to bodily diversity (*De principiis*, III.vi.4) *and* making provision for some kind of diversification of bodies into eternity (II.iii.2–3).

49. E.g. Murphy, "Evagrius Ponticus and Origenism," 253–69.

17

In the substitutionist variety of the participationist view, flesh is swapped out for a spiritual substance. The resurrection discontinues the present composition of the body in order to build a better specimen, though the body continues with its underlying foundation. Ultimately, the view falls back not so much on its quasi-material identity as its formal identity, the "shape" lent to the body as it is reconstructed with spiritual building blocks. The flesh as such, this present body, is at best a shadow of what is to come, and has no real connection with the life to come. The "real" body lies beneath the body, as a germ, carried along with the soul in the upward arc of evolution and return to God, waiting to be stripped of flesh and reclothed in spiritual garments. Perhaps because it was too closely related to middle Platonism and Gnostic mystagogy, Origen's version of participatory resurrection was sidelined as a real option for the Church, though not entirely expunged.[50]

Most of the greatest thinkers, whether orthodox or heretical, continued to come out of Alexandria. That learned Egyptian city would continue to be the epicenter for concepts of salvation through participation. Indeed, Alexandria would be ultimately responsible for the genesis of the theologoumenon known as deification (*theōsis*).[51] At its heart, the doctrine of deification teaches that salvation has to do with participation in the divine life of God. In deification (or "divinization") humans are not made God, or made into a rival deity, or consubstantial with Him. Rather, they are transfigured into His likeness, made "partakers of the divine nature" (2 Pet 1:4). By participation in God through Christ by the Holy Spirit, believers receive the grace to enjoy some of God's own attributes. When applying this potent theological idea to the general resurrection, deification could mean that even human flesh could be transformed in its proximity to the divine. The resurrection of the flesh means something more and less than bodily reconstruction: it is the "raising" of the whole psychosomatic person into the life of God.

---

50. Origen may have been marginalized, but his ideas were not; a battery of important thinkers of Alexandria over the next centuries continued to dialogue with his work (see Schmemann, *The Historical Road of Eastern Orthodoxy*, 158ff.). Philosophical baggage of Alexandrian thinkers sometimes required their teachings to be reinterpreted and "inorthodoxed," as in the case of Pseudo-Dionysius the Areopagite (Kharlamov, "'The Beauty of the Unity and the Harmony of the Whole,'" 394). Origenism was therefore never confined to late antiquity or to the East, as illustrated by John Scotus Eriugena's program in the ninth century (see Cooper, *Panentheism*, 47–50).

51. Russell, *The Doctrine of Deification in the Greek Patristic Tradition*, 115.

Athanasius of Alexandria (c.295–373) did much to expand the concept of deification,[52] and therewith to reinterpret the resurrection of the flesh. The central purpose of his writings as a bishop and theologian was to unite the Church in the belief of Jesus Christ's full deity, a task necessitated by Arianism's description of the Son as a being of inferior substance to the Father. Athanasius argues at length that only if Jesus Christ is of one being with the Father do we actually know God and receive His salvation. Yet Athanasius's fight for a high Christology is not without a contention for full humanity. The Word became *flesh*. That is the only way His deity could benefit our humanity. He in His highest being condescended to the lowest human place in order to sanctify us from the bottom up. What is naturally His must be united to what is naturally ours if His life is to be communicated to us. Put more forcefully: "He became human in order that we might become divine."[53]

Athanasius employs the scandalous word "flesh" to make sure that the whole human being is redeemed. His is a *sarx*-Christology from beginning to end, and his soteriology operates in and through the flesh. Flesh is the "deepest" and most representative medium of humanity, explains Khaled Anatolios, who describes Athanasius's allusions to *nous* (mind), *psuchē* (soul), and *sōma* (body) not as "parts" so much as "existential and relational" dimensions.[54] The body is certainly lower than the soul or the mind and has less similitude with God, but that is precisely why it of all things must be redeemed. In fact, while the soul pilots the body, the body is the place of action and transmission, "the crucial existential locus for the exercise of human freedom."[55] *Sarx* is a kind of conductive medium for internal and external relations.

If the Logos, the Son of God, has abased Himself and made Himself present to us in the flesh, then certainly the flesh will be the recipient of salvation. Athanasius involves the body in the *communicatio idiomatum*, i.e., the communication of predicates. Christ "deified" (*etheopoieito*) the body and "rendered it immortal."[56] He made it so that we might rise with-

---

52. He speaks more about deification than any previous writer and coins new terminology (Russell, *The Doctrine of Deification in the Greek Patristic Tradition*, 167–68).

53. *Autos gar enēnthrōpēsen, hina hēmeis theopoiēthōmen* (Athanasius, *De incarnatione*, liv).

54. Anatolios, *Athanasius*, 61.

55. Ibid., 62. Similarly, Athanasius takes up a kind of ascetic logic in his belief that only the fleshly body can bring salvation to the soul; the soul, hungry for God, requires a "steady" or "stabilized" body (Lyman, *Christology and Cosmology*, 146–47).

56. Athanasius, *De decretis*, xiv; cf. *De incarnatione verbi dei*, ix.

press trumps event

out a trace of corruption, just as His body showed none.[57] The flesh with the soul enjoys a glorious future in God.

The concept of deification bears obvious fruit in Athanasius's presentation, but something strange happens on the way to the doctrine of the resurrection of the flesh: his writings downplay corporeality even as they place it front and center. The flesh is drawn into the divine life—but is this the same as saying that the flesh is *raised*? Rather, one gets the feeling that Athanasius has turned the doctrine into the *ascension* of the flesh:

> When the flesh was born from Mary the Theotokos, [the Logos] is said to have been born, who furnishes to others an origin of being, in order that he may transfer our nature into himself, and *we may no longer, as mere earth, return to earth, but as being joined to the Logos from heaven, may be carried to heaven by him.* In a similar manner he has therefore not unreasonably transferred to himself the other affections of the body also, that we, no longer as being men, but as proper to the Logos, may have a share in eternal life.[58]

The ascension of the whole person via the Logos is Athanasius's concern, a movement starting from earth but very definitely leaving it.[59] Resurrection has become a spiritual process initiated by the incarnation, played out in the spiritual life, and ultimately culminated in the drawing of the whole self to a final destination in heaven. The coming resurrection in its concrete, physical form becomes a rather insignificant event, having been overshadowed by the greater mystery of deification. Yes, Athanasius confesses the resurrection, resurrection of even of the frail aspects of human existence, but the deeper reality seems to be an overarching spiritual evolution in which, "from the beginning without ceasing, [Christ] raises up every human and speaks to every human in their heart."[60] There is a "raising" for Athanasius, yes. But has this participatory resurrection in any way reanimated the flesh?

If we permit ourselves to skip ahead to Maximus the Confessor (c.580–662), it is because he arrives at a creative synthesis of the thought of the Cappadocian fathers, Evagrius Ponticus, Cyril of Alexandria,

57. Athanasius, Festal Letter xi.14.

58. Athanasius, *Contra Arianos* xxxiii.3, cited in Russell, *The Doctrine of Deification in the Greek Patristic Tradition*, 183, emphasis added.

59. Tempering a more dualistic Platonic view, Athanasius has the flesh addressed so that the person may start "living away from a historical, material setting and moving toward the noetic, eternal world" (Lyman, *Christology and Cosmology*, 145).

60. Athanasius, Festal Letter xxvii.

Pseudo-Dionysius, and many others who precede him. What the Alexandrians did with Christology, Maximus applies to theological anthropology, giving the doctrine of deification "its greatest elaboration and most profound articulation."[61] While in many ways Maximus takes up the mantle of Origen, he pursues the participationist line toward a holistic, mystical view of body and soul, thereby "sifting out the more questionable metaphysics."[62]

Following Gregory of Nazianzus, Maximus teaches that the human being goes through three births: the natural in childbirth, the spiritual in baptism, and the final in the resurrection of the dead; one receives being (*einai*), well-being (*eu einai*), and, ultimately, eternal well-being (*aei eu einai*). Deification is the result of this relationship with God. While humans already possess being and even immortal being (of the soul) in their essential nature, goodness and wisdom can only be imparted to them by grace.

The communication of the divine nature happens through God's presence. Jesus Christ once condescended and came to earth to be with us, Maximus affirms, but the Lord also promised His proximity after His departure to heaven (Matt 28:20), an abiding presence which initiates the deification of us even here on earth. His presence is what secures our presence with Him in the age to come. When the Lord is "fully revealed" the saints will participate in Him; Christ's revealed presence is what it means to have the immortality of the resurrection. Like many before and after him, Maximus makes creative use of Neoplatonic hierarchies: the telos of all things is to return to a state of "simplicity," with the effects of various syzygies restored to their causes, and triads united into a whole.[63] But unlike some of his predecessors, Maximus rejects the preexistence of souls and withholds speculation about the *apokatastasis*. There is no parabola of Origen here; Maximus has a single escalating line moving from the humble, natural state to a lofty participation in the divine life. By contemplation and acts of love the believer makes an ascent into God's own kind of life, an ascent which culminates in the final resurrection-birth. In such a manner, resurrection and ascension come together in Maximus.

Despite occasional ascetic comments against flesh(liness), Maximus promotes a holistic view of the body with the soul. Soul does not antecede or succeed the body, for parts only exist with their respective counterparts. In fact, the flesh—everything about the human—is saved, for Christ's

---

61. Russell, *The Doctrine of Deification in the Greek Patristic Tradition*, 262.

62. Louth, *Maximus the Confessor*, 24.

63. See Russell, *The Doctrine of Deification in the Greek Patristic Tradition*, 270ff.

incarnation took place "in order to save the image and immortalize the flesh," says Maximus, albeit "to present nature pure again as from a *new* beginning, with an *additional* advantage through deification over the first creation."[64] In another place he adds that God fills Christians

> with his own glory and beatitude, giving them and granting them that life which is eternal and unutterable and in every way free from every mark constitutive of the present life, which is made up of decay, for it does not breathe air nor is it made up of blood vessels running from the liver. No, *the whole of God is participated by the whole of them,* and he becomes to their souls like a soul related to a body, and through the soul he affects the body, in a way that he himself knows, that the former might receive immutability and the latter immortality, and that *the whole man might be deified,* raised to the divine life (*theourgoumenos*) by the grace of the incarnate God, the *whole remaining man* in soul and body by nature, and *the whole becoming god* in soul and body by grace and by the divine brightness of that blessed glory altogether appropriate to him, than which nothing brighter or more exalted can be conceived.[65]

The soul obtains immutability in its deification, and the body, glorified with and through the soul, obtains immortality. This is its transformation out of decay. But the whole, which is and remains human by nature, "becomes god" by grace. Adam Cooper concludes his study of Maximus' view of the body recognizing that little is said about the resurrection body itself, though the Confessor has lots to say about how "the passible and corporeal become entirely transparent to divine glory." In this purview, "the very integrity of the material order lies in it being transcended."[66]

Strengths of such a mature doctrine of deification are many, not least that it depicts the whole person as the object of salvation. Deification softens anthropological dualism as both body and soul become partakers in the divine nature. I might raise three concerns, however. First, the Alexandrian emphasis on the unity of the divine and human natures tends to generate views that eliminate or absorb the flesh altogether. While Alexandrian theologians clamped down on more egregious Christological heresies (Apollinarianism, Eutycheanism, and other variations

---

64. Maximus, *Quaestiones ad Thalassium,* liv, cited in Russell, *The Doctrine of Deification in the Greek Patristic Tradition,* 289, emphasis added.

65. Maximus, *Ambiguum* vii, in Russell, *The Doctrine of Deification in the Greek Patristic Tradition,* 276, emphasis added.

66. Cooper, *The Body in St. Maximus the Confessor,* 253.

of monophysitism), the slope of the theological field tended toward a mystical slip of the human into the divine. For theological anthropology, it would eventually require Gregory Palamas's fourteenth-century distinction between "essence" and "energies" to guard the line between Creator and creature; per Gregory, deification involves participation in the latter alone.[67] Second, in a related way, the view does not escape the Platonic priority of soul over body. Both are supposedly subject to deification, but the body is still treated as something to be contained and immobilized. Bodily living does not carry on into the eschaton. Rather, participationists such as Origen, Athanasius, and Maximus seem to desire to override the body with wholly new, pneumatic properties such as impassibility, immutability, and perhaps even invisibility.[68] Third, and most dire, the doctrine of deification effectively displaces the doctrine of the resurrection of the flesh. In fact, *any* kind of doctrine of the general resurrection becomes a footnote in this type. Jesus Christ's resurrection may retain a central motif (as it does in Orthodox liturgies), being the revelation of His divine power and the bestowal of that victory to His people. Nevertheless, what matters to adherents of the participationist view is that *theōsis* has been initiated and is in process now. The movement of glorification will come to completion, yes, and that completion is resurrection. But for the second trajectory *ascension* has become the master-concept, and participation its beating heart.

Observations about the Two Trajectories

The Church, bound by apostolic tradition, was all along the way required to articulate its belief in the resurrection of the dead in bodily terms. Early theologians stated the corporeality of the resurrection body in stark terms, preferring the phrase "resurrection of the flesh" over "resurrection of the body" or "resurrection of the dead." Theologians from the third to the thirteenth centuries attempted to repackage the doctrine of the resurrection of the flesh in more systematic ways. In moving beyond the primitive view they both added to and subtracted from the doctrine. Two trajectories,

67. For an explanation of the Palamite distinction and its legacy, see Olson, "Deification in Contemporary Theology," 186–200.

68. Even Maximus says that in the coming age "it is no longer a matter of humanity bearing or being born along existentially, since in this respect the economy of visible things comes to an end with the great and general resurrection wherein humanity is born into immortality in an unchanging state of being" (*Ambiguum* xlii, cited in Blowers and Wilken, ed., *On the Cosmic Mystery of Jesus Christ*, 95).

largely divergent along West-East lines, emerged. Jerome and Augustine and Thomas championed the collecting-the-flesh type, preserving the doctrine in rather material ways even as spiritualist notions were added. Origin and Athanasius and Maximus developed the participation-of-the-flesh type, holding onto the doctrine in a roundabout way through the total-person transformation effected in deification. I might offer a couple of observations about the collectionist and participationist options.

First, the two trajectories disagree about the ordering of the themes of continuity and discontinuity in the resurrection. The collection view insists upon sameness of flesh before and after the resurrection, securing human identity by bringing together a person's exact particles on the last Day. The collection view tries secures a wholesale continuity of matter and form, and only after reconstitution looks to add the "clothing" of bodily transformation (i.e., immortality and immutability). The body is first gathered, then aerated; made the same, then made different; continuity leads into discontinuity. Conversely, the participation view begins with the theme of discontinuity. New life in Christ is fundamentally an ascension beyond fleshly identity. In salvation one is raised to a heavenly existence, a higher existence through participation in the divine. The transformation trickles down, however, reaching each part of earthly existence, seizing even the flesh, including it and preserving it in the divine life. Transformation has within itself a sense of preservation. The body is aerated, then preserved; made different, thus the same; discontinuity leads into continuity.

Second, it needs to be stated that both of these traditional views, at least in their classical articulations, are addicted to immutability. Without exception they hope for an escape from flux, from the processes of corporeal existence. Each one desires changelessness, and suspects in other views a perverse love of mutation. Time, space, and movement are treated as penultimate dimensions honorable only insofar as they come to termination and calcification. This may be the saddest inheritance of the Church with regard to the doctrine of the general resurrection. In the millennium of thought between third to thirteenth centuries, theologians approached the doctrine of the resurrection looking for ways to terminate or transcend the corporeal mode of existence rather than see it fulfilled in a temporal, tangible, and concrete existence. I do not mean to insinuate that a millennium of spiritualizing theologians destroyed a formerly pure doctrine of the resurrection of the flesh. But I am suggesting that these thinkers, trying to imagine bodies of flesh reanimated to live once again on the New Earth, flinched.

Barth and the Two Trajectories

At first glance Barth does not fit into any classical program in the collectionist family or the participationist family. His novel approach to the resurrection does not employ the same terminology or metaphysical categories. Yet, as is characteristic with Barth, beyond first appearance his doctrine of the resurrection of the flesh is deeply ecumenical. Champions of either of the two views could hypothetically claim Barth as an ally or, at the very least, a valuable dialogue partner. Western theologians can certainly find in Barth consonant language and ideas. I will argue, however, that his three favorite descriptions of the resurrection of the flesh—eternalization, manifestation, incorporation—resonate especially well with the more Eastern, participationist trajectory. To understand that strange harmony one must start at the beginning of Barth's own remarkable work.

2

Young Barth's Resurrection Dialectic

NO THEME RESOUNDS IN Barth's early theological writings more than the resurrection of the dead. It appears everywhere as a kind of grid, or trope, or DNA sequence of sorts. A little surprising, then, is the fact that his intellectual biographers, while judging the resurrection to be the connective tissue of Barth's early work, rarely examine the resurrection of the dead with any detail.[1] Along the way scholars have preferred to describe Barth's early work (usually from 1914 to some point in the 1920s) as "theology of crisis" or "dialectical theology." These titles hone in on the philosophical nature of Barth's approach, attending to the categorical opposition between the divine and the creaturely. "Theology of crisis" and "dialectical theology" also work well as literary descriptions, since most of his writings during this decade are tumultuous and dynamic. Yet while not inaccurate, philosophical and formal analyses can overlook the extent to which Barth sought, even in his early ministry, to speak about the content of theology: God. One challenge for Barth scholarship, then, is to understand his early work as more fully doctrinal.

The purpose of this chapter, then, is to examine young Barth's exploration of critical-dialectical theology, except to narrate the examination with the resurrection in the foreground. I intend to show how Barth uses the doctrine as the central concept by which God's self-revelation operates

---

1. For a catalogue of these instances, see Dawson, *The Resurrection in Karl Barth*, 11f. Such thematic neglect may be understandable with regard to Barth's mature dogmatics (after all, he is operating with a battery of concepts by that time), but not for his early work. In fact, I would argue that the resurrection of the dead is the *only* developed biblico-theological concept he has in hand before 1924.

and is explained. Used programmatically, the resurrection of the dead describes the basic dynamic of the event of God's revelation to humans.

Anyone who dares to go this road with Barth needs to be prepared for rather serious theological reconfiguration, as he introduces some very counterintuitive notions of the resurrection of the dead. The reader does well to set aside for the moment traditional concerns about Christian eschatology. Barth is concerned with "God-encounter" more generally, not just the conditions of humankind when confronted by the Coming One at the end of time. Put as simply as possible: for Barth divine revelation has a resurrection quality. Every contact with God triggers something cataclysmic, something apocalyptic. When God unveils Himself to a human, that "dead" person is "resurrected," lifted up to God's own world. When the Lord displays Himself, a mortal human is caught up in the divine event and raised into genuine knowledge of God. Again, God's immanent Otherness takes up ("resurrects") a human's mortal, fleshly existence into His own life. Put more technically: God's self-communication is a sublation, a dialectic that dissolves and establishes anew. These dense concepts from young Barth require some unpacking.

While theology is ultimately in view, this chapter covers Barth's thought chronologically. Up front I recall Barth's early ideological influences, which I suggest can be summed up in three categories: pietism, romantic idealism, and religious socialism.[2] Through these schools of thought Barth cultivated a nascent dialectic, that is, a "movement" triggered by the breaking in of God. After the background narration, I look at three stages of how he articulated his theological program within the rubric of the resurrection of the dead. First, he *eschatologizes* his dialectic. From around 1915, Barth latches onto the resurrection as a template for all interaction between God and the world. The movement of the kingdom of God, inaugurated by the Coming One, is an immanent, revolutionary principle which springs to life. Second, Barth *radicalizes* the dialectic. From 1919, he portrays divine revelation as an absolute miracle, as the impossible touching of the divine and the creaturely, namely, as the resurrection of the dead. In the divine moment a violent epistemological revolution takes place: God's self-disclosure obliterates religious knowledge and raises the believer to divine understanding. At the radicalizing stage it is difficult to gauge Barth's implications for the actual, future resurrection

---

2. I make no attempt at a thorough biography of the young Karl Barth, which has been done (and done well) by others. See especially Busch, *Karl Barth*; McCormack, *Karl Barth's Critically Realistic Dialectical Theology*; Frei, "The Doctrine of Revelation in the Thought of Karl Barth, 1909–1922"; Torrance, *Karl Barth*; Chung, *Karl Barth*.

of the body, though this situation would begin to change around 1924. At that time, in a third stage, he *hypostatizes* the dialectic of revelation. While still linked to the moment of revelation, the resurrection of the dead is given some room to stand as its own doctrine. The coming resurrection refers to the lifting of humanity into God's eternal presence, the final "moment" when humanity is unified with Him and revealed as such.

I do not want to wander far from the ultimate aim of this study, to isolate Barth's views on the resurrection *of the flesh*, the doctrine itself. But—and this is the peculiar genius of Barth at work—the material content emerges from the formal. The structural function he gives to the resurrection of the dead early on begins to produce ontological themes. Even his youthful works insist upon the "bodily" or "fleshly" nature of the resurrected person, and he takes steps to illuminate the doctrine in that respect. His early writings show forth some of the tender shoots he would cultivate in his mature dogmatics. And with these beginnings, Barth's first difficulties with securing a rich sense of human corporeality appear.

EARLY FORMATION (1886–1914)

Karl Barth was hardly the first theologian in his family. A pastoral vocation went back several generations in both paternal and maternal lines, and many others in the family were known for their warm Christian devotion. Karl's father, Johann Friedrich ("Fritz") Barth, was of pietist stock. He emphasized personal regeneration, love for Jesus, and the life of the soul with God; he sought lively holiness over dusty orthodoxy; he practiced the study of Scripture, personal discipline, and Christian fellowship with all seriousness. What set him apart from his pietistic peers, however, was Fritz Barth's receptivity to philosophical training and his eagerness to walk the *via media* between modernity and the more doctrinally orthodox, "positive" religion.[3] A man of many talents, he taught New Testament, Church

---

3. Eberhard Busch (*Karl Barth & the Pietists*, 11f.) summarizes Fritz Barth's concern over pietism's sectarian, anti-intellectualistic, legalistic, and enthusiastic tendencies, even while praising pietism's priority of life over doctrine, its view of spiritual rebirth, its close connection of justification and sanctification, and the idea of the coming kingdom of God. For a review of the pietist movement in its English, Reformed, and Lutheran expressions, see Stoeffler, *The Rise of Evangelical Pietism*. Karl Barth's own, chiefly antagonistic history of pietism written in the late 1920s can be found in *PTNC*, especially pp. 77–86, in which he describes it as the internal side of the absolutism of the age, but see Fulbrook's *Piety and Politics* for a more nuanced analysis of this alleged connection. Hereafter I use "pietism" for the general movement and "Pietism" for the original Lutheran movement.

history, and dogmatics for much of his career at the College of Preachers in Bern, all the while facing criticism from the left and the right. Naturally, he bestowed upon his children an amalgam of the rational and experiential, the philosophical and the doctrinal; and everything immersed in the pietistic insight that true religion lives from, by, and in the presence of God. That his eldest son, Karl, mounted in his office a framed picture of his father for most of his career "hints that the father's theological pilgrimage was in a real way a model for the son."[4]

Not that Karl was a model child. He was a rabble-rouser at school and in the neighborhood, getting into street fights with other boys and exercising his precocious personality at every turn. His interest in religion came to the surface under the thoughtful catechizing of Rev. Robert Aeschbacher in Bern, who was able to channel such strenuous energy in a new direction. Within a short time Karl declared that he would study theology. Fritz Barth's joy over the vocational decision turned to frustration, however, as his son requested to attend university in Marburg, a bastion of progressive, liberal theology. Professor Barth succeeded in sending his son to more moderate schools in Bern and Berlin, but after several years Karl's pleas to study in Marburg were granted.

It is difficult to pinpoint young Karl's Christian conversion, though in his first days as a student he experienced something significant while reading Immanuel Kant on good will: "I made a rule for myself: the simpler the better. . . . [W]hat I now looked for in books and from my professors was the true knowledge of simplicity."[5] Marburg was characterized by liberal Christianity's anthropocentric basis at the expense of "unreasonable" orthodox doctrines, but this was not what impressed Barth, who elsewhere had already studied under liberal professors like Adolf Harnack. What was special about Marburg was its professors' understanding of religion as a

---

4. Green, "Karl Barth's Life and Theology," 13. In a dramatic reappraisal of pietism late in life, Karl Barth reminisced about the juvenile hymnbook he sang from as a child, one compiled by Abel Burckhardt, whose presentation of the biblical narratives in their immanence was enough "to carry us through all the serried ranks of historicism and anti-historicism, mysticism and rationalism, orthodoxy, liberalism and existentialism—and to bring one back some day to the matter itself" (IV/2, 113). At his most generous, Barth would ask if the Pietists and Moravians "might be vindicated to the extent that they actually intended the reality, the coming, and the work of the Holy Spirit, and that on that basis they might emerge in a positive-critical light" (Barth, "Concluding Unscientific Postscript on Schleiermacher," 135). By 1960 Barth also would come to a posture of major agreement with one of pietism's figureheads, Count von Zinzendorf (Busch, "'Hochverehrter Herr Graf nicht so stürmisch!,'" 252).

5. Sermon, 13 Oct 1912, cited in Busch, *Karl Barth*, 35.

simple, original, ethical consciousness. Barth sat under Neo-Kantian philosophers Hermann Cohen and Paul Natorp, who in different ways sought to radicalize Kant's understanding of intuition, explaining all knowledge as a primal production of the "I" rather than a responsiveness to objective, external phenomena.[6] At the same time Barth caught the wave of a revived interest in the thought of Friedrich Schleiermacher (1768–1834). Schleiermacher, especially in his early work, had categorized religion as a primal feeling (*Gefühl*) prior to all other knowledge and action, a basic encounter with God in consciousness. Barth was attracted to this romantic simplicity, and came to view pietism itself as retrograde form of religious individualism.[7]

For Barth these ideas fused together effortlessly in the teaching of Marburg professor Wilhelm Herrmann. Like Schleiermacher, who a century earlier had declared himself a Moravian of a higher order, Herrmann taught piety philosophically and philosophy piously. Moreover, Herrmann himself was engaged in a fruitful appropriation of critical strains from Lutheran and Kantian thought. From Luther's two-kingdoms doctrine Herrmann championed a total de-identification between historical-knowledge and faith-knowledge. Working with Kant's distinction between phenomena (a thing's appearance) and noumena (the thing as such), Herrmann maintained a split between historical expression and the primal basis underlying it. That is, in matters of religion, one is ultimately concerned with the inner experience of God before and independently of its expression in the world. Herrmann espoused the anthropocentrism of the liberal tradition but took up an amplified *sola fide* in order to de-historicize the Christian religion.

By his own admission, Barth swallowed Herrmann's teachings whole.[8] Romantic idealism (by which I mean the sustained absoluteness of primal idea over particulars, even as the idea unfolds into all the particulars[9]) met Barth's hunger for simplicity. It was his conviction that

6. Much like Kant, Cohen relegated religion to a practical function. God was understood to be the "glue" holding together logic, ethics and aesthetics, a category of relation. John Lyden ("The Influence of Hermann Cohen on Karl Barth's Dialectical Theology," 167–83) argues that a straight line can be traced from Cohen to Barth with regard to the concept of the inscrutable "origin." Natorp's answer was more complex, modifying Schleiermacher's idea of religious feeling to cast religion as an inwardness which animates thinking, willing, and the perception of the beautiful (McCormack, *Karl Barth's Critically Realistic Dialectical Theology*, 46–48).

7. Busch, *Karl Barth & the Pietists*, 23.

8. Busch, *Karl Barth*, 45.

9. Cyril O'Regan in *The Heterodox Hegel* claims that the difference between

Herrmann, in tandem with Schleiermacher, provided the *terra firma* of experience sought by pietists and liberals alike. Even more impressive to Barth, Herrmann and Schleiermacher channeled religious feeling in an explicitly Christocentric way, explaining that, for all the interiority of the primal experience of faith, the vehicle of this experience is Christ—not His external appearances presented in Scripture but "the inner life of Jesus" as it impresses itself upon the individual's consciousness. A Christian is edified by inner contact with God through Christ; edified, that is, through the Christ-*idea* one finds moving in oneself and in the authentic, ethical lives of those who are also touched by His inner life. The letter—even if it be so sophisticated as the purified Ritschlianism of Ernst Troelsch—kills, but the Spirit gives life.

With regard to Easter proclamation, Herrmann taught that biblical testimonies concerning the revivification of Jesus' body are "a thick mist of legends." Instead one must see that "*the glory of his inner life* breaks through all these veils," for "*the essential contents* of that record . . . have the power to convince the conscience that that life is an undeniable fact."[10] If there is any proof, any "help of the appearances" for us today, Herrmann argued, it is the fact of the Church's birth and its ongoing communion. By ecclesiastical experience we affirm Jesus as risen in His trans-historical personality.[11] For Herrmann, resurrection is not a theory about the afterlife (either Jesus' or our own) so much as it is a way of talking about the living power of God available through the individual's perception of the Christ.

Barth, initially appointed in 1909 to a post as assistant pastor in a German-speaking Reformed church in Geneva,[12] followed the Hermannian line by teaching that Jesus' death and resurrection are the perennial

---

Schleiermacher and Hegel can be described as the difference between the "archaeological" and the "teleological" when addressing the intersection of faith and reason. Each is Anselmian in his own way, but Schleiermacher's thinking seeks to be "primitive" where Hegel's is "representative" (p.37). I venture to say that these are the very poles around which Barth gravitates for the rest of his career, and is what I mean henceforth by "romantic idealism."

10. Herrmann, *The Communion of the Christian with God*, 183, emphasis added.

11. Herrmann, *Systematic Theology*, 126. Cf. Forrest, *The Christ of History and of Experience*, 159–61.

12. Barth had not read Calvin seriously until working in Geneva. He says about his picking up of *Institutes of the Christian Religion*, "I did not experience any sudden conversion, and at first thought that I could very well combine idealist and romantic theology with the theology of the Reformation" (cited in Busch, *Karl Barth*, 57).

fount for the religious consciousness.[13] Barth impressed upon his first confirmands that Jesus' resurrection is the eruption of faith in Christian disciples, an attitudinal shift, an inspiration discovered, a belief that Jesus had completed His conciliatory work at the cross. The resurrection is *a spiritual event in believers* certifying Jesus' significance for us and leading us to follow in His path.[14] Consequently, Christians should not claim anything about Jesus' bodily renewal. That, if anything, would be to historicize his resurrection. It would deny the infinite power available through Jesus' inner life. Barth's 1910 parish magazine article at Easter claimed that any evidence for Jesus' revivification is inadequate for faith, which by definition is quite independent of proofs and counterproofs. Liberated from external facts, Easter belief is the living power of Jesus, the power to be free from the influence of the visible and "provable," freedom bestowed by the influence of that which is not verifiable by normal science, namely, *das persönliche innere Leben Jesu*.[15] Parroting Herrmann, Pastor Barth taught that "[t]he historical Jesus becomes the resurrected living Christ in the congregation of Christ."[16]

Barth maintains silence about the doctrine of the general resurrection, though he wagers an occasional murky thought on immortality. Since according to his philosophical commitments any theological statement has to be grounded in religious consciousness, not historical world-order, any kind of hope for personal afterlife must derive from an extension of the transcendence one experiences in the here and now. If anything, Barth harkened back to Kant, who in place of the resurrection postulated the unprovable but "necessary" tenet of the immortality of the soul as a buttress to his ethics in *Critique of Practical Reason*. At one point he regurgitates Kant's thought with a mystical hue, teaching that the individual's living from "good will" completes itself in a "measureless future" through the

---

13. Karl Barth, "Mit Christus Gestorben," church newsletter, 18 Mar 1910, in *GA* III.22, 33–36.

14. Karl Barth, "Konfirmandenunterricht, 1909/10," in *GA* I.18, 48–50.

15. "Ob Jesus gelebt hat?," letter from Karl Barth to Wilhelm Loew, 30 Apr/1 May 1910, in *GA* III.22, 37–45. Barth therefore appreciated the criticisms leveled at the Easter traditions by Reimarus, Strauss, and Harnack, though he was wholly uninterested in their attempts to explain the missing body.

16. Cited in McCormack, *Karl Barth's Critically Realistic Dialectical Theology*, 76. Likewise, Barth in 1913 equates the resurrection with the "irresistible impression" of the Savior's life upon Peter, an impression left even before Easter morning!: "Jesus had been resurrected before He died—long before" (Karl Barth, sermon, 29 June 1913, in *GA* I.8, 323–24).

passage of death, since by that good will one has lived in God's goodness.[17] But Barth's reluctance to codify thoughts on immortality into concrete doctrine follows the lead of Schleiermacher and Herrmann.[18]

Along with pietism turned to romantic idealism, a third ideology impacted young Barth: religious socialism. Sensitive to the plight of the common workers from a young age, he was introduced to a Christian version of socialism by his catechizing pastor. During his university years Barth also was exposed to the thought of activist Leonhard Ragaz. Barth's early lectures, articles, and sermons have brought to light just how formative religious socialism was to him. It gave him a framework to think through the Church's identification with the poor. It permitted him to stand back from world forces, whether the self-justification of nationalism or the faceless avarice of capitalism. More germane to this study is the way religious socialism imparted to him a response to the privatization of pietism. In Barth's assessment, pietism's obsession with one's inner, authentic spirituality spawned legalism, which in turn slipped into a kind of cultural stratification, which in turn baptized the inequalities of bourgeois capitalism. Socialism permitted no such privatizing decay. Similarly, socialism emphasized the whole person, body and soul together,[19] rejecting the crass my-soul-is-going-to-heaven-when-I-die theology of otherworldly Christians. Socialism could do the same for introverted romantic impulses, forcing the ethical feeling to correspond with the ethical deed.

Barth had plenty of opportunities to express his political views after taking his second pastoral post in 1911, this time in Safenwil, an industrializing village in the Aargau canton. A large portion of his parishioners suffered the loss of their lands while transitioning to textile jobs with miserable wages. Almost immediately the "Red Pastor" took up socialist causes in that area, organizing protests, lecturing on workers' rights, and helping to establish unions. I am not convinced that Barth can be called "a

---

17. "Konfirmanden-Unterricht 1910–1911," *GA* I.18, 73–74. No wonder Barth was criticized by the Safenwil church leadership committee for his short, meager funeral sermons (Busch, *Karl Barth*, 62).

18. E.g., Schleiermacher, *The Christian Faith*, 709–14; Herrmann, *Systematic Theology*, 93–96, 129.

19. "With its 'materialism' [socialism] preaches to us a word which stems not from Jesus himself, yet certainly from his Spirit. The word goes like this: '*The end of the way of God is the affirmation of the body*'" (cited in Hunsinger, *Karl Barth and Radical Politics*, 29). While the socialist edge fades into the background, Friedrich Oetinger's phrase crops up again in 1919, when Barth preaches that "the end of the way of God is embodiment" (Karl Barth, sermon, 20 Apr 1919, in *GA* I.39, 162), and again in 1924 (*RD*, 194) and 1926 (*UCR* III, 416).

liberation theologian" in either his early or later years, but at Safenwil one finds in him an anticipation of liberation theology's critique of the worldly powers, even of the absolutism of theological liberalism. Irrespective of its overall political utility, religious socialism sensitized Barth to God's judgment on human arrogance in its manifold forms. It taught him to question the present order and to long for another. From it Barth was equipped with a revolutionary, anti-bourgeois spirit, making him wary of anything that smacked of quietism or absolutism. More than pietism or romantic idealism, socialism primed him for the impending crisis of World War I.

Later in life Barth would described the horrific event which occurred in October of 1914:

> One day . . . stands out in my personal memory as a black day. Ninety-three German intellectuals impressed public opinion by their proclamation in support of the war policy of Wilhelm II and his counselors. Among these intellectuals I discovered to my horror almost all of my theological teachers [including Harnack and Herrmann] whom I had greatly venerated. In despair over what this indicated about the signs of the time I suddenly realized that I could not any longer follow either their ethics and dogmatics or their understanding of the Bible and of history. For me at least, 19th-century theology no longer held any future.[20]

Liberal theology, in its speculative and historicist forms alike, Barth renounced. He recanted self-grounded ethics. He turned from the totalizing, so-called scientific approach to the Scriptures. Yet observe what Barth does *not* say in the quote above, viz., that he rejected the nineteenth century's subjective epistemology, its reliance on personal encounter of God as the foundation of "religious individualism." Still—and this was his true revolution—Barth realized at that time that *the anthropocentric foundation* had to be dug up and replaced with a new cornerstone. Romantic Idealism (built atop the Enlightenment and pietism) had been too uncritical, slipping into the deleterious absolutism of the nineteenth century and the Great War. But did the whole edifice have to be discarded? What if the philosophical apparatuses of Kant, Schleiermacher, and Herrmann were to find traction upon a different, still more basic, axiom? How does one speak confidently about God in His immanence—yet critically about the human consciousness to which He is immanent?

---

20. Barth, *The Humanity of God*, 14. Cf. Barth, *The Theology of Schleiermacher*, 264, which also mentions his rejection of German exegesis and preaching.

ESCHATOLOGIZING THE DIALECTIC (1915–19)

The months after the announcement of war were a period of inner agitation for Barth, an agitation reflected in the themes of judgment and spiritual warfare peppering his sermons. Through this season he professed confidence in the providence of God, but it was painfully clear to him that his theological paradigm had been fragmented quite seriously. What could one say against Herrmann and the Kaiser's theologians, all of whom insisted that religious experience dictated the German holy war? Barth had cultivated an ability to think outside the box by affiliating with the socialist cause, even going so far as to join the Social Democratic Party in January 1915. But socialism itself was insufficient: its inability to prevent Prussian imperialism aside, it was doing little to articulate a new theological paradigm for Barth. By the end of 1914 the European socialists were already split between Ragaz's confident, vocal, activist ideology, and Kutter's tempered, patient, contemplative approach. Barth found himself sympathetic to, and frustrated with, each side. Socialism itself was caught between activism and quietism, between an "over-realized Christianity" in ethical action (Ragaz) and an over-encumbered negativity (Kutter), between the Yes and No of God. Was this not the very problem of the religious consciousness itself, God's immanence in His transcendence? However much these two dimensions seemed at odds, the positions had to be reconcilable, if only in God.

In this dark hour a friendship blossomed between Barth and another young pastor by the name of Eduard Thurneysen. He, like Barth, was grappling with religious socialism and its response to the war. He too was going through the birth pangs of a paradigm shift. The two ministers regularly traversed the miles between their churches in order to smoke and converse. At one such rendezvous it was Thurneysen who murmured under his breath what they were both thinking: that they needed a new foundation, something "totally other."[21]

It was Thurneysen who arranged a personal meeting with the man who would catalyze Barth's thinking: Christoph Blumhardt. Blumhardt, a spiritual director in the German village of Bad Boll, was a Schwäbian Pietist in the Lutheran church. Even more than his father, Johann, he was a prophetic voice for his generation. In eschatological fashion he claimed that the kingdom of God had drawn near, and that it depended upon faithful hearts to receive this movement of the Holy Spirit. A staunch opponent

---

21. Cited in Busch, *Karl Barth*, 97.

of those who would spiritualize the kingdom, Blumhardt had become a member (indeed, an officer) of the Social Democrat Party, resulting in the loss of his ordination and pension. He never fully subscribed to the socialists' secular theorizing or their violent methods, and he ultimately left the party after 1906 to pursue the kingdom of God in an overtly theo-political mode. He continued to support the socialist cause as a "parable" of the coming kingdom, though in his later years he came to see the world as a problem more than a site of promise.[22] What remained unshaken was his tremendous confidence in the power of the Victor, Jesus Christ. Optimist and cynic rolled into one, the prophetic Blumhardt seemed to bridge the gap between pietism and socialism, between biblical Christianity and revolutionary politics, between waiting and hastening.[23] But what really captured Barth was how Blumhardt moved between the two poles in the spirit of *eschatological immediacy*. "Blumhardt always begins right away with God's presence, might, and purpose," Barth wrote in September 1916; "he starts out from God; he does not begin by climbing upwards to Him by means of contemplation and deliberation. God is the end, and because we already know Him as the beginning, we may await his consummating acts."[24]

Barth and Thurneysen made the trek to Bad Boll, visiting with Blumhardt for the better part of a week in April 1915. While the precise content of those days remains a mystery, it is not difficult to imagine what kind of things they might have heard from the cheerful, apocalyptic pastor. Consider a message from Blumhardt a year earlier:

> All those who believe, all those who truly penetrate into the reality of Jesus' life, will no longer see death but pass into eternity like shining lights. Thus a light will also shine on the earth. This light must come from beyond the earth, from heaven. It must come from the place where Jesus Christ now rules and triumphs and judges. A day must break in upon the earth. Yet this day

22. Collins Winn, *"Jesus Is Victor!"*, 147.

23. Cf. Barth, "Past and Future," 40–45.

24. Barth, afterword to *Action in Waiting* by Christoph Blumhardt, 219. "Very naively, but with axiomatic certainty, they [the Blumhardts] were thinking of the reality of the risen and living Jesus himself, acting and speaking as a distinctive factor no less actual today than yesterday . . . the Jesus who has already come and will come again, and who is thus present to his people and—unknown to it—the world" (Barth, *The Christian Life*, 259). To Barth's mind, Jesus' broad and futural presence opened up the future: "In the midst of this hopeless confusion," Barth later relayed, "it was the message of . . . Christian *hope* which above all began to make sense to me" (quoted in Busch, *Karl Barth*, 84).

cannot come from the earth; it cannot be brought about by new human thoughts, new inventions or great deeds of men. This new day must come from eternity.

We all live in eternity, Blumhardt concludes, "Yet the eternity in which Jesus Christ lives is a higher eternity, a brighter one, one which penetrates more deeply into our lives. For Jesus Christ is the one who rose from the dead."[25]

A few observations are in order. From the above quote we see that Blumhardt supposes a *disjuncture between time and eternity*, and that light shines only by God's breaking-in, for "it cannot come from the earth." Second, salvation is a *participation in eternity*, where those who "penetrate into the reality of Jesus' life" enter into this state. Still, thirdly, this victory has *social ramifications*, for it is society that is illuminated; this light will shine "*on* the earth." Eternity is not a heaven-going or a spiritual reality apart from earthly action; on the contrary, it is intensely social and bodi-ly.[26] Fourth, all of these things are *future-oriented*, summed up under and mediated by the profound truth that Jesus Christ is risen from the dead. In His resurrection He comes to bring eternity to time. Indeed, one finds in Blumhardt a relentless appeal to the resurrection of Jesus as the basis for all God's work in the present time, so much so that the Easter miracle is almost indistinguishable from the work of the Spirit in the Church age, and the Second Person in His glorified state indecipherable from the Third Person.[27] What results from this move, in any case, is that the present time must be understood as dominated and governed by a final truth, the truth from the future, the truth that *Jesus ist Sieger*. The "already but not yet," the perfect amongst the imperfect, is controlled by the presence of the risen Word. Christoph Blumhardt (along with the writings of his father[28]) had given Barth a kind of resurrection framework.

---

25. In Lejeune, *Christoph Blumhardt and His Message*, 235.

26. "Believing does not mean thinking; belief is being, and being means that things happen" (cited in Collins Winn, "*Jesus Is Victor!*," 116). This world-connected dyna-mism extends to the doctrine of God for both Blumhardts, as drawn out in Bodamer, "The Life and Work of Johann Christoph Blumhardt," 59ff.

27. Cf. Collins Winn, "*Jesus Is Victor!*," 121f.

28. Barth read Zündel's biography of J. C. Blumhardt in June 1915 and found it deeply compelling. The elder Blumhardt became more influential to Barth's work in *KD*, though in the short run the mantle of influence fell on the junior Blumhardt, whose eschatological theology concerned itself with the healing not so much of the body as the body politic (ibid., xv).

From the Blumhardtian thoughts came something of a dialectic, a back-and-forth movement of theological thought. Jesus Christ in His resurrection-movement necessitates a contrast between heaven and earth, but His coming also heals everything and leads it toward divine unity. The otherworldly resurrection-power of Jesus punctures the world in order to heal it from within. As sinful human hearts receive His transcendent grace, they see and act from a spiritual perspective. Eternity breaks into time through the Word of God, reorienting human existence to the future.

Barth's preaching brimmed with victorious optimism upon his return from Bad Boll.[29] Truly, in the months and years ahead he would exploit many of Blumhardt's themes and watchwords, encouraging his congregation to rejoice in the Victor, to hasten and wait for the perfect kingdom of God, to look for the future rather than hold onto the religious past, to pray "Thy kingdom come," to know that "world is world, but God is God." Through Blumhardt the resurrection of Jesus became for Barth a touchstone of the critical otherness of divine intervention in the world. Consider Barth's Easter sermon in 1917, in which he contrasts the resurrection-world with our own world. In our own world "King Mammon stands before us and pounds his claws at us, making us into joyless, hounded slaves," where, devoid of eternity, our wistfulness is "a religion in which we truly have an intoxication, a chloroform, but no real consolation, no serious help."[30] Against our present world the resurrection of Jesus comes, subjecting the enemies of God, taking them captive. What Jesus perceived and embodied through His life and death was the newness of God able to conquer this world. Easter, then, is the proclamation of this victory: "Hear the Easter message: This world is no more! A new world has erupted, as on the first Creation-day!"[31] The future of God has drawn nigh with grace and judgment, for this King is for the world even in His opposition to it.

Interestingly, Blumhardt's eschatological preaching led Barth to re-weigh his pietist heritage. Barth had inherited his family's library, and over the course of the Great War he read attentively the works of F. C. Oetinger, J. A. Bengel, and, perhaps most seminally, the millennial theology of J. T.

29. The prophetic Word given to us today, he said to his congregation, contains the future. "For in God today and tomorrow are one. He who has recognized [*erkannt*] what he is today knows also what he will be tomorrow. . . . The truth of the world is verily the world of eternity. And since we have heard its Word, we have total clarity about all that is before us" (Karl Barth, sermon, 25 April 1915, in *GA* I.27, 168).

30. Karl Barth, sermon, 8 Apr 1917, *GA* I.32, 138–39.

31. Ibid., 140.

Beck. He appreciated their intense, eschatological outlook, though their slip toward hyper-subjective Christianity continued to feel problematic. Barth's opinion of pietism was not helped any by the arrival of a revivalist by the name of Vetter. To Barth, Vetter's revival seemed mechanical, self-ish, and psychological in nature, and the memory of it undoubtedly was part of the reason Barth lambasted pietistic religiosity over the next few years. Such Christianity had nothing to do with the glorious disruption of the resurrection.

Barth and Thurneysen agreed that they must seek out a new basis, to begin again at the beginning, not through a rereading of Kant or Hegel, but by returning to the Bible itself.[32] Barth had occasion to develop his thoughts on the resurrection through his first major writing project, a commentary on Paul's epistle to the Romans. In 1916 Barth took to writing it, not for publication but (much like Schleiermacher with his *Speeches*) in order to explain himself to his circle of friends. After some early fits and starts, it was completed in a rush and put into print at the very end of 1918.[33]

One finds in the first *Römerbrief* a flurry of attacks on romanticism, idealism, religious socialism, and pietism—though the last of these, inter-preted as religious individualism, receives the brunt of Barth's polemic. The sin of pietism is its insistence that the *lone soul* should become an end in itself, that salvation is the salvation of the *individual*, that redemption is only a heaven-going for the *self*, that religion is a divorcing oneself from the world in order to be set *apart*. "Better to be in hell with the world church," Barth rails, "than in heaven with pietists of a lower or higher order, of an older or more modern observance," for Christ Himself did not seek inner peace but descended to the place of torment.[34] The selfishness of religious individualism breeds the legalistic pride characteristic of the carnal nature. Offered grace, the religious person settles for law; sensing liberation, he ensnares himself; being addressed from without, she turns inward; finding God, such a person devours oneself. The religious consciousness is, to use Barth's preferred epithet, a "contradiction" (*Widerspruch*). But God is not religion. Rather, God contradicts the world's contradiction through His

---

32. It lies outside our scope to examine this rich biblical reeducation to which Barth submitted himself, but see Burnett, *Karl Barth's Theological Exegesis* and Donald Wood, "'Ich sah mit Staunen,'" 184–98. Likewise, this study can only appreciate in passing the formative role of the task of preaching upon the early Barth (see *GD* §2 and Migliore, "Karl Barth's First Lectures in Dogmatics," in *GD* I, xx–xxv).

33. Not 1919, its listed date of printing (Busch, *Karl Barth*, 106).

34. 1*Rö*, 363, in *GA* II.16.

passion: He dies our death, then comes with resurrection power, which alone "makes the *contradiction* of our present situation understandable, tolerable and fruitful."[35]

In 1*Rö* Barth describes God's judgment of humanity in temporal terms. There can be no confusion of eternity and history, but there really is a conjunction of God and the world in Jesus Christ. The resurrection is the Day of the Lord, the overcoming of sinful present-time with a "new world-time," "an end of all time," an eschatological reality in which one must conclude that "time has been halted by eternity."[36] Humans as such cannot cross into eternity at will. They are judged by the risen Lord.

1*Rö* also contains positive elements about God's resurrection judgment. The Coming One's intersection with time can be apprehended by faith. Moreover, humans get to be a part of the revolution of the kingdom of God; they usher it in by participating in its mysterious growth. Through the resurrection God's presence is implanted into history, growing there in supernatural contemporaneousness with history, weaving a critical but rejuvenating force into the fabric of all occurrence. It is an immanent start to world transformation, for, despite its miraculous origin, the heavenly kingdom sprouts up *within* the world as an alternative to the world's possibilities. Quite concretely, Jesus Christ *is* the embodiment of eternity, and His resurrected life, extended to believers, provides eruptions of intervening power in which time's self-destructive patterns are overridden. Thus the kingdom of God can be said to have entered the stream of time, contradicting "mechanical" religion with something "organic."[37] The young Barth holds that the law of the Spirit has now overtaken the law of sin and death "as the developing energy [*die wachstümliche Energie*] of the coming world of God";[38] God has planted a "life seed [*Lebenskeim*]" in us.[39] Those who abide in Christ sustain genuine spiritual growth even as their true life is hidden by mortality. What is more, the life seed must and will sprout forth its shoots out to the world. Religious introversion, then, can have nothing to do with the moment of faith, which, though conceived inwardly, is resurrection power with outgoing movement. Even though the risen Christ alone has union with God, Christians through Christ live

35. Ibid., 322.
36. Ibid., 86.
37. Ibid., 21, 90.
38. Ibid., 298.
39. Ibid., 310. Cf. *WGWM*, 25.

in the kingdom of God, understanding "that each of their epochs (even theirs specifically) has immediacy to God."[40]

All of this Barth accomplishes by playing off of the Pauline ethical antithesis between flesh and Spirit, except now flesh is the way of religious individualism, and Spirit the way of divine possibility. The latter must subsume and conquer the former. Such victory of the Spirit over the flesh is apparent first in the resurrection of Jesus Christ, who

> participates in two worlds, two histories, and the one is the other enclosed [*abgeschlossen*] and overcome [*überwunden*] through Him. . . . What He *was* is left behind. As He completed his course as a part of that old world, His actual, inner being broke out forcefully in His resurrection from the dead . . . proclaiming Him as God's Son, in whom the history of an alternate humanity has been inaugurated.[41]

Negatively, the death of Jesus signals the negation of the old world, the termination of the vanity of human striving, achievement, and possibilities. Positively, the resurrection of Jesus proposes a new world in the midst of the old, a victorious force for a new humanity. The resurrection, then, is a kind of counter-principle to the inbred religious world. Being the power of the Origin (*Ursprung*) of all things, the resurrection invigorates the creation for external action even as it leads all things back into oneness with God.[42]

A similar sentiment appears in Barth's Easter Sunday sermon of 1919. Still in an organic view of the kingdom of God, he preaches about the fact that earthly existence has its limits,

> But that which has borders also has a Beyond. A Beyond, that which we are not able to observe, but which nonetheless is necessarily part of the whole, not as the warp, but as the weft [*Einschlag*] in the fabric. There is no this-world without a Beyond, as there is no fabric made only of warp. This-world without the Beyond, time without eternity is supreme dubiousness, questionableness; it is the mortal, the corruptible, the perishable. Therefore eternity is a new thing, a totally other, which must come into time. The final weft in time is the content of the Bible. A different, new, upper world with new, other orders and relations, a world in which death is no more, takes a step into our

---

40. Ibid., 106–7.

41. 1*Rö*, 13, in *GA* II.16.

42. Cf. Brazier, "Barth's First Commentary on Romans (1919)," 391–92.

world to interlock [*verschlingen*] it in itself, so that it becomes the whole.[43]

Even here Barth can speak of eternity as "totally other," though the antagonism between heaven and earth is mollified by a sense of constructive relationship. The divine presence injects the present world-process with a countervailing force so that the world will not disintegrate. The resurrection is the heavenly dimension, the genuine knowledge of God which holds together the world by overtaking its self-centered religion. Eternity is weft to time's warp: that, we might say, is the gist of the dialectic in Barth's early understanding of Easter.

As Barth would soon find out, his dialectic was doubly problematic. On one front 1*Rö* was too radical, opposing the divine and the earthly so thoroughly that the world of the Spirit seemed to sneer at history as such. Its dualism seemed to orphan the appearances of religious history in favor of fantastical spiritual realities. Unsurprisingly, biblical historians the likes of Adolf Jülicher and Karl Ludwig Schmidt labeled Barth a Marcionite. On the other front, Barth's eschatological language was not radical *enough*, giving the impression that the resurrection enters in as the divine side of a necessary world-process. How are we to understand God's world as *totally* other if it grows "organically" in the contaminated soil of world history? With good reason Graham Ward says that "Barth's approach to dialectics in the first edition of *Romans*—whilst emphasizing *Krisis* and *Diakrisis*—is much more Hegelian" than the second edition.[44] That is, 1*Rö* leaves the door open for the idealistic possibility of the happy resolution of dualism into monism.

I would add a third difficulty: the dialectic of 1*Rö* permits little to be said about the final state of humanity. God's future comes to this earth, sprouts, and overrides the earth, but it does not offer hope beyond death. The commentary prefers the phrase "the power of the resurrection" to "the resurrection of the dead" so as to draw attention to the transformation of

---

43. Karl Barth, sermon, 20 April 1919, in *GA* I, *Predigten* 1919, 155.

44. Ward, "Barth, Hegel and the Possibility for Christian Apologetics," 56. I might offer here a cautionary note about finding too much Hegel in the early Barth, if only because of the fact that he did not read him carefully until his professorship at Münich. Chung's observation about Barth's ineradicable romantic sensibility is also important: "Unlike the Hegelian dialectical method, where a mutual mediation of all positions and negations appears as the synthesis in a historical immanent process, Barth conceives that synthesis as Origin is not identical with the dialectical movement in thesis and negation. Rather, Origin is the condition of the possibility as well as the realizing, creative reality of Yes and No" (*Karl Barth*, 185–86).

the present world. Around this time Barth says, "One is taken with the vision of an immortality or even of a future life here on earth in which the righteous will of God breaks forth, prevails, and is done as it is done in heaven" (*WGWM*, 26). But by this he hardly means to describe the immortality of the soul or the resurrection of the flesh in the temporal, actual "afterwards"; he means the possibility of the power of the future coming in to change the present. In this theology of hope little room is left for a doctrine of final glorification. There is only the Easter "echo" of Jesus' disciples "who listen, watch, and wait" (*WGWM*, 31). Resurrection is faith-based transformation and praxis for this life. No more is mentioned.

If Barth accomplished something of importance in this stage, it was his efforts to drive an initial wedge between the eternal wellspring and its religious apprehension, between the divine *Ursprung* and the human *Gefühl*. By attributing to Him a wholly different ground outside the bounds of history, 1*Rö* sang "a very hymn in praise of the Godness of God."[45] Grounded in the pietist's sense of the seminal presence of God and the romantic idealist's sense of the encompassing subjectivity of God, but tempered by the socialist impulse and the apocalyptic optimism of Blumhardt, Barth was walking on, if not holy ground, fertile ground.

RADICALIZING THE DIALECTIC (1919–24)

The next five years for Barth were the most productive (and complicated) of his life. This study will be content to show how he radicalized the dialectic of his theology, that is, how he focused the divine and the earthly terms to show forth an unmistakable *difference*. God is God and humanity is humanity. Interestingly, Barth starts from God's immanence, the reality that He has made contact with us. But from this initial contact-point of immanence almost everything Barth says about the event of revelation has to do with God's total transcendence, His judgment upon human existence, the ripping away of the heavenly from the earthly, the contrast between the living Lord and mortal creatures. In the writings of this tempestuous period, not for a second will Barth allow the earthly to rest in naïve unity with the divine, or the human spirit to blend with God's. And during this period "the resurrection of the dead" is Barth's all-important formulation. It best captures the dynamic of the movement of the living God upon dead humanity.

---

45. Hartwell, *The Theology of Karl Barth*, 9.

Almost immediately after the publication of his first commentary, Barth sensed the inadequacy of its language. It needed to establish a stronger qualitative difference between God and humanity, so the two could not be confused at any point. The fabric analogy could not work, for the warp and weft making up cloth are interlocking threads; they are parts of a larger whole; they are functionally indecipherable. Not so for the kingdom of God with the kingdoms of this earth. God is not the German people. God is not the Kaiser's war or the Russian revolution. God is not the pietist's fervor or the contemplative's feelings or the Church's plans. God is God, utterly distinct from world's machinations. God is God, and any confusion with the world is sheer idolatry.

The force with which Barth pounds the distinction between God and the world sometimes covers up the basic issue he is interested in addressing: the possibility of speaking of God's very real immanence. The difficulty with immanence stems from the nature of revelation itself: God approaches the world with dangerously close proximity, so close, in fact, that idols can spring up all around. Yes, divine disclosure is the gift of the heavenly Father *to* us; it is Christ *with* us; it is the Spirit *in* us. But how can we receive the Father's gift without thinking of ourselves as gods? How can we receive Christ without subsuming Him into our history? And how can the Holy Spirit draw near without us mistaking Him for our own spirits? God is "in" us, yes. But "in" cannot mean "of." Immanence never comes without transcendence. God's *within* is also His *beyond*. If Barth agonizes at this stage of his life, it is because of his intimate discernment of this problem.

With the problem of immanence in mind, Barth formulated the Tambach lecture of September 1919. Titled "The Christian's Place in Society," the turgid presentation was much more about *God's* place in *creation*. Impressively, it contains most of the core ideas of 2*Rö*. The lecture begins with the premise of "Christ in us," which, sounding very much like the organic eschatology of 1*Rö*, is "a formative life-energy within all our weak, tottering movements of thought, a unity in a time which is out of joint" (*WGWM*, 273). But it becomes clear that Barth is heightening the sense of the total transcendence of God in His intercourse with creation. God's kingdom is not the would-be victory march of the evolving dominant culture, neither is it equivalent to one single contravening movement pitted against the establishment. He is *the* movement, *the* Mover, and therefore the One who sets Himself apart from all movements in time. Not even for a moment can the Origin be confused with historical phenomena (even if those phenomena be so sacrosanct as Christian socialism or the family or heartfelt religion), for "[t]he so called 'religious experience' is a wholly derived, secondary, fragmentary form of the divine" (*WGWM*, 285). God alone is the original. To pursue the world for a second without this transcendent consciousness, to consider things as such, is to pursue "dead" facts uncontained in the eternity which holds them together and gives them meaning.

Barth's preferred language here is, much more than 1*Rö*, that of resurrection. It is the movement *par excellence*: "I mean a movement from above, a movement from a third dimension, so to speak, which transcends and yet penetrates all these movements and gives them their inner meaning and motive," says Barth. "I mean the movement of God in history or, otherwise expressed, the movement of God in consciousness, the movement whose power and import are revealed in the resurrection of Jesus Christ from the dead" (*WGWM*, 283). God enters history by entering "consciousness," and this appearance of God (or deity of Christ) in our primal imaginations is what resurrection is. As the Lord comes from His self-contained holiness into consciousness (and from there to society), humans participate in the meaning and power which is nothing less than "the bodily resurrection of Christ from the dead" (*WGWM*, 287). For Barth, resurrection is the God-instantiated invasion of deity *into the world of flesh*—and the "bodily" resurrection for that reason alone. Unfortunately, this latter insight is not spelled out, and he fails to make clear why "resurrection" is the best way to describe the human's encounter with God in this "movement."

What Barth makes clear at any rate is that there is a severe dialectic inherent in God's activity in the world. God is the fount and the end of all movements, "the revolution which is before all revolutions," an original preceding and guaranteeing the synthesis of all historical theses and antitheses in time, a basis out of which "both thesis and antithesis arise" (*WGWM*, 299). In revelation one is called to see from this original position, and from it to love the world and have peace about its motions even while rejecting all such motions as inherent expressions of the kingdom of God. God really does perceive the world as a whole, and really does hold the fragments together. In this monistic sense, Barth chimes, "We can permit ourselves to be more romantic than the romanticists and more humanistic than the humanists" (*WGWM*, 303). But everything about us must be undone in order to rise to this level of understanding. In the power of the resurrection believers accept "the annulment of the[ir] creaturehood," that is, "the subversion and conversion of this present and of every conceivable world, into the judgment and the grace which the presence of God entails" (*WGWM*, 288, 318). Only in the presence of the transcendent God may a person, annulled and reconstituted by faith, see and enjoy the summation of history.

During this time Barth's Platonism is perspicuous. Under one umbrella he places Kohelet and Socrates, the pietists and Schleiermacher, Bach and Michelangelo, Paul and Socrates. They all perceive the unperceivable, Barth says. They all met God and were able to say something theological because they understood the crisis at hand.[46] Somehow they all perceived God's Idea, Jesus Christ, in whom is the awareness of immediacy to God. They comprehended the transcendent form which lies beyond the appearances even as it surrounds and is in them. Barth's older brother Heinrich, a professor of philosophy, was certainly responsible for impressing Platonism upon him in the form of a critical *Ursprungsphilosophie*.[47]

Perhaps even more influential upon Barth during this time were a number of biblical studies he conducted, including major ones on Romans, Ephesians, and 1 Corinthians. While his studies of Ephesians and Romans helped fill out his thoughts on the unification of the world in its transcendent Origin, it was 1 Corinthians that contributed the most to the language of his dialectical method. In November 1919, just two months after the Tambach lecture, a startled Barth wrote to Eduard Thurneysen about his study on 1 Corinthians 15, saying, "The chapter is the key to the whole letter . . . and out of its last wisdom comes disclosures about this and that, striking several of us lately like pulses from an electric ray."[48] Was the resurrection of the dead a skeleton key to Scripture—if not to all theological method? Undoubtedly, Barth had been primed for a shift in his dialectic, goaded by his philosophical readings, reviews of 1*Rö*, and his disappointment with the absolutist turn of socialism into Bolshevism.[49] Still, why did 1 Corinthians 15 precipitate a new theological approach?

---

46. That he accords revelation to all these crises, pagan or Israelite or Christian alike, indicates that Barth's *is* a "theology of crisis," counter to claims that Barth intended to present only the crisis of theology (e.g., McCormack, *Karl Barth's Critically Realistic Dialectical Theology*, 209–16).

47. See ibid., 218–26, for the influence of Heinrich Barth.

48. Karl Barth to Eduard Thurneysen, 11 Nov 1919, in *GA* V.3, 350. By no accident, the imagery comes from Plato's *Meno*, in which Socrates' teaching holds the listener in thrall like an electric ray (cf. *ER*, 271).

49. For the first two factors, cf. *ER*, 3–4; for the last, cf. Chung, *Karl Barth*, 165ff.

What we can say is that Barth found in the phrase "the resurrection of the dead" a way to relate God and humanity in the event of revelation. God is the resurrection; we are the dead being raised. In "the resurrection of the dead" we hear grace and judgment. We hear God's Yes and God's No. We hear unity with God and separation from Him. We come up against the terms of life and death. The eschatological phrase captures the unique paradox of God's interaction with the world. In short, Barth mobilizes his radicalized dialectic via an existentialized interpretation of the phrase, "the resurrection of the dead."

The first strong expression of Barth's radicalized dialectic appears in "Biblical Questions, Insights, and Vistas," his speech at the Aarau Student Conference in April 1920. He begins by reminding his listeners that Scripture is not concerned with the historical so much as the divine basis behind history. Therefore historical and religiously emotional inquiries are incapacitated in their approaches to the Bible. Instead one must approach the Bible as "the document of the axiomatic" (*WGWM*, 52) and the "key to the mind" which conceives the inconceivable origin (*WGWM*, 62). Barth's interest in Scripture is based on interest about its theme.

To apprehend God, Barth argues, one must go beyond human limit. And that limit is mortality, death. By definition one cannot go beyond that limit—but the believer hopes for transcendence. With Franz Overbeck's *Todesweisheit* in mind, Barth muses on mortality as the marker of the divine source of life.

> To understand the New Testament Yes as anything but the Yes contained in the No, is not to understand it at all. Life comes from *death*! Death is the source of all. *Thence* comes the New Testament's knowledge of God as the Father, the Original, the Creator of heaven and earth. (*WGWM*, 80–1)

Søren Kierkegaard's existentialism speaks of this paradox too. The miraculous leap of faith happens at the very precipice of being. Faith means "death" for all our possibilities and powers—but there we find God. The resurrection of the dead gives us confidence that "life" indeed comes from "death."

Remarkably, Barth finishes the lecture with something resembling an Easter sermon. He lists off five meanings of the resurrection: the sovereignty of God, eternity, the new world, a new corporeality, and humanity's "one experience." Barth's thoughts are rather jumbled at this point. Still, the most important critical feature of his work in 2*Rö* and *AT* is here evident, viz., that while eternity "comprehends" time, time is not eternity.

Finitum non capax infiniti! The dead must really die in the presence of God if they are to share in His life.

Barth's language about the resurrection of the body in "Biblical Questions" is impenetrable. He speaks of a new and bodily future, but "future" in this case means the divine perception of the present, a perception mysteriously shared in revelation. Bodily resurrection, then, is a statement about a higher order of life lived even as one goes through the vicissitudes of life in the flesh:

> As [the body] participates in the incomprehensibility, the vexatiousness, and the darkness of our existence, it must *also* participate in the new possibility beyond the boundary of our existence. . . . A change of predicates takes place between the sowing in corruption and the raising in incorruption (or, otherwise expressed, the raising into a consciousness of God). The subject remains the same. But since the subject is born anew . . . and is conscious of itself in God, *ultimately* there can remain in it no "below" what[so]ever. (*WGWM*, 93, emphasis added)

In rather Athanasian language, Barth describes a double participation: a human participates in the human nature, but is also "born anew," becoming a participant in the divine nature. The ego in revelation is a double-subject; it must affirm itself in flesh *and* "itself in God." It needs the purification and unity which are characteristic only of ultimacy. Unfortunately, Barth does not describe this final state. The "resurrection of the body" is the expression of the penultimate double-existence: the physical human being in time caught up and transcendentally perceived from the divine vista of revelation.

What comes to fruition as early as 1919 is Barth's radicalized dialectic, a movement of God in the world in which the world is subverted in order to conform to its glorious Origin. Since Barth's idealistic structure fits within the family of Platonic patterns, one might state his dialectic philosophically: eternity judges and enfolds time; the Idea relativizes and includes the appearances. But to dwell upon philosophical formulations is to misrepresent Barth. He preferred a biblical-eschatological formulation derived from the Pauline texts: revelation is *the resurrection of the dead*. The thesis ("dead" humanity) is confronted by its totally-other antithesis (the Spirit), the latter raising the former to a higher reality (God's resurrection of the dead). In this radical schism and ultimate unity, no qualitative parity between God and humanity remains. Barth has effaced any organic quality about this meeting of the two worlds; God's self-disclosure has a miraculous character, the "raising" of those who are metaphysically and epistemologically "dead." Barth's radicalized dialectic comes to articulation through his fusing together of resurrection with revelation.

Here we might pause and attempt a definition of "revelation," since the term becomes so obviously important through this radical period. By "revelation" Barth intends to speak of something beyond mere scientific knowledge (be it derived from normal investigation of history or the sacred texts) or mere religious experience (whether psychological or social epiphenomena). Rather, by it Barth means the personal self-disclosure of God, the supernatural "moment" of connection when God communicates Himself to the human consciousness. It is the "event" of God's manifest presence, the encounter between God and that which is not God. If revelation is religious knowledge, then, it is so only as miraculous human awareness of the transcendent One, the impossible perception of God Himself. Where modern philosophies hoped to "get" knowledge about God "naturally" (through empirical or psychological sources) for the sake of some kind of religious science, Barth spoke of it as God "giving" knowledge of Himself "supernaturally" (that is, on His own terms) for the sake of covenant. Barth unpacks this concept of revelation in his later constructive dogmatic projects, yet his basic sense of revelation as a divine, miraculous, and richly communicative encounter is in effect from about 1919.

To return to how revelation is played out in eschatological terms, we move to *Die Auferstehung der Toten* (*The Resurrection of the Dead*). This jump calls for an explanation, though. Why treat these lectures, delivered in 1923 and published in 1924, before 2*Rö*, published in 1922? My answer is this. First, we have observed how Barth's meditations on 1 Corinthians in 1919 preceded his rewriting of the Romans commentary, and that his radicalization of a dialectical method/epistemology/ethics/ontology formed around 1 Corinthians 15 in particular. Secondly, as Barth indicated, were it not for some incompleteness in his notes he would have lectured on the resurrection of the dead—"the presupposition [*Voraussetzung*] of Christian theology"—in the first year of his professorship at Göttingen.[50] I think it reasonable to conclude that the core idea of *AT* had coalesced before or at the same time as Barth's writing of 2*Rö*, which was prepared from 1919 to 1921.[51] Thirdly, there is the practical consideration of treating the clearer example of *AT*'s dialectic before the more abstruse 2*Rö*.

50. Karl Barth to Eduard Thurneysen, 16 Feb 1921, *B–Th* I, in *GA* V.3, 469.

51. Textually this can be seen in the overflow of the two works. At times one wonders if Barth is saying that 1 Corinthians 15:50—"flesh and blood cannot inherit the kingdom of God"—is the thesis verse of Romans too! Reciprocally, at the crux of Barth's argument in *AT* is a thorough correlation with the sub-themes of the book

As others have observed, *AT* is a peculiar book in a peculiar genre.[52] Both less and more than a biblical commentary, its real value is its novel assertion that chapter fifteen is the epistle's "very peak and crown" (*RD*, 101).[53] The content of the chapter is not arcane speculation on revivification. Rather, "[t]he ideas developed in I Cor. xv. could better described as the *methodology of the apostle's preaching*, rather than eschatology, because it is really concerned not with this and that special thing, but with the meaning and nerve of its whole" (*RD*, 109). The entire epistle is an outworking of ethical and doctrinal matters in light of the invasion of God's kingdom.

Barth understands Paul to be presenting *the* ultimate paradox when he says "the resurrection of the dead." The immanence of God in revelation, which identifies us as mortal by marking the untransgressable boundary, is also that which ushers us into eternal life. Barth puts it memorably when he says,

> The dead: that is what we are. The risen: that is what we are not. But precisely for this reason the resurrection of the dead involves that that which *we are not* is equivalent with that which *we are*: the dead living, time eternity, the being truth, things real. All this is not given except in hope, and therefore this identity is not to be put into effect. The life that we dead are living here and now is not, therefore, to be confounded with *this* life . . . time is not to be confused with eternity; the corporeality of phenomena is not to be confused with *this* reality. (*RD*, 108)

Barth's radical parsing of this present life and the life to come means no resolution of the dialectic of heaven and earth. We humans are always the dead, even when resurrected (that is, when we become the recipients of revelation). In putting it this way, Barth levels a hard word at religious persons who would claim that intimacy with God means possession of Him. Instead, God's gift of grace is "given in hope." It cannot ever be mistaken

---

of Romans (*RD*, 118–19). 2*Rö* and *AT* were, for all intents and purposes, conceived simultaneously. The disjuncture between intellectual development and actual publication tends to throw off researchers. For instance, A. Katherine Grieb's otherwise helpful essay ("Last Things First," 50ff.) contextualizes *AT* in too restricted a period, 1923–24.

52. See Webster, *Barth's Earlier Theology*, 76ff. For a summary of *AT*, see Dawson, *The Resurrection in Karl Barth*, 33–63, or the more superficial presentation in Mueller, *Foundation of Karl Barth's Doctrine of Reconciliation*, 74–111.

53. Likewise, the resurrection of the dead is "the gospel," "the source and truth of all that exists," "the nerve of Christianity," "the meaning of the Christian faith," even "a paraphrase for the word 'God'" (*RD*, 87, 108, 123, 165, 192).

as personal property of this life. Christian men and women—even if they be the most religious of Corinth—are caught in the paradox: sinners saved by grace, temporal people promised eternity, penultimate creatures set in death *and* life.

The resurrection of *the dead*: Let us first look at the negation of the thesis in the dialectic. By Barth's evaluation, the epistle is thoroughly pejorative. The No of God comes against every religious expression of the Corinthian church, whether in their special knowledge or petty alliances or impressive charismata or their musings on immortality. They mistakenly assume that their experiential, religious culture is the eschaton itself. Against them comes the iconoclastic force of the resurrection. Paul begins his fifteenth chapter by reminding them that the glorious resurrection of Jesus was and is the center of the gospel, and that this truth did not come by historical verification but *kata tas graphas* (vv. 3–7). Barth proffers the unusual interpretation that Paul, in mentioning scriptural verification of the resurrection, is not offering any kind of historical apologetic in these verses. Furthermore, Barth concludes that the empty tomb of Jesus is "a matter of indifference," since belief and skepticism are each possible before the historical data (*RD*, 135). Faith alone apprehends the resurrection life of Jesus. But the Corinthians have misunderstood the nature of faith. They have failed to honor the fact that God is God, and in denying His distinct glory, they deny the resurrection *of the dead*. In vaunting their own spiritual knowledge they have insanely claimed for themselves a life of spiritual ultimacy (in more conventional terminology, an over-realized eschatology). Because they confuse *Christ's* resurrection with their present religious life, they do not hope for their *own* coming resurrection. They even think that their deaths will be a mere continuation of this life. It is quite the contrary, says Barth about Paul's message: "Dying is pitilessly nothing but dying, only the expression of the corruptibility of all finite things, if there be no *end* of the finite, no *perishing* of the corruptible, no *death* of death" (*RD*, 159). How much better would it be if they had placed their religion under God's judgment! Then "the general victory of Christ announced in the resurrection" would be theirs even in "the crisis of every human temporal thing" (*RD*, 167–68). Outside of the crisis there is no hope.

From the other side, Barth says just as forcefully *the resurrection* of the dead, the synthesis which preserves the thesis. First Corinthians 15 proclaims the positive production achieved through the negating force of revelation. If God points out the dichotomy between His world and the

Corinthians', He also makes it clear that they are claimed by it and placed under its *promise*. Christ is raised, and so shall we be raised—each in one's own order. What is salvation, then? Here Barth's monistic vision hinted at earlier becomes more explicit. To be raised from the dead means to have life *in* God, to *enter* His kind of existence, to *share* in the eternity proper to His life. The truth of God is "the change in the predication, which signifies return from creaturehood [*Kreatürlichkeit*] into primordiality [*Ursprünglichkeit*]," albeit "effected [*vollziehen*] nowhere else than by and in the palpably visible bodily life of man" (*RD*, 199 = *AT*, 116). The resurrection cannot be the mode of existence proper to the creature, since flesh and blood cannot inherit the kingdom of God. Nevertheless, the dead creature can be made alive again, granted total newness, given an outside life, clothed with eternity. Resurrection from God overcomes "the unabolished [*unaufgehobene*] mere humanity of our existence" (*RD*, 210 = *AT*, 124), not in full now, not as a given ultimate, but really and truly. The eternal Yes of God will be revealed as God's final word to those currently in time.[54]

More specifically, and to his great credit, Barth interposes a line of continuity within this radical discontinuity: the body. Again and again he insists that the *fleshly* human being is the object of the resurrection, the human in all his or her own tangibility, fragility, limitation, and death.

> The corruptibility, dishonour, and weakness of man is, in fact, that of his *corporeality*. Death is the death of his body. If death be not only the end—but the turning point, then the new life must consist in the repredication of his corporeality. To be sown and to rise again must then apply to the *body*. The body is man, body in relation to a non-bodily, determined, indeed, by this non-bodily, but body. The change in the relationship of the body to this non-bodily is just the resurrection. (*RD*, 191)

Not to leave it at that, Barth goes on to reject the notion of "pure spirituality" (*RD*, 194). The *sōma pneumatikon* of 1 Corinthians 15:44 is, paradoxically, the triumph of God in the body because it is His triumph over the body. For all its repredication, the body is still body in its resurrected form. It is not a new body, but a renovated and re-powered body. Though Barth only flirts with the idea, he says that if there is a replacement—and

54. John Webster reminds those who believe Barth's early theology afflicted with an abstract, anti-creaturely pre-temporality that, in *RD*, "the centre of gravity is not God's primal decision but the parousia as the full manifestation of the redeemer and his redeemed creation" (*Barth's Earlier Theology*, 88–89).

what follows stands in bold contradistinction to a hulking philosophico-theological tradition—the resurrection is the *replacement* of the soul. Consider a fascinating passage:

> Instead of the human soul, the Spirit of God appears in the resurrection. That which persists is not the soul (the latter is the predicate, which must give place to something else), but the body, and even that, not as an immortal body, but in the transition from life in death to life. It is not that [discontinuity], however, which Paul wants to indicate here, but the positive aspect. Exactly in the place of that which makes me a man, the human soul, is set . . . the Spirit of God. . . . But exactly in *this* place! To wish to be God's *without* the body is rebellion against God's will, is secret denial of God; it is indeed, the body which suffers, sins, dies. We are waiting for our *Body's* [sic] redemption; if the body is not redeemed to obedience, to health, to life, then there is no God; then what may be called God does not deserve this name. The truth of God requires and establishes the Resurrection of the Dead, the Resurrection of the Body. (*RD*, 196–97)

No longer the engine of the human, the soul must give way to the Spirit of God.[55] The *body*, though good as dead on this side of eternity, is marked as the point of continuity. The *body*, the person as the recipient of revelation, is the true point of revelatory contact and thus the true point of identity. Barth, then, permits this one small dimension of continuity in the midst of discontinuity, an ember kept lit by God in its sublation, so utterly insignificant as to be wholly significant. *The flesh is the subject* caught up in revelation and slated for redemption, *this* human life in its physical-social existence. Bodily life as such ("flesh and blood") cannot inherit the kingdom of God—but it is nevertheless the *place* of redemption. The palpable, active, social thing the body is in all its fleshly infirmity is the very self God chooses to raise to Himself.

"Flesh" plays an especially important role in matters of resurrection, I think, for fleshliness is the very thing that guarantees the eternal distinction between Creator and creature. Flesh always defines the creature, even as it is caught up into the life of God. That insight is crucial, for on a close reading of Barth, one gets the sense that salvation is union with God. A

55. The latter must die away penultimately in this age and fully in the next, for the soul "is really only the place holder for the divine Spirit of Christ" (*RD*, 198). Had Barth continued along this line, a fruitful dialogue would have been possible with the work of N. T. Wright on the *sōma pneumatikon* (e.g., *The Resurrection of the Son of God*, 347ff.).

saved human is a human resolved in God. Though we cannot synthesize God into our existence, Christ recapitulates us into the divine. "Christian monism is not a knowledge that is presently possible, but a *coming* knowledge," says Barth. "To set right what is in disorder, to abolish what is provisional, to overcome dualism, to bring about the 'God who is all in all,' *such* is the mission and significance of Christ" (*RD*, 170). At face value Barth's claims sound like an impending absorption of the human into God. That is why he perpetuates the crisis of revelation so zealously: to protect against any *achieved* or *undifferentiated* monism. And truly, the "flesh" is Barth's critical concept to hold open the space between God and redeemed humanity. *This human body* in its earthly existence is the indissoluble recipient of resurrection grace. Were concrete flesh compromised, the Christian *apokatastasis* would slip into a mystical *henosis*.

But has Barth posited the frangible flesh strongly enough in *AT* to ward off absorption? Has he spoken of the body in such a way that it retains its bodily predicates in the state of final redemption? In his account of the book, David Fergusson puzzles at Barth's "excessive restraint" about the human life in the eschaton. He concludes that Barth, for all his deference to God as the proper subject of theology, "telescopes" the eschaton into an instant of revelation in such a way as to make the final things resistant to narration.[56] Where have the historical, bodily, temporal qualities of the redeemed person gone? Barth would probably respond by saying that serialized narration involves speculation, and that specification about human life in the eschaton too easily becomes historicized and mythological, thus undoing the sense of newness with the resurrection.[57] He would also defend his agnostic posture by saying that theologians have no way of speaking about the final state *in* God, since that would mean *speaking conclusively about God*—an impossibility.[58] These defenses notwithstanding, I think Fergusson's concern about a "muted" corporeality points us in the right direction.[59] If Barth insists on detemporalizing the final state and compacting all fleshly history into God's eternal Moment, then *it is incumbent upon him to account for the distinctive creatureliness of the creature caught up in this Moment*, even if he has ruled out narratable specificity.

56. Fergusson, "Barth's *Resurrection of the Dead*," 70–72.

57. Cf. Bolt, "Exploring Karl Barth's Eschatology," 225.

58. "*That God may be all in all* . . . is the beginning and the end. We have, of course, no words to express this; for if we had, it would not be what it is" (*ER*, 327). Because pure in-Godness is a totally otherworldly arrangement, the individual's future "eludes expression" (*ER*, 223).

59. Fergusson, "Barth's *Resurrection of the Dead*," 71.

I appreciate Barth's claim that the body is the place of revelation (and therefore redemption), but his unwillingness to say more is troubling. Does the second Romans commentary clarify?

2*Rö* can been viewed as the consummate work of Barth early period. But unlike *AT*, the Romans commentary suffers from a diffusion or overload of dialectical concepts. Which concept (and corresponding text) is the center? Barth and his co-laborer Thurneysen suggested a number of keys to the epistle over the years, never coming to a firm conclusion.[60] Part of the problem with their suggestions, I think, is that they sought a single word or idea to summarize the gospel: "grace," "faith," "*theou*," "election," etc., each of which failed to denote the full sense of *dialectical movement*. A two-sided term was needed. The "resurrection of the dead" is only one of many dialectical devices used in the commentary, but let me make the suggestion that it has a subtle and special place in 2*Rö*. Barth's treatment of the programmatic passage in Romans 1:3–4 suggests that the resurrection of the dead serves as a compass of sorts for the rest of the commentary.

Of course, the resurrection appears as an important idea in the epistle to the Romans at several junctures (4:16–25; 5:9–11; 6:1–11; 8:9–11; 8:18–25). But in 2*Rö* Barth calls attention to the resurrection of the dead right away, in Romans 1:3–4, insinuating that it structures Paul's thought from the very fore. Easter is the miraculous frontier of all contact between heaven and earth: "The Resurrection from the dead is . . . the transformation: the establishing or declaration of that point from above, and the corresponding discerning of it from below" (*ER*, 30). "Resurrection from the dead" posits a *distinction* of "above" and "below" even as it sets in place a real *communication* between God and humanity.

How Barth arrives at this differentiation and unity is derived from the text itself. He capitalizes on the loose parallelism of the verses, which I have amplified and diagrammed below in the Greek and a fairly literal English translation.

---

60. With the first edition Barth toyed with the idea that the *pistis theou* of 3:3 was "the key to the whole" (in Barth and Thurneysen, *Revolutionary Theology in the Making*, 38). In 1921 Barth opines that the mystical baptism into Christ in the first half of Romans 6 is the "axis on which the whole letter turns" (p. 59), a thought to which Thurneysen apparently did not subscribe entirely, since years later he would say that "grace," and therefore Rom 1:16–17, was the "great theme" for Barth (p. 19).

A *tou huiou autou*
B *tou genomenou*
C *ek spermatos Dauid*
D *kata sarka,*
B' *tou horisthentos hoiou theou en dunamei*
D' *kata pneuma hagiōsunēs*
C' *ex anastaseōs nekrōn*
A' *Iēsou Christou tou kuriou hēmōn*

A His Son,
B who came
C from the seed of David
D according to the flesh,
B' who was appointed the Son of God in power
D' according to the Spirit of holiness
C' from the resurrection of the dead,
A' Jesus Christ our Lord

Barth's fresh translation of the Greek into German (2*Rö*, 3) shows, I think, greater attentiveness to this structure than what is conveyed in most translations, including the one substituted by Hoskyns in the English version.[61]

A *seinem Sohn,*
B *geboren*
C *aus Davids Geschlecht*
D *nach dem Fleisch,*
B' *kräftig eingesetzt als Sohn Gottes*
D' *nach dem Heiligen Geist*
C' *durch seine Auferstehung von den Toten,*
A' *von Jesus Christus unserm Herrn*

Which can be translated back into English as:

A His Son,
B born
C out of David's line
D according to the flesh,

---

61. *ER*, 27. Hoskyns generally chooses to use preexisting English translations in the place of a re-translation from Barth's German (*ER*, xiv–xv), an error in this instance.

B' powerfully installed as the Son of God
D' according to the Holy Spirit
C' through His resurrection of the dead,
A' Jesus Christ our Lord

The first noteworthy thing in these verses is the *singularity* expressed. For all the iconoclastic negativity with which readers are battered in 2*Rö*, Barth's key assertion is positive and unitary. Everything said here is held together by a single person, the man who is the content of the gospel, Jesus Christ: "In this name two worlds meet and go apart" (*ER*, 29). This singularity is called for by the text, since A and A' form an inclusio: God's Son is Jesus Christ our Lord. And who is this resurrected Lord but the selfsame man from the fleshly line of David? This *One* brings together heaven and earth in Himself. He is the risen-dead-one. By extension this suggests another singularity, that we who are caught up in the one revelation of God remain ourselves (and can only be our true selves) in the grace of God.

Nevertheless, Barth's translation makes sure to point out the *contrast* between the two worlds, the differentiation precipitated by the gospel of Jesus Christ. The Spirit powerfully installs (*kräftig eingesetzt*) Jesus as the Son of God, in bold relief against Jesus' being born (*geboren*) of the earthly seed of David, which, for all its religiosity, is earthly, inglorious, limited, sinful, characterized by death. Human life is *kata sarka* (D), the visible world known to us, whereas the invisible world, *kata pneuma* (D'), is that Primal Origin which is unknown even in its being made known. The resurrection creates and facilitates this *diastasis*. It does not weave together the worlds; it exposes the difference between them.[62]

Third and most importantly, Barth finds here a radical *transformation* in the event of revelation. Observe how much Barth reads out of *horisthentos* (B'). His translation and use of the verb suggest an elevation, a re-positioning of Jesus through the resurrection. He is "appointed,"

---

62. With the rewriting of *Der Römerbrief* Barth's textile language converts to something far more violent and polemical: the *Einschlag* of his 1919 Easter sermon becomes the *Einschlagstricher*. Implantation becomes impact. Weft becomes bomb-crater. The resurrection is the "effulgence, or, rather, the crater made at the percussion point of an exploding shell [*die erstaunlichen Einschlagstrichter und Hohlräume*], the void by which the point on the line of intersection makes itself known in the concrete world of history . . . . Through His presence in the world and in our life we have been dissolved as men and established in God" (*ER*, 29–30 = 2*Rö*, 5–6). "A specter that devours [*verschlingendes Gespenst*] every living thing," Barth shouts, "that is what the resurrection seems like as it is thrust into history, the presupposition in Jesus as it is thrust into the cohesion of circumstances, the paradox of faith as it is thrust into humans' spiritual lives" (2*Rö*, 90).

"installed," "ordained," "raised up to prominence." This is surprising at first, since Barth goes on to speak of the resurrection mostly in the noetic, revelational, seemingly non-ontological sense ("declared"). Something more is afoot. Jesus' crossing from Good Friday to Easter is an active *transposition* of that which is flesh as it meets the frontier of death, which by grace is also the frontier of the Spirit. For us the revelation of God means that our religious, historical-psychological human lives must be "dissolved" (*aufhebt*) and "established" (*begründet*) in God.[63] It seems to me that Barth sees the *einsetzen* of 1:4 as a kind of composite synonym for the *aufheben/begründen* pair. We in all our worldliness are dismantled and taken up, "appointed," by the grace of God.

A pause here. The limitations of the English language are painfully apparent with the verb *aufheben* (noun: *Aufhebung*), the semantic range of which leads to renderings like "to dissolve" or "to abolish." A better, precise reproduction is the technical "to sublate."[64] The crisis Barth has in mind here, just as in *AT*, is a dialectical movement. Sublation in the most generic sense involves the confrontation of one force (thesis) with a second (antithesis) in which one dominates and raises the other into a higher reality (synthesis). Sublation is not an obliteration or extinction, but a "taking up" of the negated object into a new order in which the negated thing is somehow sustained. For Barth a very certain kind of sublation takes place, of God's world radically dissolving and establishing ours. This is why Barth keeps the positional sense of *horisthentos*: because resurrection is God's election to take historical existence, to conquer it and reconstitute it divinely. The world *kata pneuma* lights upon the world *kata sarka*. Knowledge of the unknown God is given. Justification is granted to sinners. The dead are resurrected.

A final observation is that humanity's connection to God is entirely *resurrection-facilitated*. Barth identifies the resurrection of the dead as nothing less than the linchpin of all human knowing and being. The human world and God's world touch only at the eschatological frontier.

---

63. E.g., *ER*, 30, 35, 36, 79, 139, 141, 158, 162, 165, 218, 289, 298, 344, 417. Cf. Lowe considers this pair "a fundamental trope" which "provides a way of speaking of *krisis* without becoming entangled in opposition" (Lowe, "Barth as the Critic of Dualism," 385).

64. Or "sublimate." The misleading language of revelation as "the *abolition* of religion" is Garrett Green's chief reason for retranslating *CD* §17 (in Barth, *On Religion*, viii–ix). With Hoskyns (*ER*, xiv), I wonder if the English "dissolve" at least holds the potential of being helpful when understood in its chemical sense, as when a solute is dissolved in a solution, the former preserved in some sense as it is restructured in the latter.

Barth's translation calls attention to this. Notice how he treats the *ex* of C' as being an instrumental preposition, something closer to the Greek *dia*, translating it "through" (*durch*).[65] The resurrection is the pivotal instrumental power by which the human Jesus is appointed and presented to us as the Son of God. And it is the event by which we as human recipients are negated and re-posited on a new foundation. Breaking the parallelism of C and C' actually underscores the resurrection, setting it apart, making it the arbitrator of the first and second *kata* and the whole sublational process. But this emphasis comes at the cost of adding confusion as to whether the resurrection is a predicate of the Son or the Spirit. Just whose resurrection is "His" (*seine*) resurrection, the Son's or the Spirit's? And if both, then how? The risk involved with Barth's axiom is that it becomes overly axiomatic, thereby too generic a concept for Trinitarian dogmatics. But for the Romans commentary it has real utility. The resurrection of the dead offers the possibility of hanging the Yes and No of God upon a single hinge.

The No and the Yes, hiddenness and revealedness, judgment and grace: the paradox comes together in the resurrection. In fact, all of Barth's talk about the resurrection can sometimes distract from the point that his dialectic is a thorough re-articulation of Martin Luther's theology of the cross. Regin Prenter describes Luther's *theologia crucis* as "theology in its totality, that is, theology in so far as it is at all capable of understanding the unity underlying the antitheses in the divine works: God's righteousness under his judgment, his grace under his anger, the life which he bestows even in the midst of death, his power to turn the present evil into a thing of good."[66] From this line of thought Barth reads Romans as a document of the violent intersection of two kingdoms, as divine presence in the midst of seeming absence, as a furious relation between veiling and unveiling, as Good Friday with Easter behind it.[67] Recall that during this time Barth is reading and rediscovering Luther along with Kierkegaard (a radical Lutheran), as well as Nietzsche and Overbeck (lapsed Lutherans). It is not an oversimplification to say that Barth in 2*Rö* (and *AT*) has taken the *theologia crucis* tradition and repackaged it in the language of resurrection.

---

65. Barth may be superimposing Rom 8:11 to acquire this meaning (see *ER*, 287).

66. Prenter, *Luther's Theology of the Cross*, 2. For the degree to which Barth became staurocentric through it, see Bradbury, "Identifying the Classical *Theologia Crucis*, and in This Light, Karl Barth's Modern Theology of the Cross,'" 123ff.

67. This seminal thought stays with Barth, who mounted a print of Matthias Grünewald's triptych above his desk for many years. Among other things, the triptych portrays an agonizing, dying Christ on the front, which opens up to a resurrection scene behind it. For a brief interpretation of the triptych, see I/2, 125.

Mixed with Paul, Plato, and Kant, this more Lutheran approach to revelation operates like nuclear fission.[68] Fission, because the insertion of God's world into ours splits apart what is Spiritual and what is fleshly. In the midst of the ensuing explosion, apotheosis—the undifferentiated unity of God and creature—is impossible.[69] Nevertheless, if fission, then one is supposing on some level an *original unity*. In fact—and this must not be overlooked if one is to understand young Barth—he feels driven to posit the split between the divine and the earthly with such force *precisely because he starts from the assumption that God is immanent*. The two worlds are blasted apart *precisely because they are already conjoined in revelation*. In that seminal moment time has been comprehended by eternity; they touch; they are one. Consider how Barth says, "The unity of the divine will is divided only that it may be revealed in overcoming the division. But it is only too easy to confuse this invisible occurrence in God with that observable series of psychophysical experiences in which it is manifested" (*ER*, 189). The proximity of Spirit and flesh in revelation tempts humans to identify the two, but any such idolatrous identification elicits a fission from God that is not mercy but wrath. But mark well: Barth delivers his devastating critique from the very position of unity so prized by the romantics—and yes, he argues, however violently, *toward* that same unity.[70]

Barth's fission of the romantic nucleus is exactly the thing at work when he invokes the resurrection of the dead. Epistemologically, the resurrection means revelation in concealment, the unveiling of deity in the veiling of the cross. Ethically, resurrection means the carving out of a hollow canal of religious activity with the living water of God. Forensically,

---

68. Cf. Busch, *The Great Passion*, 22; Grube, "Reconstructing the Dialectics in Karl Barth's *Epistle to the Romans*," 127–46; Oh, "Complementary Dialectics of Kierkegaard and Barth," 497–512; McCormack, *Karl Barth's Critically Realistic Dialectical Theology*, 216ff.

69. This insight is reflected in Barth's remark in December 1920 that he had moved from Osiander to Luther by rewriting the commentary (Barth and Thurneysen, *Revolutionary Theology in the Making*, 55).

70. Therefore Torrance's claim that Barth's early dialectic was an "attack upon . . . immanentist thinking" (*Karl Barth*, 63) is misleading. Barth's attack happened from within, for at this stage (even all along?) he himself was a sort of immanentist. Bultmann is much more attentive when he pens that 2*Rö* had "touches of romanticism in places" and "traces of the transcendental philosophy of Cohen," suggesting to Barth that he should be more gracious with Schleiermacher (Bultmann to Barth, 31 Dec 1922, in Barth and Bultmann, *Letters 1922/1966*, 4–6).

resurrection means *iustificatio impii*, the justification of sinners.[71] And ontologically, when Barth says resurrection he means the stark differentiation of mortal creature from immortal Creator even as humans participate in deity.

With that said, let us return to the question of the possibility of eschatology proper. Has young Barth left room for any statement about one's personal future, particularly the resurrection of the body at the end of time? Part of the problem here is that he has practically invented a new tense, "the eternal future" (*futurum aeternam* or *futurum resurrectionis*), to take the place of the temporal future. Even so, at various times he is willing to speak of an absolute future in which all penultimacy is made ultimate and all dialectical movement finished. He has been unwilling to suppose a new history to be initiated in the chronological future, but he is willing to induce from the moment of revelation that God can and will resolve all historical movement in His own eternity.

A handful of examples will demonstrate this. Barth holds that through revelation "we are aware of a final consummation and comfort and pride" (*ER*, 153), "a final one-ness, a final clarity and peace" (*ER*, 178). For this "final advent" we wait with ardent longing (*ER*, 223). Resolution cannot occur on this side of eternity, but there is a reality in God waiting to be revealed in a conclusive way. Barth is unopposed to the thought of *this* monism. The resurrection of the flesh is blasphemy if construed as an achieved earthly reality, but in the Beyond "time is swallowed up in eternity, and the flesh in the infinite victory of the Spirit" (*ER*, 285). Accordingly, with every duality of this existence removed, men and women will experience "direct, genuine, and eternal life" (*ER*, 308). They will be revealed in their eternal egos, their identity *in God*.

Again, as in *AT*, Barth's talk of recapitulation begs the question as to how human preservation is possible. Does the obliterating critique of the *Aufhebung* genuinely preserve the corporeal thing in its Yes? Why are we not to conclude that the fleshly phenomena are simply reintegrated and absorbed into their Primal Origin, as planets into a black hole? Distinctive creatureliness seems questionable if creaturely "positions . . . have been dissolved," with every earthly agent "at peace, reconciled, redeemed, and resolved" in God's unity (*ER*, 329). Barth does not make the situation any

71. The Barth of the second Romans commentary can be understood as transposing the song of the *sola fidei* of the Reformers into an eschatological key. The resurrection of the dead has the same character as the forgiveness of sins. Resurrection is an alien deification, a salvation which comes only from without and has no native provenance in us. Resurrection is imputed.

better by calling Jesus Christ the new ego.[72] How does the creaturely "I" keep any of its parameters once human identity, at present in its dialectic, is fully translated into Christ?

And yet again, in 2*Rö* just as in *AT*, Barth turns to the flesh to prop open some line of continuity of human identity in the midst of radical discontinuity. God will not destroy or absorb the creature. His "judgment" does not necessarily remove the fleshly realities:

> [M]aybe the lightning leaves these things untouched; or refines and purifies them; carbonizes them; or transmutes them into other substances; or perhaps it consumes and destroys them altogether—and yet, not altogether: *Non omnis moriar!* In every case, they are subjected to a radical testing. What we were is proved by its relation to what we are, whether it stands on this side or on that side of the gulf which becomes visible through the revelation and observation of God, whether its quality be life or death. (*ER*, 227)

Since the fleshly person is the one to whom the eternal God reveals Himself, there exists the possibility that this very same fleshly person is preserved eternally. In the sublation of God, the human subject is related to its Origin. Nonetheless, return to its Origin never undoes the reality that the "I," this tangible body, this clod of atoms, is the one to whom God manifested Himself. The subject slated for redemption is flesh and not sub-deity. Thus, Barth concludes, "The more coldly we speak of the resurrection of the body the better" (*ER*, 289).

One cannot escape the feeling that Barth's eschatology in the early 1920s suffers from debilitating murkiness. Along philosophical and theological lines, he describes the resurrection power as a bringing all things into the eternal Deity. To compensate for it, however, he imports a qualitative distinction between the divine and human so great as to have all things temporal "dissolved" in the acids of eternity if they are to cross over the chasm and abide in God. Barth hints about a final resting place in God after the resolution of the temporal dialectic, which would suggest a looming absorption of humans into a divine monad. However, we have noted a stubborn counterpoint, that Barth maintains the resurrection of the flesh, the flesh as the subject, the flesh as the stuff claimed by God, the stuff preserved by Him, even in eternity. The flesh, we might say, guarantees the

72. E.g., *ER*, 181, 269, 297, 312f., 438. Taking from Romans 5 and his study on Ephesians, Barth casts Jesus as the true Adam in the strongest sense, as an *Anthropos*, as the idea of the individual, as the eternal "I" in God. For more on Barth's over-determination of the unity between Jesus Christ and the rest of humanity, see chapter 5.

irreducibility of the subjected subject. For all its radical re-identification, flesh is the continuity of human identity between this temporal world and the eternal.

HYPOSTATIZING THE DIALECTIC (1924–32)

The resurrection of the dead as a dialectical trope all but disappeared in 1924. From the outside the change comes as surprise, given that 1924 marked the high-water point of that structure with the publication of *AT*, heralding Barth even more as a leading exponent of the so-called *dialektische Theologie* movement. There were good reasons for him to repackage his approach, however. Barth found himself overwhelmed by the task of teaching, having arrived at the university at Göttingen at the end of 1921 woefully unprepared to instruct his students in an orderly, systematic way. That challenge was multiplied many fold due to the fact that he was supposed to teach Reformed theology, about which (apart from a modest knowledge of Calvin) Barth was ignorant.[73] While other theologians were cleaning up the shrapnel from their own bombarded playgrounds, he was attempting to process the Protestant theologians of the sixteenth and seventeenth centuries. Of course, he managed to complete 2*Rö* in a short time, and a biblical studies course most semesters permitted him to teach on Ephesians, James, and, significantly, to write his *Erklärung* of 1 Corinthians. But he was expected to teach doctrine, and by orders of the (Lutheran) university, Reformed doctrine. So at the end of 1924, with trepidation (and not a little resistance against the administration's sectarianism), Barth took up the challenge of building a systematic theology over the course of three semesters. The series he called, with a nod to Calvin, *Unterricht in der christlichen Religion.*[74]

Before turning to these lectures, it will be helpful to note some of the failures of Barth's "eschatological" approach. First, the resurrection dialectic was *overly critical*, more suitable for deconstruction than the building of a framework of thought. The early work cleared the field of its confusion of revelation and religion, but it did not lend itself to dogmatics. Secondly, the eschatological approach was *too exclusively Pauline*. The

---

73. The irony increases when one considers that Barth had just confessed earlier that year to Martin Rade that he was quickly moving toward Lutheranism (Karl Barth to Martin Rade, 31 Jan 1921 in *Karl Barth—Martin Rade*, 154).

74. The first half of this Institutes (that is, the first cycle-and-a-half of Barth's courses) appears in English as *GD* I.

apocalyptic thread he detected in his exegetical work on Paul's epistles did not shine through as forcefully in other apostolic writings, let alone ancient and modern dogmatics. Third, we note that such a dialectic was unwieldy. People did not subscribe (or could not understand) such a formulation, and his novel interpretation of 1 Corinthians 15 received weak applause.[75] Fourth, there remained something strangely *anthropocentric* to the old dialectic. Are we really intent on speaking of God if we, at every point, need to mention "the dead," humanity's existential limit? Contrary to the purpose of 2*Rö* and *AT*, all of Barth's talk about the human frontier and faith gave the impression that humanity is the *Sache* after all![76] In a roundabout way these early commentaries were overly concentrated on the subjective aspect of revelation. His early Christology was anemic and seemingly subordinate to the work of the Spirit—and the Father was hardly mentioned at all. The objective reality of revelation and the objective possibility of revelation Barth left unaddressed. Perhaps he had not escaped the nineteenth century so much after all!

Seemingly overnight Barth repositioned his axis away from eschatology: "I regard the doctrine of the Trinity as the true center of the concept of revelation" (*GD* I, 131). It, not the resurrection of the dead, is "the presupposition of all the doctrinal presuppositions of Christian preaching" (*GD* I, 95). The shift from the resurrection of the dead to the doctrine of the Trinity seems unlikely until one considers that Barth's primary aim in *AT* and 2*Rö* was to show how God remains the subject of revelation even in His immanence. According to Barth's explanation, God's unique God-ness is exactly what the doctrine of the Trinity teaches, that God is God three times over in revelation, as a) the transcendent Revealer b) who reveals Himself historically in Jesus Christ and c) who turns to us personally in the Holy Spirit. The seminal thought of Christian revelation addresses the threefold "inexhaustible vitality or the indestructible subjectivity of God in his revelation" (*GD* I, 98). The core unity in revelation is that between

---

75. The fact that Barth's intellectual biographers to this day overlook the significance of the conception of the resurrection of the dead indicates that the idea was a muddled one. But, aside from the charge that it did not make clear the inner relation of faith and history, it got warm reception from Rudolf Bultmann (*Faith and Understanding* I, 66–94).

76. This is evinced in Barth's willingness to find the resurrection in every philosophy and religion that subscribes to some form of Platonism, a *Religionsgeschichte* which, if not natural theology, is sibling to it. I find his early existential presentation to be an ongoing flirtation with a kind of apophatic natural theology, which (understandably, I think) misled Brunner into thinking they were in agreement. The Barth of 2*Rö*, however, is not the Barth of "Nein!"

God and God and God—*not* between God and the religious consciousness. A trinitarian perspective also proved a better launch point for bal-
anced, constructive dogmatics,[77] for from the start God's immanence and
transcendence are available in all three Persons, not lopsided toward the
Spirit as in Barth's early axiom in the resurrection of the dead. By making
this shift Barth leaves behind Schleiermacher (who relegated the doctrine
of the Trinity to a postscript in his *Glaubenslehre*) and joins a more pedi-
greed theological tradition.

Not that Barth ever sought to resolve the crisis between Creator
and creature! As Daniel Migliore contends, dialectical thinking marks
the treatment of every doctrine in *UCR*.[78] The project at Göttingen is one
directed first and foremost to ministers undertaking the task of preaching, and preaching operates out of a sense that a mere human is daring to
speak about the living God. In fact, a full third of the dogmatic program
is devoted to prolegomena, which tries to capture the sense of compre-
hensibility in incomprehensibility, the paradox inherent in the event of
the sovereign Word of God as it is spoken and heard among humans. For
instance, Barth in §3 invokes a potent Latin phrase, *Deus dixit* ("God hath
spoken") to explain revelation as the unconditioned supremacy of God
which comes to others as "a special, once-for-all, contingent event" (*GD* I,
59), but "as qualified history, [with] no such links with the rest of history"
(*GD* I, 61). The negation of human experience implicit in God's affirming
Word comes through even clearer in "Man and His Question" (§4). God's
address to a person unveils the contradiction at the heart of a person's
earthly existence: "In his subjectivity he cannot be glad for a moment, because not for a moment is he secure, because notoriously he is constantly
what he is not and is not what he is" (*GD* I, 75). Barth's eschatological tone
has vanished, but the dialectical language remains.

Just as important is Barth's developing Christology (§§6, 27–29). The
convergence of time and eternity (epistemologically: God's veiledness and
unveiledness) are given a basis and fulfillment by the incarnation. Incarnation, Barth claims, is the prototype of revelation, the objective encounter of God with humanity, the presupposition of revelation. The hypostatic
union of Jesus Christ is the *unity* the Romantics desire but cannot attain,
Barth says, for "the restoration of the original relation between God and
man with no distance or alienation or antithesis" solves humanity's quandary (*GD* I, 155). Full communion is the reality of God's Son alone, for He

---

77. Cf. McCormack, *Orthodox and Modern*, 84.

78. Migliore, "Karl Barth's First Lectures in Dogmatics," xxx.

is true God and true human. The actual union of the God-human comes with an internal fissure, however. Jesus' deity is not His humanity; Jesus' humanity is not His deity. The historical Jesus as such is not inherently divine or deified. Likewise, for all of humanity's homecoming in the divine union of revelation, no blending with God is possible, no apotheosis occurs in the union. Barth instead affirms the "dialectical distinction and unity of the divine and the human in Christ" of the definition of Chalcedon in AD 451 (*GD* I, 154).

But Barth goes beyond Chalcedonian Christology. Through Heinrich Schmid's collection of scholastic Lutheran theologians and Heinrich Heppe's compendium of scholastic Reformed theologians, Barth discovered a line of medieval Christology, namely, the dual concept of *anhypostatos-enhypostatos*. Alexandrian in nature, the original terminology was an attempt to set forth the *priority* of the divine nature over the human nature without disintegrating the latter, though Lutheran and Reformed theologians alike had molded the terms for their own uses.[79] What the terms came to mean (or, rather, how Barth interpreted them) was this: Jesus Christ's humanity is not a person and does not subsist in itself (*anhypostatos*), but is fully dependent upon the divine Logos for its existence. The human nature has no life in itself. It requires the grace, the initiative, and the power of the divine. The negative thrust of the term protects against Ebionite thinking, including Neo-Protestant historicization. Stated positively, Jesus' humanity, being assumed and sustained by the Logos, is genuine, alive, and has being (*enhypostatos*). "It has personhood, subsistence, reality, only in its union with the Logos of God," wherein the flesh is reified, given concretion, raised to life (*GD* I, 157). The positive thrust distances one's Christology from docetism, and Barth found in the concept an establishment of humanity in the midst of its dissolution. Humanity was put in its place, rightly ordered, negated and affirmed, in this union.

Up to this point Barth's dialectical language gravitates around the subjective event of revelation, the illumination by the Holy Spirit, "the resurrection of the dead." But now Barth has put into place the objective basis for this encounter, sanctified unity and difference, through the person of

---

79. F. LeRon Shults claim that these terms were adopted and distorted by Protestant scholasticism before being passed to Barth, who distorted them further. In my opinion, Shults tends to miss the Alexandrian forest for the Leontian trees in the search for terminological exactitude. Yet Shults points out two important observations about the Alexandrian family: that the Lutherans wanted the same thing as Leontius, and that Barth follows the Lutheran usage more closely than the Reformed ("A Dubious Christological Formula," 442, 445).

Christ. This is the *Realdialektik* (the central, objective dialectic) of the Christian faith: the God-man, Jesus Christ, the prototype of all revelation. From this point on Barth relies more upon the concrete, inner relations of the Son rather than the (rather cloudy) time-eternity dialectic.[80] While his theology was far from maturity, Barth has set aside the resurrection dialectic in order to pursue a more objective basis in a Chalcedonian, Alexandrian Christology. The hypostatic union of the incarnation is the original dialectic; the pneumato-eschatological "raising" in the subjective Moment of revelation is but an echo. The person of Jesus Christ *is* the resurrection of the dead, where revelation to us in the Spirit "only *proclaims* the resurrection of the dead" (*GD* I, 155, emphasis added). Since Christology had moved into the heart of Barth's program, eschatology could and would become methodologically ancillary.

Barth's eschatology could finally have its own content, though it seems he hardly knew how to articulate an eschatology that was not simultaneously a doctrine of revelation. Barth's first systematic theology ends with a discussion of "eschatological limits" (*UCR* III, 420), a dogmatic postscript appearing to be, at first glance at least, little more than philosophical aftermath. But Barth goes on to devote four sections to the last things: §35 "Hope," §36 "The Presence of Jesus Christ," §37 "The Resurrection of the Dead," and §38 "The Glory of God." In these four chapters one again discovers that remarkable feature of Barth's theology, viz., that he frames eschatology entirely within the rubric of revelation. The doctrines of the *eschata* are simply the unpacking of that which is the case in God's disclosure to us in the here and now. The doctrines of the end time are the exposition of human nature caught up in the event of revelation. Eschatology describes our being and knowledge in the manifest presence of God. If Barth's doctrine of the Word of God forms a prolegomena by explaining the penultimate condition of humanity in the presence of God, then his doctrine of the end time forms a postlegomena as a prospective statement about the ultimate condition of humanity in the presence of God. Since Barth never lived to complete *CD* V, The Doctrine of Redemption, these sections are tantalizing and suggestive. Let us entertain a few of his insights.

Barth continues to define eschatology as the encounter with God at the perimeter of our earthly limitations. Eschatology speaks of *the coming God*, and is therefore not overly concerned with *the last things*, whether

---

80. This is one of the major features of the periodization from Bruce McCormack (*Karl Barth's Critically Realistic Dialectical Theology*, 19–23, 327ff.).

historical-sociological projections, geological-astronomical calculations, historical predictions, parapsychology, ontological speculation (be it from Plato or Kant or anyone else looking for a necessary postulate to bolster ethics), or mythology. The history of Protestant dogmatics has suffered the double failure of rank speculation and over-spiritualization. Rather, eschatology is supposed to speak about God's eternity touching our frail reality. Like his saying that Christianity is "altogether thoroughgoing eschatology" (ER, 314), Barth comments:

> Eschatological contents in their fullness are the whole of Christianity. The eschatological question in particular goes under the cloak of the promise which hides fulfillment. If it is already really there in that cloak, then the hour of its pure manifestation [reinen Erscheinung] is also coming, close to this already advanced hour. (UCR III, 464)

The doctrines of the End are the fullness of the Christian faith. In this life God's promise is veiled by the dialectical encounter, but the final resurrection is revelation with perfect clarity, the "pure manifestation" of the promise, the Day of full disclosure, utter fulfillment.

What are we, in the end, as "fulfilled" creatures? I suggest that §36 of UCR is the key to Barth's early eschatology. The doctrine of the final state is really only an outworking of the idea of the presence (Gegenwart) of Christ, that is, of our being present with Him in His eternal contemporaneity, His eternal Now. This is what is meant by "parousia." Toward this explanation, Barth appeals to a robust concept of eternity. Jesus Christ lives in the state of exaltation, which is His whole person displayed in the eternality and glory of the Father. He comes to us as the crucified and resurrected Lord whose in-temporality is also granted an overarching existence through all of time. In fact, we can only profess Him as the eternal Lord: if Reconciler, also Creator and Redeemer. These three moments—creation, reconciliation, redemption (or past, present, future)—appear to be dispersed throughout time according to our fleshly perspective, though in eternity God's movements they are "an undivided, unbroken act, actus purissimus." Were we permitted to behold this meta-display (Zentralschau), were we to exercise unfettered participation (Teilnahme), we would understand the perfect, pure, eternal act that is Jesus Christ's (UCR III, 435). We would understand that all things belong to Him, and that all things, sub specie aeternitatis, are given a share in the eternity which surrounds and upholds them. We would be standing in Christ's presence. To be present with Christ in that way will be to have perfect comprehension of God, of God with

It's Jesus presence we long for — not something else He brings for us

humanity, of eternity with time, is the promise of the resurrection. Just as Christ is being revealed as true human in fellowship with true God, so humans will fellowship with God, not in an extended chronology, but in the *fullness* of time, at "the eternal, terminal, final Hereafter [*Nachher*] of all time" (*UCR* III, 453). We will be revealed as those gripped in the unifying power of eternity, the Today of Jesus Christ. His parousia will be the unveiling of life in God, an eternity for all.

Not that we see such unity from this side, warns Barth, for the state of the creature in time is a glory with God veiled by death. Humans are caught in the here but not yet. We are forced to exist, think and speak in dialectic. But the presence of Christ draws nigh, and when it comes definitely, there will be "a replacement [*Ersetzung*]" of this temporal "interim" (*UCR* III, 456). The last hour approaches—not as an episode of time, but as that which comes at the frontier of time, at time's collapse. Does this transition from contradiction to unity occur at physical death, then? Is the collapse of an individual's time coincidental with eternal life? Barth's answer is unsatisfying. He says that we cannot be rigorously dogmatic at this point, since death is still a phenomenon on this side, though we need not fear termination, and may even look forward to Christ's *final* presence at our *final* breath, for "these two hours . . . can no longer be distinguished" (*UCR* III, 458).

While Barth differentiates parousia, the resurrection of the dead, and the glory of God (the Last Judgment), these are minor conceptual variations. His doctrine of the general resurrection corresponds to, and is really just a subset of, the presence of Jesus. In fact, "the new presence of Jesus Christ *is* the content, the *whole* content, the one and all of Christian hope" (*UCR* III, 466). Barth's prioritization of the parousia over the resurrection reflects the fact that he thinks it better to speak of Jesus Christ's coming, to hope for His presence, to long *for* Him, rather than to pine for something *from* Him. The general resurrection's content is really just an extended meditation on what it means to be fully and finally *present with Christ* in the pure sense.

Barth, having established that true life is life in eternity, makes reminder once again that believers do not yet possess such life. Jesus Christ's risen presence has brushed against them in time just enough to bring their existence into contradiction. They are alive in Him and dead in the flesh simultaneously. "So long as time endures," they are not defined fully by the Moment of revelation, not yet fully in the Spirit, requiring the Church to assume the role of the *ecclesia militans* (*UCR* III, 469). However, the presence of Christ promises an *absolute* Moment in which, Christ having appeared unequivocally to the saints, "their collective life with Christ will be *truly* direct, immediate, on display" (*UCR* III, 469).

Redemption involves subtraction and addition.[81] The resurrection of the dead involves a kind of subtraction, for it only happens with the cessation of time, according to Barth. While time is not exactly evil, it is the veil of death and dying under which humanity is kept from its eternal presence with Christ. The mode of time must be taken away conclusively, the seal of deathliness must be broken, the veil must be lifted. Thus Barth's thought keeps its negative thrust: the resurrection of the dead will be the abolition of every current world-order, "the removal [*Aufhebung*] of all impeding, obfuscating, retarding not-yet" and "the demolition [*Abbruch*] of the tent" (*UCR* III, 470). On the flip side, the resurrection of the dead can just as well be understood in positive terms. It is a summation: only by the conclusive removal of the contradiction of the flesh to the Spirit can all earthly existence be gathered, unified, and come to resolution in God. Only in this ultimate sublation will there be "no expectation, no privation, nothing unresolved," each moment of time characterized by "completion and also sequence, history as eternal history, a striding from prosperity to prosperity" (*UCR* III, 466).

The whole of time must be *resolved* so that humans may live in eternity.[82] Then all of time, rather than being extended, will be "rolled up" like a carpet (*UCR* III, 447–48). Barth again discourages speculation about life in the final state, but he agrees with the basic Augustinian conviction that the end will hold out for us the *visio Dei*, the intimate perception of God, and the *fruitio Dei*, the enjoyment of God. These things need not be objectified or examined too closely, suggests Barth, since the consummation of all things is ultimately a matter of *God's* glory.

Just as in *AT* and *2Rö*, Barth issues a strong a word about the flesh in *UCR*. Corporeality is the point of continuing creaturely identity, even as eternity dissolves and reconstitutes human existence. Barth reaffirms his commitment to corporeality by making four related points. First and foremost, he says that a human remains creature in the resurrection:

> Redemption does not means that the person ceases to be himself, and something else comes to be. One will *not be God*. God

81. Cf. Johnson, *Karl Barth and the Postmodern Foundations of Theology*, 130.

82. This supposedly allows for a communitarian expression of the eschaton, since in this inclusive picture of eternity the resurrection is obtained "simultaneously, or rather co-eternally, by all the dead" (*UCR* III, 474).

> *remains* the Creator, and humanity *remains* the creature. The
> creaturely limit is *not* lifted [*aufgehoben*] by the lifting [*Aufhe-*
> *ben*] of the eschatological frontier. (*UCR* III, 478)

Secondly, nothing substantial is superadded in the resurrection. The veil
drops and one simply becomes what he or she already is.[83] In the power
of one's unity with Christ, one "only needs to become the subject of the
predicates which on this side of the parousia is Jesus Christ alone" (*UCR*
III, 479). Thirdly, redemption lands the person in the same region as
one lived beforehand, for the New Jerusalem is placed upon earth. And
fourthly, "the most remarkable and incomprehensible thing" is that the
resurrection will not happen in another time, but in this one (*UCR* III,
480)! Time is ended—but miraculously safeguarded. In all this Barth casts
a fantastically difficult vision: humanity must be transported out of its own
mode and translated into the consummate state in the presence of God,
yet in such a way that the fleshly existence is wholly preserved. Each atom
stays in place, so to speak.

PRELIMINARY CONCLUSIONS

We have trekked a long path to get to this point. We found that Karl Barth's
triple education in pietism, romantic idealism, and religious socialism
contributed to his conception of an "eschatological present." Though re-
luctant to speak about the end times early in his career, he took up eschatology as a way to articulate the revolutionary immanence of God's
power on the earth. For Barth, speaking of the kingdom of heaven as a
coming force connoted the *critical* yet *unifying* power of God's movement
in history. Having started a battle in 1*Rö* against religious individualism
with eschatological-epistemological weaponry, Barth wielded an even
more severe dialectic in the early 1920s. The resurrection of the dead was
made the touchstone for Barth's dialectical approach. The dissolution and
establishment of the old world by the new world of God guides Barth's
epistemology and ethics, although as an "existential" statement about the
predicament of humanity it also points beyond the crisis to a final ontological reality, unity with God which somehow preserves human identity,
even human identity in the flesh. Once Barth had shifted the weight of

---

83. This passing point makes clear why Barth does not think his eschatology is
speculative, I suggest. All that is being said about the future is that which is already
given in the present Moment of revelation. Nothing is added. Christ simply makes
reality "realized" as we enter His unbroken—but familiar—presence.

prolegomena onto the doctrine of the Trinity, the resurrection of the dead could surface as its own material doctrine. From his concluding lectures of *UCR* in 1926 forward, Barth would teach that humanity is slated for the absolute expression of the resurrection of the dead, that is, taken fully into the *presence* of Christ so that time (with its existential contradictions) is resolved.

Because of its deep importance, let me revisit an equation at the heart of Barth's thinking on the resurrection of the dead: resurrection = sublation. Everywhere in his early work Barth chooses to articulate his dialectic eschatologically and his eschatology dialectically. The verb *aufheben*, translated technically as "to sublate," permeates his discourse. The term is important because of its enormous semantic range: "to lift," "to cancel," "to raise," "to evolve," "to abolish," "to comprehend," or, in Barth's complicated sense, "to dissolve—and establish—and in its establishment to preserve that which it has dissolved." Sublation (*Aufheben*) describes the dialectical movement of ideas or forces in their relative positions, confrontations, and resolutions; in its more pedestrian form, the meeting of a thesis with its antithesis which leads upward into a synthesis. Sublation is associated most often with Hegelian idealism, but in young Barth's case it gathers a somewhat different meaning from his heritage in pietism, romanticism, and (neo-Marxian) religious socialism, as well as older Platonic philosophy and radical Lutheran theology. By the time he was through with it, Barth's dialectic would barely resemble the Hegelian idea of world-evolution in the Spirit. Nevertheless, Barth's critical *diastasis* never erased the positive note, the beautiful synthesis which could only be the conquering placement of the rebellious creature into the simple presence of God. In the end, the dissolving No could be understood as a subordinate and completed moment in the establishing Yes of God.

Barth's connection of resurrection with sublation comes with another quasi-equation: resurrection = revelation. Resurrection and revelation alike are the event of the human before the personal disclosure of the living God. Each is the event of eternity pervading time so as to raise time to itself. Each is the event of communion in the contemporaneous presence of Jesus Christ. *Die Auferstehung ist die Offenbarung ist die Aufhebung.* Barth's basic equation of resurrection, revelation, and sublation would hold for the next decade.[84] Functionally intact through volume I of *KD*,[85] it would inform Barth's thinking to his final days.

To grasp the Barthian equation is to have a solid anticipation of the remainder of the rest of this study. Everything eschatological in Barth's early years is seed for a mature doctrine of resurrection in *KD* III and IV. The resurrection of the dead will come to mean "lifting into divine duration," that is, *eternalization*. It will mean "removal of the veil," that is, *manifestation*. And it will mean a "raising into union with God," that is, *incorporation*. These three themes start to surface in Barth's early work and become the dominant expressions of the general resurrection in his mature work.

Finally, we detected in the first few decades of Barth's life a concern for embodiment. From the beginning of his interest in the resurrection (regardless of his exact use of it), Barth makes pains to describe it as the resurrection *of the flesh*. God's Word is spoken to those in the flesh, thus the flesh is raised. Barth holds fast to this point in *AT*, 2*Rö*, and *UCR* alike, and for sustaining this note of the Christian hope he should be commended. But his description of the sublative force of the resurrection calls for a healthy suspicion. In the next three chapters I interrogate Barth to trace the consequences of his program and to weigh the extent to which the flesh he speaks of as raised is truly flesh. Just how can eternity's dissolution of time be, in the end, an establishment of time? How can the translation of the creaturely mode of existence into the divine be a preservation of the former when all is revealed? And when the "pure" presence of humans with God is achieved, will fleshliness hold open space for the differentiation of individual persons? These questions are best directed at Barth's mature work, to which we now turn.

---

84. There is little decisively new material added between *UCR* and *Die Christliche Dogmatik im Entwurf* (1927), concludes McCormack (*Karl Barth's Critically Realistic Dialectic Theology*, 375). Let us only observe that Barth achieves his characteristic schematization in the latter, speaking of revelation's objective being (§9), objective possibility (§14), and subjective possibility (§17). I have also elected not to narrate Barth's fruitful debates with Erik Pryzywara and Roman Catholicism during the late 1920s; for this, see Johnson, *Karl Barth and the Analogia Entis*.

85. Also for expedience I have opted to bypass the rather rich developments in *CD* I/1 and I/2, though see John Drury, "'From Crib and Cross to Resurrection and Ascension." I also mention in passing the obvious parallels between resurrection and revelation as Barth describes the Word of God revealed (*KD* §5) as spiritual, personal, purposive, contingently contemporaneous, powerful to rule, "worldly," etc.

3

The Resurrection of the Flesh
as Eternalization

THE CHRISTIAN HOPE INVOLVES a profession in "eternal life" in connection with resurrection. Therefore any full account of the resurrection of the flesh has to account for the question of time, viz., how time relates to eternity. Is eternity like chronological time as we know it, just an unending future? Or is eternity something different, a transcendence of time itself? How one imagines foreverness is intimately related to how one imagines the redeemed body. Through his mature work Barth came to articulate the resurrection of the flesh in several ways, but his first mature expression involves this very question, the issue of the bodily human in time and eternity.

As we discovered in the last chapter, Barth early on had plenty to say about the relation of time and eternity. Turning to his later theological output in *Church Dogmatics*, especially volumes III and IV, we find that the topic is still near the foreground. He continues to address temporality near the head of his dogmatic projects, and thoughts about time always lie close to the heart of his doctrine of God. One might say that Barth prefers to approach metaphysics in terms of time, using the temporal category as "*the* ontological dimension."[1] That being the case, we understand Barth's doctrine of the resurrection by understanding how Jesus' temporal life is related to eternity at Easter, and how our own future involves a very specific conception of eternal life. For Barth, the idea of risen flesh is in concert with an idea of risen time, best captured in the word "eternalization."

---

1. Roberts, *A Theology on Its Way?*, 70.

I explore the theme of eternalization in four steps. We begin with God's eternity, which Barth casts as a "pure duration" expansive enough to encompass all of time and be "simultaneous" with it. Second, Jesus Christ's own being in the resurrection is that of a limited, temporal existence which has been gifted with eternal simultaneity by the Father. God fulfills time by claiming it in Jesus incarnate life, then, in the resurrection, He grants Jesus' delimited historical existence an eternal mode. Third, Barth says that time, as opposed to the wholeness of eternity, bears a wound of limitation: it is fragmented, fleeting and uncollected, a sequence with no durability, a degenerate and dying movement. The solution, and our fourth step, is the resurrection of the flesh. As a corollary to Jesus' resurrection, God intends to confer to humans (in their limited lifespans) the eternal Beyond: "Resurrection of the flesh . . . opens the perspective of human life to eternity: you will find human life in eternity."[2] God's very pantemporal comprehensiveness will be our own, says Barth—even as this eternalization will sustain as its basic template the same bodily existence each person lived in his or her own earthly life. The resurrection of the flesh bestows a trans-temporal duration to the boundaried history one enacts between conception and death, and supposedly does so without annihilating one's history in space-time. Barth therefore makes a creative reconnection of embodied history and eternal life, though along the way I must register concern about the Platonic closure of time endemic in such a vision of the future, and about the extent to which this conception invites a romanticization of death.

THE FREEDOM OF GOD

In the last chapter we found that Barth adjusted his eschatological dialectic in his early career, though he continued to describe the tense communion between eternity and time in revelation. He always intended to speak of God who is free in His own pan-duration, free *from* the world's time, yet also (and thereby) free *for* the world's time. For all the transcendence of God's eternity, it is also a transcendent graciousness wrapping around time. The Deity fills time and exceeds it; He fills time *because* He exceeds it. "It could be said of Barth's God, with little exaggeration, that he is radically transcendent *in order to be* radically immanent."[3] That is God's freedom.

2. Barth, *The Faith of the Church*, 136.

3. Gunton, *Becoming and Being*, 195.

To understand the importance of eternity for Barth going into *KD*, I think it wise to pick up where the last chapter left off, noting his changing articulation of the concept. Beginning with the period in which he radicalized his sense of eschatology, bringing eternity into an overtly critical relationship with time (1919–24), we saw how Barth implemented the thought-language of Luther, Kierkegaard, and Overbeck. Perhaps even more influential on Barth's thinking with regard to the issue of God and time was the influence of Kant.[4] First, Kant had argued that God was not an object of perception, and that any argument for His existence (or non-existence) along empirical lines was sheer sophistry. Likewise, God could not be made a category of pure reason—though He could be spoken of through practical reason, as the unconditioned reality which guarantees ethics ("unconditioned," meaning God never becomes an object to the creature within the causal order of phenomena). Barth adopts the basic schema of difference between the unconditioned God and the conditioned human even as he holds open the possibility of revelation of the divine Subject through faith.[5] More germane to our point here, Kant held that time itself was not an independent reality but an *a priori* intuition of the human. Rather than being an objective feature of the universe, time (like space) is a thought-category supplied by the human mind in order to understand the world.[6] Barth works within Kant's basic paradigm, making time and eternity two very different categories of *perception*. "Time" is the limited and conditioned category of thought provided by the human mind, where "eternity" is God's perfect and unconditioned knowledge. "Time" is the human's partially successful attempt to comprehend the universe and the vain attempt to understand God. On the other hand, "eternity" is God's perfect grasp of all things. In His unconditioned reality He perceives and sustains all things. Furthermore, Barth extends the Kantian paradigm to speak of time as a *sinful* human claim about self-being (the Cartesian *cogito ergo sum*), when God's comprehensive claim on us is that which alone guarantees being (*cogitor ergo sum*[7]). In any case, if we speak of an antithesis of time and eternity in Barth's early critical work, we must do so against its Kantian background.

---

4. Note Barth's admission that he has rewritten the Romans commentary under the influence of Plato and Kant (*ER*, 4).

5. Cf. Barth's 1929 lecture on Kant in *PTNC*, 252–98.

6. See Immanuel Kant, *Critique of Pure Reason*, Transcendental Doctrine of Elements I.2; second div., II.ii.3.b.

7. See *RD*, 46, though its coinage is Franz von Baader's.

After 1924, Barth repackaged his concept of revelation into a trinitarian format with greater emphasis on Jesus Christ as the Word of God, though this did little at first to resolve the tension between the unconditioned and conditioned, between eternity and time. The perceiving God, grasping all, is free from time. That freedom is expressed in His unity, His simplicity, His aseity. But, construed as a total independence from the creation, "freedom" could suggest a distance of God from chronology. For instance, in the mid-twenties Barth still agreed with Schleiermacher and Biedermann about the "absolute timelessness and spacelessness" of the divine (*GD* I, 434), a life which is omnipresent by virtue of the fact that it is *outside* all time. In revelation God does not become temporal, though He does invite the human into a paradox: communion with God "means standing in this *antithesis*," being taken out of time even as one remains in time.[8] Only paradox can result. As for God, He remains the unconditioned One, the ever-Subject-non-object, He who seizes us and is not seized, the Totally Other.

Barth justified this devouring view of eternity by invoking the Reformed scholastic Polanus' description of God as *nunc stans*: God's "standing alongside" is multidimensional enough to "coexist" with the earth and cloak it, for He "contains in Himself the meaning of time." A thousand days in God's time are but a watch of the night, says the psalmist, meaning that eternity *duratio quae tota simul est*: eternity is the duration in which all things are simultaneous.[9] God's omnitemporality is His power to be gracious to us in our time. His presence says Yes to us even in its No.[10] Through this teaching Barth clearly wanted to avoid portraying God's freedom as a kind of transcendent prison away from time, though one gets the impression that for Barth God's coexistence with the earth means not an accompanying as much as a puncturing of the time-space continuum at each intersection.

Even the first volume of *CD* militates the absolute difference between God's mode and our own. In Barth's theology of the Word of God, God is

8. Barth, *Epistle to the Philippians*, 114.

9. *UCR* II, 161–2 = *GD* I, 436. By this neither Polanus nor Barth mean that eternity is the summation of time, but that eternity crosses over each present in such a way that all can be present to it.

10. While Barth does not develop this conception of simultaneity (*Gleichzeitigkeit*) until *CD* II/1, Richard Burnett calls attention to the fact that the Yes of simultaneity can heard in the stormy No of each edition of the *Römerbrief* (*Karl Barth's Theological Exegesis*, 107ff.). Dawson finds the same feature in *RD* (*The Resurrection in Karl Barth*, 62–63).

said to interject His own transcendent moment into consciousness so that revelation may occur. In the moment of revelation a believer understands God as the living Lord, that is, as the One who lives trans-temporally. In *CD* I/2, especially §14 "The Time of Revelation," Barth, again spurred by Kantian thought, presses for a sharp distinction between eternity and time.[11] God in His freedom can "have time," even "have time for us," but in no way does this time cease to be eternity. Jesus Christ in His freedom can become incarnate, though His identity is never given over to spatio-temporality. He is the Son of God, flesh and blood in union with His deity. In the grip of eternity, time gives way to "mastered time," "a present that is not a present without also being a genuine perfect," "a genuine, indestructible present" (I/2, 52). Eternity creates its own time by entering and overruling the sinful human activity of sense-making. Time is "overtopped and dominated" by the eternity of the incarnate Son (I/2, 66). God's perfect mode means for the earth "suspension, the total relativising of all other time and of its apparently moved and moving content" (I/1, 131). God perceives His creation, and on that basis alone is there really objective spatio-temporal reality. Nonetheless, only an eternal perception sees things rightly. Over the years Barth made it explicit that he did not intend to portray eternity and time as oppositional concepts,[12] though a kind of violence hangs over their relationship in his writings, even through *CD* I.

Some readers have observed a significant modification to this relationship in Barth's thinking as he wrote out his mature dogmatics.[13] I would be more specific and say that his leaning towards a more time-positive eternity had its decisive transition in the mid 1930s, as he finished *CD* II/1.[14] There we find Barth making sure to note the freedom of God at every point in perfect alignment with the love of God, expressed together in Jesus Christ. God's eternal being *is* His freedom to love, His transcendent freedom exercised by His willingness to be with us. In the

11. Barth appeals to Kant's antinomies as evidence that time belongs to (broken) human apperception, that we do not know what true time is save by the Word of God (I/2, 47–49).

12. E.g. *GD* I, 435; Barth, *How I Changed My Mind*, 48. However, it is certainly with some sort of repentance that he reflects on how he and other eschatologizing theologians unwittingly capitulated to something like the pre-temporality of the Reformers (and even the supra-temporality of the Neo-Protestants), positing an idea of "qualified time" with eternity equidistant from every point of time (II/1, 635).

13. Cullmann, *Christ and Time*, 60, 62ff.; Nielson, "Karl Barth—A Brief Introduction," 3.

14. *Pace* those who would locate the shift at the beginning of *CD*, e.g., van der Kooi, *As in a Mirror*, 359.

midst of writing out this doctrine of God, Barth's mind underwent a seismic rearrangement via a new perspective on election, one gleaned from Pierre Maury in 1936. Stated briefly, Barth came to view predestination as a decision within God Himself, as God's own *self*-election as the means of covenant with the creature.[15] Specifically, Jesus Christ, the very Son of God, ordained Himself and was ordained as the concrete toward-ness of God to humanity, the One in whom all are determined. In the one God-man Barth can even postulate (supralapsarianistically) that the Father establishes His "double election," Jesus Christ under reprobation for the sins of humanity and Jesus Christ chosen for the glory of humanity. Though he does not spell it out until *CD* II/2, Barth's revised doctrine of election makes itself felt as he pairs the perfections of God's eternity and glory at the end of II/1.

The payoff is this: the contradistinction of eternity and time is mediated within God's own being. If God is the predestined basis of His own temporal creation, then time in its creational dimension can be spoken of and embraced simply because it is, in the most important sense, the time belonging to the eternal Son. History unfolds in the first place because it is already enfolded in Christ's pleromic presence. Time is good because it exists as something already "in" and coming "from" God's inner life. What we find in the elected Jesus Christ is that time, in a very concrete sense, is *proper to* God's being by virtue of His eternal decision. He exists as "the prototype and foreordination of all being" (II/1, 611), the One who shows eternity as the absolute basis of time, and therefore absolute "readiness" or "preparedness" for it (II/1, 618, 621). By the power of His eternal being-in-decision God has made time compatible with eternity. Doctrines of creation and anthropology follow after this insight about election, not alongside or independently of it. By couching the doctrine of creation within the covenantal purposes of predestination, time *qua* time can and may and must be called good, for it is, under the banner of predestination, already from and in God. Jesus Christ's election sets the covenantal Alpha and Omega in place for creation to play out.[16]

The antithetical, Kantian framework is made obsolete when Barth comes to understand God's "native" perception this way. Creational time can be spoken of as fundamentally good because it is foreordained and contained as a mode of God's perception, not simply the sinful human

---

15. See Barth's foreword in Maury, *Predestination and Other Papers*; cf. McCormack, *Karl Barth's Critically Realistic Dialectical Theology*, 453–63.

16. Creation takes priority "formally" and "historically"; covenant takes priority "materially" and "substantially" (III/1, 232). Cf. Berkouwer, *The Triumph of Grace in the Theology of Karl Barth*, 55–57.

thought-category. God's intuitive powers comprehend from above *and* from below; His own being spans unconditioned *and* conditioned reality. With a rewired doctrine of election Barth had found a way to make eternity the basis, core, and telos of temporal process.

Barth continues his claim that eternity is not time and time is not eternity, but the difference now becomes that eternity alone has "duration."

> Eternity simply lacks the fleeting nature of the present, the separation between before and after. Eternity is certainly the negation of created time in so far as it has no part in the problematical and questionable nature of our possession of time, our present and our beginning, continuation and ending. But eternity is not the negation of time *simpliciter*. On the contrary, time is absolutely presupposed in it. (II/1, 613)

Endurance, durability, a holding onto the succession of things: God grasps each moment present within the all-embracing Now of His unique consciousness. For the mature Barth, God's freedom is best described as *reine Dauer*, "pure duration."[17] "Pure," not in that eternity avoids time through a heavenly transcendence; rather, "pure" in that eternity has in itself all times at once, "pure" in that God possesses all moments, the past and present and future together. Rather than omitting the fluidity (*fluere*) of time, God incorporates it into His standing (*stare*). The mature Barth is henceforth able to integrate a certain Hegelian sense of *nunc fluens* into the Augustinian *nunc stans*.[18]

With the doctrine of election as the foundation, Barth seeks to re-explain eternity, this time using medieval sources, especially the sixth century philosopher Boethius. The key feature of pure duration, he says, is *simultaneity*: "The being is eternal in whose duration beginning, succession and end are not three but one, not separate as a first, a second and a third occasion, but one simultaneous occasion as beginning, middle and end" (II/1, 608), a "simultaneity and coinherence of past, present and future" (III/2, 526). Where humans experience time in a fragmented present, in God "all beginning, continuation and ending form a unique Now, steadfast yet moving, moving yet steadfast" (II/1, 617). In the divine life there is no distance between times.[19] The ages do more than appear before

---

17. II/1, 608 (= *KD*, 685), et al. Barth prefers to speak of durational eternity, though Gunton's preference of "eminent temporality" may be the more helpful term (Gunton, *Becoming and Being*, 179ff.).

18. Hunsinger, *Disruptive Grace*, 187–89.

19. Readers find in simultaneity a more sinewy version of Barth's earlier conception

His omniscience; they are held in His ever-present hands. Consequently, Barth feels comfortable invoking the scholastic term *sempiternitas* to describe the everlastingness of God, the everlastingness which sums up of all time in His omnitemporal Now. After all, is it not written that Christ is and reveals God the Alpha and Omega, *ho ōn kai ho ēn kai ho erchomenos, ho pantokratōr* (Rev 1:8)? God freely rules over time and space in such a way as to grace them, making them a part of the great instant of His eternity.

Barth goes on to elaborate by calling upon the doctrine of the Trinity as a sort of diagram of the way in which eternity embraces time. God can be said to have a threefold eternity, one in which He is pre-temporal, supra-temporal, and post-temporal. The eternal God exists pre-temporally, before anything else was, in His self-sufficient being. Though this pre-time was the "pure time" of the Father, Son, and Holy Spirit (II/1, 622), it was also the time of the election of the Son to take flesh, and therefore of God's will to create and ordain all things. Secondly, in reiterating what was said about simultaneity, God has His supra-temporal[20] existence in which He accompanies the whole of time. Eternity carries on with a before, now and after, but in perfect harmony and confluence. Proffering a maternal image, Barth explains that "every epoch, every lifetime, every new and closing year, every passing hour: they are all in eternity like a child in the arms of its mother" (II/1, 623). Rather than distancing Himself, God co-exists with the creature in the sense that He surrounds it and makes it to co-exist with Himself.[21] Far more remarkably, by the incarnation God lives *in* time, diachronically, and so enacts a covenantal history at the heart of time, the Jesus-history in which all other histories participate.[22] Thirdly, eternity

---

of the "contingent contemporaneity" of God's Word (*GD* I, 145–48; I/1, 145–49, 205f.).

20. Sensitive to the non-temporal, anti-temporal tone of "supra-temporality" (*überzeitlich*), Barth acknowledges possible parallel German terms such as "co-temporal" (*mitzeitlich*) or "in-temporal" (*inzeitlich*), though he defends his choice by arguing that "supra-temporal" keeps with the truth that eternity "embraces" (*umschließende*) time on all sides (II/1, 623 = *KD* II/1, 702).

21. Cf. III/2, 523; III/3, 12.

22. The history of the world has a representative history in Israel and the Church, and, more importantly, the history of God's people has its ultimate history bound up in the history of Jesus Christ (II/1, 625; cf. IV/1, 508–13; IV/2, 760). When Barth says, "He Himself is time for us" (II/1, 612), one does not go too far in saying that Barth understands time and space "as forms within God," and that in the incarnation, "God *becomes* the mystery of time" (van der Kooi, *As in a Mirror*, 360). He enters into the imaged existence of which He Himself is the form, and so all other image-bearers in space and time already participate in Christ on some level. Jesus Christ's becoming flesh is "the actualization of the eternal God's *essential* temporality into the relative temporality of the creature" (Guretzki, *Karl Barth on the Filioque*, 155).

means post-temporality, the rear bracket of time, in which God already resides in the future, even the future when there will be no more time given. He dwells in the place to which all things are moving teleologically. At that end-point, when all creation meets Him there, He will strip away the concealment of time to reveal the glory of His already-accomplished reconciliation (II/1, 630). These three forms, pre-temporality, supra-temporality, and post-temporality, like the triune God, should be thought of in their perichoretic unity.[23] Time itself is spun out and caught up, as it were, in the waltz of God's triunity.

For all its improvements, Barth's mature conception of eternity has received sharp criticism over the years. Oscar Cullmann commends Barth's revisions, but does not see him freed from a Platonic idea of spiritual timelessness. God's all-temporal quality abstracts Him too much from history as we live it.[24] Cullmann says we must hold to a more biblical concept of "linear time," by which he means only that we must remain agnostic to God's eternal being and remain fixed to the narrative of redemptive history.[25] Richard Roberts puts forth a more sweeping critique by claiming that Barth's temporal quality within eternity is no more than a useful fiction. In his attempt to eradicate natural theology Barth construes eternity as a totalizing force, a black hole that never lets time stand on its own. Though Barth uses the incarnational structure of the person of Jesus Christ to ground all other being, historical existence is granted as real only to the extent that it is "the very self-explication of the divine being, a gigantic celestial tautology, the *circulus veritatis Dei*."[26] In Roberts' appraisal, eternity's all-encompassing clutch means not sustenance but stranglehold. Barth's re-temporalized eternity "is nevertheless

---

23. Barth does not make perspicuous the extent to which these three forms of eternity correlate to the three hypostases. His weak prohibition against making too much of these concepts opens the door for Robert Jenson's "communicative" Trinity in which the divine persons have one-to-one identification with their distinct (but perichoretically shared) temporal categories (Jenson, *God after God*, 191f.).

24. Cullmann, *Christ and Time*, 62–66. See also his critique of W. Kreck in Cullmann, *Salvation in History*, 62. Cullmann's objection is blunted by his failure to show how Barthian "qualitative difference" necessarily means "timelessness," though it counts for something that he cannot detect sufficient evidence in the Scriptures to underwrite Barth's view of eternity.

25. Cullman, *Christ and Time*, 11f. In response, Barth charges Cullmann with playing dumb about presuppositions, harboring a pre-established conception of time into which he inserts Jesus as the midpoint (III/2, 443).

26. Roberts, *A Theology on Its Way?*, 61.

not in *substantial* coinherence with our time."[27] Thus Roberts continues to fear in Barth "a logical implosion into timelessness," an incipient docetism.[28]

Given that Barth does so good a job covering his bases as he re-inscribes God's eternal transcendence as a predestinary, trinitarian gift to time, Cullmann and Roberts have probably overstated their objections. God's freedom from time is a freedom to embrace time. Still, in my estimation, Cullmann and Roberts begin to get at the biblical and theological perils of submerging time in divine omnitemporality. While eternity should be construed as a mode that does not lose anything by washing over into time, the converse is not necessarily true. Time may be too fragile a thing to be plunged in the ocean of eternity.

Laying aside this diffused objection, we are now prepared to understand Barth's understanding of the resurrection in the temporal-eternal categories he invokes. Indeed, what we detect from here parallels his theology proper: in the resurrection eternity gives its freedom *to* time. That gift—the gift of simultaneity—is exactly what Barth sees in the Easter miracle. Christ, though human, possesses total duration in the resurrection. In the Risen One we behold time freed by eternity.

THE ETERNALIZATION OF THE RISEN CHRIST

The resurrection of the flesh means the fulfillment of time, a fulfillment which begins with and flows from Jesus Christ, the firstborn from the dead. In Him God's freedom addresses our limitation. In Him we discover our human representative who is actually judged and destroyed, but who is afterwards appointed by the verdict of the Father to an enduring life. The Father grants the slain Son immortality, which Barth understands to be a freedom to dwell contemporaneously with every time. For Jesus Christ, eternity has the "texture" of His earthly history, and His earthly history in return enjoys the freedom of omnitemporality.[29] In Jesus we find the solution to human deficiency: eternalized time.

---

27. Ibid., 76.

28. Ibid., 26. For one rejoinder, see McDowell, *Hope in Barth's Eschatology*, 126, 146.

29. From here forward I will use "texture" as an important way to describe the earthly-temporal dimension of Barth's actualistic ontology. The term has been used in passing in Torrance, *Space, Time and Resurrection*, 144. For more on Barth's "actualism" see chapter 4.

Barth devotes considerable attention to Jesus Christ's resurrection in *CD* IV/1, §59.3 "The Verdict of the Father." Since Dawson exposits this subsection at length,[30] my task will be to explain Barth's complicated idea that the resurrection is for Jesus an appointment to a kind of transcendent time. What we are told to see here is the Christian hope: durable, completed, contemporaneous life.

I start by summarizing Barth's five points about the "Beyond" (*Jenseits*) of the resurrection in §59.3: 1) The resurrection of Jesus is *God's free act alone*, 2) a *new episode* marked off from the cross, 3) though *identical to the cross in substance*, 4) constituting a *historical event* in time 5) *of the selfsame Jesus Christ* who went before.[31] These five points can be interpreted in various ways, but for our purpose here let us take a step back and see these points with eternity and time in mind. Consider how the emphasis of the points includes aspects of both divine "non-history" and human history. Point one emphasizes that God alone is the agent, and that therefore the Beyond of Jesus' life means something no human has ever seen or heard or experienced, being wholly of God's world. Points three and five secure the stability of the person before and after the resurrection, the eternal Jesus Christ. Points two and four explain how the stability of this eternal person still leaves room for genuine history. Put more generally, Barth depicts eternity as preceding time (point one), uniting the times (points three and five), but also exercising lordship in such a way that it, for all its transcendence, can run concurrently with time (points two and four).[32] Easter must be spoken of as an event characterized by divine transcendence and historical immanence, for the Beyond of the Risen One overtakes history even as He moves in it.

As seen in the first two points above, Barth is concerned to recognize God's freedom in the gift of resurrection. In IV/1 he concentrates on the first Person, narrating the drama of the cross and resurrection from the perspective of the active Father and the passive Son. God's active freedom meets Jesus' passive condition. The human has no way to grasp the fullness of life, but God may, through a supernatural act, bestow it upon the human. For all intents and purposes, Barth says, history ended with Jesus

---

30. E.g. Dawson, *The Resurrection in Karl Barth*, 113ff.

31. IV/1, 297ff.

32. David Ford extends an interesting interpretation, matching points one and five (referring to the agency behind the event), points two and four (clarifying the nature of the event), and point three as the substantial unity of the resurrection and the cross: a chiastic structure with point three, the Crucified One = the Resurrected One, at the heart (Ford, *Barth and God's Story*, 40–42).

on the cross: He suffered death, was buried, descended into hell. So both Son and Father are there at Joseph of Arimathea's tomb, but only God the Father acts. He alone is the active agent. Easter Sunday "is unequivocally marked off from the first happening [Good Friday] by the fact that it does not have in the very least this component of human willing and activity" (IV/1, 300). The Father lives, the Son is dead, and, put starkly, "To be dead means not to be" (IV/1, 301). Jesus was not playing dead. His history was over. Barth wants to acknowledge the reality of this terminus, this end of human power at the end of life. Therefore the awakening of the dead Son was God's act, from above, outside of Christ. There is something like creation going on at Easter as the Father organizes the *tohu wa-bohu* again. His miraculous act on that Sunday is not collaboration or correction. It is, practically speaking, creation out of nothing.[33]

We might expect Barth to qualify his statement so as to speak about Jesus Christ strictly according to His human nature. But no, even according to His divine nature Jesus Christ participates in the event by His passivity:

> We obscure and weaken the character of the resurrection as a free pure act of divine grace (in contrast to the character of His death on the cross suffered in obedience), if appealing to His divine sonship we describe it as His own action and work. No, not simply as man, but even as the Son of God Jesus Christ is here simply the One who takes and receives, the recipient of a gift, just as in His death on the cross it is not only as man but as the Son of God that He is wholly and only the obedient servant. The fact that as very God and very man He is worthy of the divine gift of new life from the dead does not alter in the slightest the fact that He did not take this new life but that it was given to Him. (IV/1, 304)

With His last breath the Son entrusts His spirit into the Father's hands, then says no more, for in His voluntary dying He trusts the Father. Jesus "delivers Himself up" to the Father's "decree and disposing" (IV/1, 306). This is the Son's willful offering, to offer His dying time to God in hope. In the economy of salvation we see the Son exercising His prerogative to condescend into judgment and death. He is free to assume time and to play the part of the obedient, passive one before God. This drama enacts on earth what has ever been true in heaven, that the Son freely submits to the

---

33. Cf. I/1, 413; III/1, 17, 78; IV/1, 349.

Father.[34] Accordingly, just as the Father joyfully begets the Son eternally, so also the Father uses His eternal freedom to vindicate the beloved Son's obedience through resurrection.

To Barth's third point, that crucifixion and resurrection are to be read together. With this point Barth draws up the objective basis for the same dialectic at work in his early writings on the resurrection of the dead. The gracious act of the Father upon the Son at Easter can only be paired with Good Friday. The resurrection's new, eternal power from the Father's hand has built into it God's No to human merit. Resurrection contains within it a statement about "the dead," that is, that humans are not self-sustaining; they depend on the eternal God; standing apart from God they are rejected, condemned, and terminated. In Jesus' crucifixion humanity faced its death, and the resurrection, being that *novum* from above, reinforced the hard truth that the creature really has no claim to eternal life. Easter's distinct No echoed Golgotha. But Barth calls his readers to hear the final Yes of Easter, which is God's word of eternal welcome to the dead human. For Christ Himself it is the Father's verdict, the Father's "justification." The Father did this freely for Christ. The Son committed Himself into the Father's hands, and the Father joyfully gave new life to His altruistic child. The resurrection "was a second act of justice after the first to the extent that it was the divine approval and acknowledgment of the obedience given by Jesus Christ, the acceptance of His sacrifice, the proclamation and bringing into force of the consequences, the saving consequences, of His action and passion in our place" (IV/1, 305). To reinforce the notion of the uncoerced nature of the Father's gift to humanity's representative, Barth adds the wobbly side note that God did not have to justify the Son by raising Him and presenting Him to the world.[35] In any case, the Easter drama between Son and Father displays the kind of relationship Barth has been talking about all along between time and eternity. Time acknowledges its limitation, and eternity freely lifts time up to a new dimension.

What is the nature of this gift that the Father bestows on the dead Jesus? Is it not eternal life, i.e., the *simultaneity* of eternity? This is the payout of Barth's third point about the Beyond. As the impartation of eternity,

34. The subordination of the Son to the Father does nothing to detract from true deity of each, for "genuine miracle stands side by side with genuine miracle" (I/1, 414). The Son has *potestas* to be obedient to the Father (IV/2, 97).

35. IV/1, 306ff. Such a refusal to raise the Son would have been at odds with election, a disparity that should have been inconceivable for Barth considering his marriage of the two (see chapter 5). Note also Dawson's critique (*The Resurrection in Karl Barth*, 122f.; 220ff.).

the resurrection had the effect of bringing back Jesus Christ's voided life which had disappeared at His crucifixion. His history was restored and "rescued" (II/2, 762). But Barth pursues more than temporal restoration. He sees the resurrection as the ushering in of Jesus' omnitemporal *duration*. Christ's time was bracketed by a beginning and an end, but in the resurrection it became characterized by a "removal of the limitations of its yesterday, to-day and to-morrow, of its once, now and then" (III/2, 464), effecting "the perfection of this limited temporally restricted life" (III/2, 571), the passing away of the "imprisonment" of "temporal, spatial and personal singularity" (IV/4, 24). What took place in the resurrection was a "putting into effect . . . of what had taken place before," resulting in a pan-cosmic significance and application (IV/1, 318). Jesus "acquires" (*bekommt*) the duration which allows God to be equally available to all times (III/2, 440 = *KD*, 528). He "was made eternal and therefore always present in His resurrection and for every age from the days of His resurrection" (IV/1, 322).[36] The Crucified Jesus Christ may be known through all times, since He now comes to all times as the Crucified. His appearances during the forty days did not impress upon the disciples that their Lord was merely resuscitated, but that he had become "really but transcendentally present," overstepping the bounds of yesterday to be "absolutely present temporally" (III/2, 467). He is risen—a clarion call which Barth interprets to mean that Christ lives in the *Gegenwart* of God, the all-transcending, all-encompassing, all-suffusing Now of the divine life.

Building on the idea of Christ's duration, Barth in *CD* IV/1 hones in on the resurrection's pan-application of the sacrifice of Christ. Soteriologically, the resurrection establishes Jesus Christ as high priest forever. Instead of His ended life becoming a "dead history," the resurrection makes it to redound throughout all time, becoming "as such eternal history" (IV/1, 313), "the one truly contemporaneous divine act to us" (IV/1, 316). His atoning work did not come and go, as with the slaughter of cultic animals. It remains (and will remain forever) a once-for-all act that has become Christ's living intercession. I think it important that one not miss Barth's exchange of terms here: instead of describing Christ's priesthood in terms of an *ongoing* history with resurrection *power*, he speaks of the *concluded*

---

36. Donald MacKinnon follows the same tack, saying that in Christ's resurrection "an eternity is bestowed upon his work," according universal contemporaneity to the "stuff" or "very substance" of what had transpired historically beforehand (MacKinnon, "The Resurrection," 65).

history of Christ with resurrection *duration*.[37] Barth exposits the life of Jesus, now risen and ascended, as omnipresent in the sense that Jesus has access to all times.[38] The ransom for the whole world is kairologically full, actual, and immanent because the potency of the sacrifice of Jesus belongs to His eternal present.

The idea of the contemporaneity of Jesus has a philosophical function for Barth as well. The Enlightenment writer G. E. Lessing spoke of the impossibility of belief in the occurrence of Jesus Christ's resurrection because an "ugly, broad ditch" many centuries wide stood between it and the modern person. How could one possibly verify such a miracle, since it was nowhere in the vicinity of the present day and so could not supply immediate empirical data? Phrasing it as a maxim, Lessing concluded that "the accidental truths of history can never become the proof of necessary truths of reason."[39] While one might point out a categorical fallacy here, Lessing's cry for skepticism had the ring of common sense. Barth was well aware of this objection and addressed it on multiple occasions.[40] His answer to Lessing, however, was quite simple: the risen Jesus is present. He is not a figure of history swallowed by the past. His miraculous life and power have not been swept away by the tides of time. More to the point, His resurrection is not like other events. It perdures. The Living One is immanent in the moment of revelation; His presence, one could say, is momentous (in the expanded sense of that term). One need not invent clever ways to vault over the ugly ditch, for the risen Savior bridges His way to us in the power of eternity. Therefore, Lessing's objection is a mere "methodological question" (IV/1, 289), a technical objection which in the end turns out to be nothing more than a disingenuous delay tactic against faith (IV/1, 292, 348).

---

37. The difficulty of this concept has perhaps obfuscated and minimized Christ's priestly office (as argued in Torrance, *Karl Barth, Biblical and Evangelical Theologian*, 206f.; Gunton, "Salvation," 153).

38. By doing so he recites Luther's ubiquitarianism in the temporal key (Farrow, *Ascension and Ecclesia*, 292).

39. In the same passage, regarding the resurrection, Lessing teaches, "Since the truth of these miracles has completely ceased to be demonstrable by miracles still happening now, since they are no more than reports of miracles, I deny that they should bind me in the least to a faith in the other teachings of Christ" (Lessing, "On the Proof of the Spirit and of Power," 55).

40. E.g., Barth, *The Theology of the Reformed Confessions*, 46; *GD* I, 65; *PT*, 251ff.; I/1, 146f.; IV/1, 21; IV/2, 113; cf. Berkouwer, *The Triumph of Grace in the Theology of Karl Barth*, 139.

Another problem, but one which Barth does not address sufficiently, is how the eternalized Jesus can have His entire history in the flesh raised if that means the perpetuating of tragic components of His life. The effect of Christ's sacrifice should be available in every time, of course, but it seems obscene for us to say that Jesus' sin-bearing and suffering themselves carry on into the ages. Is not the Resurrected One immune to any kind of future death, having suffering death once and for all (Rom 6:9–10)? Did He not despise the shame of the cross (Heb 12:2)? Jesus retained His scars in glory, certainly, but even these were mementos of dying *overcome*. The perpetuation of the flesh as an eternally actualized history does not seem to allow for the skimming off of the dross of punishment for sin or the ending of the horrors of bodily torment. I therefore struggle to come to terms with the concept of an eternalized history as being a desirable kind of glorification. Yet Barth is intent on salvaging the whole history: "Because as crucified and dead He is risen and lives, the fact of His death on the cross can never be past, it can never cease to be His action" (IV/1, 315). How, then, is Jesus not eternally damned? If His history has been eternalized, if He is eternally living as the One who was dying and dead, how does He come in unfettered glory and not in perpetual suffering? If the Father's justifying word to the Word is to mean deliverance, then it must also be a leaving behind of cursed historical components. As it is, however, Barth has made no provision for the alleviation of cursedness, since the crucifixion is Christ's hidden glory and the resurrection is the glorious meaning of His dying. The empty tomb translates what happens the cross. Barth makes that clear enough. But mere translation does not sufficiently undo the hard facts of suffering, and it does not heal that which was broken. A more chronological conception of life everlasting would open up the chance to put some distance between present goodness and the horrors of yesteryear. With eternalization, unfortunately, one is simply not at liberty to leave anything in the past.

On a related topic, others have objected in general terms to a kind of false openness to the future implicit in the theme of duration. Robert Jenson's rigorous critique exposes Barth's eagerness to close off futurity by creating a vortex of the bi-une drama between Father and Son. The lack of the Holy Spirit's venture into the world as a fresh movement among human agents stems from an overrealized notion of eternity, "putting the historical event of Jesus's existence in the place formerly occupied by changeless 'Being.'"[41] Barth's account of the resurrection of Jesus and the

41. Jenson, *Alpha and Omega*, 140.

procession of the Spirit do not make for a radical openness to the world; the Church has little hope of entering into the trinitarian drama in any significant way. Similarly, Colin Gunton speaks of a lingering Platonism in Barth's work, a "partial failure" in that Christ acquires a certain static quality at His death, whereupon His actual life is rounded up and "the history of God with man is telescoped."[42] Here Barth is "not being trinitarian enough . . . [f]or if the meaningful activity of God is already completed in the past—or timeless—eternity, the outworking of the divine decision has all the necessity of a timeless concept, and our theology becomes the quest . . . for timeless truths."[43] More breathing room is needed for a fully kinetic ontology.

Without baptizing the respective projects of Jenson and Gunton, I feel their apprehension about Barth's lingering Platonism is warranted. Has Barth really escaped the lure of immutability? Has reality been dynamized in the life of Jesus only to plunge back into stasis at Easter? I am not so sympathetic to Jenson's and Gunton's fear that Christ's eternal history would mean the cutting off of human agency (at least in the penultimate age). But their concern at the very least brings up the important question in Christology: Does Barth leave room for a newness in the risen Jesus' agency, an open-endedness to His ongoing personal history?

Barth gives something of an answer in his fourth point about the Beyond: Jesus' resurrection was a genuinely historical event. The forty days of resurrection appearances were actual happenings in time and space, enacted by the selfsame Jesus Christ who lived and died in the flesh. Having started with the power of eternity, Barth now seeks to reaffirm the resurrection's temporality, saying that the resurrection event "must stand in a sequence of time and space. However different it may be in other respects, as history it must be like all other history in regard to its historicity" (IV/1, 298). Riffing off of 1 Cor 15, Barth asserts, "If Jesus Christ is not risen—bodily, visibly, audibly, perceptibly, in the same concrete sense in which He died . . . we are still in our sins" (IV/1, 351f.). Jesus Christ had to be raised in the fullness of what He was. Who is the One who has victory? The some-body who went before. Who is the High Priest of the ages? The man in flesh and bone who served God in His once-for-all role. If Jesus was historical on one side, and if He is the same person now, then He must be historical in the Beyond. In eternity Jesus is still Himself, the historical God-man. By His eternalized historical identity He has freedom to roam

42. Gunton, *Becoming and Being*, 183.
43. Ibid., 218.

within the wider boundaries of history. The super-historical nature of His resurrection allows Jesus to engage history once again. In this qualified sense, Jesus' resurrection appearances were historical.

Not to be misunderstood, Barth excoriates all backtracking into rationalism through a naked, historicized account of the resurrection. So, for instance, he rejects Enlightenment-style explanations hypothesizing that Jesus' body left the tomb by theft or because He was not fully expired (H. S. Reimarus, K. F. Bahrdt, F. D. E. Schleiermacher, R. Seeburg), as well as a psychological explanation in which the disciples hallucinated because of their grief or their overpowering messianic expectations (D. F. Strauss, Ernest Renan). Likewise, Barth refuses to label the resurrection "a myth" (A. E. Biedermann, Rudolf Bultmann) or ethical symbol (Paul Tillich), for both approaches put the New Testament accounts on a Procrustean bed, making out of the resurrection ornamental portrayals of "the non-spatial and timeless being of certain general truths, orders and relationships" (IV/1, 337).[44] Jesus Christ is not raised into an abstraction! Finally, Barth rejects the apologetical (i.e., historical-positive) accounts in the same way he rejects historical-critical explanations. Why? Because one does not encounter the resurrection as normal history. It cannot be probed and apprehended and synthesized like normal historical research. Because God alone is at work in resurrection-revelation it is better to speak of the forty days as "saga," a particular historical event indescribable except through poetic language and inaccessible to verification except through revelation.[45] The resurrection is *special history*, history suffused with eternity. No wonder the New Testament supplies a marvelous and bewildering and near-contradictory testimony to these days.

I do not care to be consumed by the historicity debate, which has received enough attention in Barth studies.[46] Our concern at this juncture is simply how the forty days, as the chief expression of Jesus' eternalized time, are portrayed as non-historical history by Barth. Non-history and history coexist in the resurrection—though it seems clear to me that

---

44. Frei takes up Barth's tenacious defense of the particular: far from a myth, the biblical narrative is "a demythologization of the dying-rising savior myth" with "an unsubstitutable individual . . . inseparable from the unsubstitutable events constituting it, with the resurrection as its climax" (Frei, *The Identity of Jesus Christ*, 174f.).

45. IV/1, 336f.; cf. III/1, 80ff; III/2, 452; Barth, *The Heidelberg Catechism for Today*, 76.

46. For resources along this line see Fuller, "The Resurrection of Jesus and the Historical Method," 18–24; Lorenzen, *Resurrection and Discipleship*, 66–71; Carnley, *The Structure of Resurrection Belief*, 46ff.; Frei, *The Identity of Jesus Christ*, 139–52; Migliore, *Faith Seeking Understanding*, 370–83.

Barth, even late in *CD*, gives the non-history of eternity the upper hand during the forty days. He remarks at the "peculiar character of this history, which bursts through all general ideas of history as it takes place and as it may be said to take place in space and time" (IV/1, 335). It is a "second history" at the place where history stops (III/2, 441). This newness dominates because Jesus Christ is alive in His eternal power, coming to the disciples not as a resuscitated man but as the One-who-went-before in transcendent duration, "the totality of the event of the existence of Jesus" (III/2, 337). Barth calls the reader to see in the forty days the history of non-history, a first and potent expression of non-history in and "at" history. The divine kairological makes residence among the chronological for these forty days.

Let me point out once again that resurrection and revelation are usually equivalent terms for Barth. Whenever God reveals Himself through the Son or the Spirit, the normal conditions of perception and reality cease to apply. This was true for Abraham, true for Moses, true for Jeremiah, true for Macrina and Anselm and Calvin. God always displays Himself as transcendent, as "future," to His saints. He abides in the Beyond and breaks into history in order to make Himself known in self-revelation, subjecting all history to the divine in-breaking. To summon the language of *Der Römerbrief*, eternity "dissolves" and "establishes" history. For Barth, the forty day period of Jesus' risen appearances to the disciples is the pinnacle of historical dissolution and establishment. The risen God-man uses His freedom to puncture time and raise these moments of historical time into His eternal presence. The seconds keep ticking on earth for the disciples: they walk, they fish and cook, they eat and dialogue—but they are *with Jesus* in His unconcealed glory. These men and women find themselves on the bridge of simultaneity upon which Jesus meets them, interacting with them in "the assumption of their time into His" (III/2, 470). They are taken up into His contemporaneous life without leaving their own sequential histories. The forty days are not the theological equivalent of an "overtime" or an "extended play" or "bonus round." Analogies fail immediately. Resurrection time is paradox, plodding forward in clock-time but suffused by eschaton. Resurrection time is paradox like the logic of revelation itself. Indeed, as Barth sees it, the forty days are the premier form of revelation, after which all revelation takes its shape.[47]

47. Because the disciples' experience cannot be verified by historical-scientific method, Barth does not say much about the forty days as the fount of apostolic authority. Nevertheless, he can join Bengel in saying that the gospel writers (and their narratives) "breathe resurrection" (e.g., *DO*, 102; IV/2, 132). The Scriptures represent the

He ascended. He didn't shrink, disappear, vaporize, vanish, relocate, submerge, evaporate, fizzle, explode, or descend.

Barth's central point, however, is that the first Eastertide is primarily the story about Jesus, *His* forty days. He makes this history and is there at the center of it. He appears bodily. The forty days are the objective occurrence of Jesus Christ, taking place as He claimed the concrete, tangible setting in Israel for His interaction with Mary, John, Peter, and the like. Only secondarily can it be about human faith in response to His revelation. In contrast, Rudolf Bultmann's interpretation of the forty days breaks apart the historical-subjective and historical-objective elements, classifying the former as faith and the latter as a mythological husk. "Objective" history must be stripped away to get to the spiritual truth. Barth charts a different course in that he affirms the objective with the subjective, and does so because it is the selfsame historical Jesus at work in history: "[I]t was because God Himself, the Creator, who was first hidden in the lowliness of this creature, in the death of this man, was now manifested in His resurrection, that it was absolutely necessary for this event genuinely and apprehensibly to include nature, and therefore to be physical" (III/2, 451). The tomb really was empty; His body really did interact with the disciples' bodies; He really ended this time with His ascension into heaven. Jesus' revelatory history is not categorically incompatible with sequential history. This Jesus is not docetic. Like the incarnation, the resurrection means that eternity has time, that the eternal man Jesus can intersect time even after His earthly years are over. Super-nature has hold of nature. In this vein, Barth's commentary on the forty days gives priority to the divine even as it affirms creation.

So far as Barth's narration of the resurrection is an rich account of Christ's *deity*, Christ's divine-transcendence-embracing-history, I believe that most criticisms fall flat. The Son's loving freedom permits a mutual transhistoricity and historicity. As the risen Son of God living in eternity He has authority to access history and, in some sense, still to live in it. As far as Christ's *divine* freedom is concerned, I have no serious objection to the possibility that God's totally-other action in the resurrection might exhibit a certain historical margin.

My concern regarding Christ in His *humanity* remains, however. Barth teaches that Jesus' human-temporal identity is exhausted in His death, and that this Jesus-history, compiled and immutable, is eternalized in the

---

memoirs of those who were directly *in* the resurrection like no one after them would ever be. On the other hand, the days of appearance to the disciples can be said to bear a certain all-importance, since Barth compresses Jesus' human history in the Beyond to the forty days instead of extending it in the heavenly session (Farrow, *Ascension and Ecclesia*, 247f.).

resurrection. But if Barth means to say that the risen Jesus adds nothing to His history in the resurrection, then it makes little sense to say He has a *continuing* history. The recapitulated Jesus may influence others—but He does not necessarily *interact*. That risen man may have *a bodily quality*—but it is not at all clear that He is a living, moving body. The risen Lord goes forth into history—but He does not *inhabit* that place in any significant human sense. David Ford seems to detect this very problem when he writes that, in Barth's picture, the resurrection appearances "have much more the character of 'sendings' into the future" than a genuine expression of eternity in time.[48] Would it not be more consistent for Barth to say that the humanity of Christ is made alive only so far it is "raised" and "put to use" by His deity? And if the risen Christ does not extend His human history, shall it not suffice to say that the living Christ is busy in the act of resurrective history-*making*?[49]

What we may say with confidence is that Barth chooses to dwell upon the point of the pliability of eternity's freedom. The divine has no temporal restraints, and therefore Jesus' incarnate life, eternally actualized by the verdict of the Father, makes Jesus' time contemporaneous with every time. Freedom is imparted to Him in that history, and therefore to Him in His body. He in His past embodiment is present to us in eternal power. Wherever and whenever Christ interposes Himself in history, there and then we find His particular presence "in the flesh." So much Barth says about the Son of God's death and resurrection—now what about our own?

THE LIMITATION OF THE HUMAN

In contrast to eternity, says Barth, creaturely time has no freedom for comprehension of moments. It has no duration. The "now" flits from moment to moment, leaving to the void a trail of irretrievable past happenings.

> What is the present? It is the time between the times. And this, strictly speaking and as we actually experience it, is no time at all, no duration, no series of moments, but only the boundary between past and future" (III/2, 514).

Even when Barth comes to speak of time as a created good, he never accords it any sense of intrinsic permanence. It is simply the flow in which creaturely things have an opportunity to act. Time is the flux and decay

48. Ford, *Barth and God's Story*, 144.
49. As in Barth, *Credo*, 109; IV/3, 212. Cf. Moltmann, *Theology of Hope*, 180f.

If the ascension takes place in time, then it also is a movement w/in space.

in which humans have their meager present. I will look at this limitation of the human, which Barth describes as a kind of wound or incapacity. Human existence transpires as a passing act, delimited by God through birth and death.

Having identified Barth's later shift, we may go back and glean insight from *CD* I/2's §14.1 "God's Time and Our Time." There Barth classifies three types of time, viz., creational, sinful, and redeemed. After II/1 these categories become inaccurate for Barth, since time, posited by God within His own being, is in its basic essence wrapped in the divine definition and thereby made good. But some of what Barth says about sinful time is still relevant to his systematic. Outside of Christ's mastery of time, creaturely time as such can only be described as a "flow from one conjectural present to another," a course fragmented and uncollected (I/2, 68). The changing phenomena fly away from humans, who can only try to grasp them in their lame, deformed consciousnesses. They seize the past through memories and ponder the coming times through imagination, but their *attentio* is abbreviated at best.[50] The movement of creation really does exist objectively because it has been made part of God's being (according to II/2), but human time (read: time-gathering) still cannot make sense of the voided past, the fleeting present, and the unknown future. Without recourse to God, human perception is a feeble subjective sequencing of time.

Barth sometimes speaks of this incapacity in terms of an injury. The risen Christ "does not extinguish time. . . . He normalizes time. He heals its wounds" (III/1, 74). For time to persist and thrive, it must lean wholeheartedly upon another, supernatural dimension. George Hunsinger is right to say that this neediness does not have to reflect a moral deficiency.

> Note that time's healing is distinct from salvation from sin. Time's wounds, as here set forth, are inherent in the good creation. They may be exacerbated and corrupted by sin, but they are not identical with it, nor are they hostile to God. When measured by eternity, they are merely imperfections, not corruptions.[51]

God does not make corrupt humans in corrupt time or commit some sort of violence against them in the act of creation. He does, however, make them unperfected, as creatures in need of a divine supplement. Thus we might substitute the more neutral "impaired" for Barth's "wounded."

---

50. Cf. Augustine, *Confessions*, XI. Though note Barth's repudiation of Augustine's intra-cognitive measurements, which he says fall into the same trap as Martin Heidegger's philosophy (I/2, 45–46).

51. Hunsinger, *Disruptive Grace*, 204. Cf. Roberts, *A Theology on Its Way?*, 29.

For all its reality, time as we experience it does not have simultaneity with other times.[52] It is imprisoned in the simple, evaporating present. It possesses no comprehensive being, no contemporaneous mode. Here we might import one of Barth's favorite metaphors about doing theology: trying to live life in time is an attempt to sketch a bird on the wing.[53] That is time's metaphysical quandary for Barth. It lacks cumulativity. It is without God's perfect dynamism. It hobbles along in its impairment, seeking that dimension which will complete it. Fragmented and supine, human life reaches out in utter dependence to Him "who alone is immortal and who dwells in unapproachable light" (1 Tim 6:16).

A chronic situation for time!—but necessarily and purposefully so. Its void is God-shaped. Limitations are evil, says Barth, only when humans pridefully and insanely assert their self-sufficiency.[54] God intends limitations to become good as they spur us to the good, for by them we are led unto Him who can bestow the eternal good. The finitude of one's own existence between conception and death can be a righteous plea unto God to subsume this frail history into a higher order. As that which presupposes and encourages dependence on the eternal God, the limited, dying quality of time is an auspicious condition, a *felix plaga*.

§47 "Man in His Time" is an important section because of the way Barth positions human life in needy juxtaposition to eternity. Having commented on the resurrection of Christ in His divine-human history (the content of §47.1 "Jesus, Lord of Time"), we may go on to look at anthropology more directly. From the resurrection of Jesus Christ, Barth asserts four aspects of human time: given, allotted, beginning, and ending.

In §47.2 "Given Time" Barth begins to spell out, by contrast with Jesus Christ's fulfilled time in the resurrection, what *mere* time looks like. Humanity has this time. Indeed, humanity "is temporality" (III/2, 522). God supplies this mode to humans in order to play out His purposes among them. He gives them room to act, bestowing and maintaining the form of their creaturely existence. But this moving-room is not the safety of eternal life; their existence is ever imperiled. Because humans have their humble being in the sequence from past to present to future, because the stream from the past to the future must be continually forded, because

52. Cf. II/1, 608; III/2, 463.

53. Human perceptions and correspondences of God in thought, word and deed are no more than "momentary view[s] of a bird in flight" (*WGWM*, 282). Similarly, Christian theology can only be a "living *procession*," a humble mimicry of the dynamism of its uncaged Subject (Barth, *Evangelical Theology*, 9–10).

54. Cf. IV/1, §60.2 "The Pride of Man."

the "now" can commence only by fragmenting away from the past and toward future, the present is the most vulnerable tense. Humans call upon memory and imagination, dim powers that they are, for temporal ligamentation. But God alone can give time in the first place, He alone can supply that concrete but fragile reality, the flux in which people may live and move and have their being.

Barth expands this theme with §47.3 "Allotted Time." God gives time, but only a set interval of time. A human is born and dies. A person's time commences and ends, and through that allotment one has his or her own bracketed history. The "rock walls" of conception and death form a "workshop" for human action and response toward God (III/2, 563).[55] Human life lives within *die Grenze*: borders which limit human time even as they define it, borders which terminate flesh even as they bracket it as a concrete history.

I think it important here that we put a name to this aspect of Barth's ontology: actualism. Actualism means that one's being can be identified directly, even entirely, with the extent of one's actions and enacted relations. It identifies one's being with one's history: "the 'I' emerges in the unique story I manage to tell between birth and death."[56] A rather unconventional metaphysical approach, actualism allows us to "sum it all up and simply say: 'My time'—I am my time!"[57] We have already seen how God has an actualized existence through the election of Himself to be the human Savior within time and space, a central truth about Jesus we will spell out further in the next chapter. Here we speak of actualism strictly in its anthropological application. All that a human does (and leaves undone) in his or her fleeting stretch of movement is that person's life.

Turning back to Barth more particularly, he teaches that something in us resists life's borders, especially death. "Human life protests against this 'only.'" It desires duration, and rightly so, admits Barth, "for if it is to fulfil its determination it would seem to need unending time" (III/2, 555–56). Covenantal life with the eternal God cries out for more, even infinitely more. Should we not see limitations as evil, then? Not at all, argues Barth. Rather, we should accept with joy the limitations inherent to

---

55. Barth's allotted time, then, is not entirely unlike the concrete spectacle of John Calvin's *theatrum gloria Dei*.

56. Mangina, *Karl Barth*, 94. "At a sheerly descriptive or phenomenological level, Barth stands firmly within this [broadly existentialist] tradition of thought. He is in his own way an existentialist" (ibid.).

57. Barth, "My Time Is Secure in Your Hands," sermon, 31 Dec 1960, in Barth, *Call for God*.

our allotted time. First of all, limitations are proper to the time had by the creature. They designate the creature as creature; they give definition to historicity. It is God's design for the creature to have its identity in limited but concrete action. Since humans are by nature not co-eternal with God, their good lies in the restricted period of their days and years. Possessing a definite beginning and end is what it means to live in the dimension of time, "a dimension which fits and suits [human life] like a tailor-made garment" (III/2, 559). Secondly, Barth says that the prospect of infinite, limitless time does not offer hope of completion anyway. Time is given in order for humans to have opportunity to reach the perfection of their relationships to God and others. Perpetual life would not advance this quest, avows Barth, as "it is hard to see how everlasting life can guarantee duration and fulfillment in relation to its determination" (III/2, 561). Only so much time is needed.[58] Barth's disregard for perpetuity has a third reason: unending time would promote humanity's endless seeking and dissatisfaction. With no possible completion and culmination to life, a person would be condemned to the hellish life of continuous want with no hope of "the peace of permanent life under God and with other men" (III/2, 562).[59] To Barth, continuation of earthly life smacks of tedium. What humanity really needs is eternal rest, a divine Sabbath.[60] The real reason for the rejection of infinite life, Barth ultimately gets around to saying, is that completion only comes by turning to God. A finite human existence needs the eternal God for vital supplementation. As the "Counterpart" to humans in time,

58. "It is understandable that [humanity] wants a sufficient measure of days and years for its development as the fulfilment of its destiny" (III/2, 560). Barth admits, though he neglects the problem of early demises. This leaves him open to a chorus of protests: Has the stillborn child had enough time? Have enough days been given to the teenage soldier consumed in a landmine explosion? What about the elderly who do not conclude with Simeon's and Anna's joy, who wait in vain for an answer to prayer? How does this hope address the horror of countless truncated lives? (Cf. Hebblethwaite, *Philosophical Theology and Christian Doctrine*, 112.) And how would Barth explain trito-Isaiah's flat equation of longevity with blessing in the New Jerusalem, in which even the dead centenarian shall be considered accursed (Isa 65:20)?

59. The same idea is at work in God's benevolent eviction of Adam and Eve from the garden (III/1, 284). To eat from the tree of life (that is, to seek perpetuation) after rebelling from the grace of God is to damn oneself without end. Yet mortal men and women, dejected and obstinate, desire the barren hope of becoming gods on their own terms. "All evil begins with the fact that we will not thankfully accept the limitation of our existence where we should hope in the light of it, and be certain, joyously certain, of the fulfilment of life in the expectation of its end" (IV/2, 468).

60. The resurrection is "a rest that fills time," "the eschatological limit" of work, "achieved culture"—and inquiries into the potential boringness of this quietude are "stupid questions" (Barth, *Ethics*, 223).

God "can encounter us and be our Neighbour on all sides" (III/2, 565). Humans must not try to be gods alongside Him. Rather, they must hold out their hands to their Maker and Sustainer, to Him who confronts and offers complete duration to them at the very borderline of non-existence. Their bounded existences call out for His unbounded one.[61] In Barth's appraisal, human life needs its divine context. Allotted time poses the question to which eternity gives the answer.

A problem looms, however. How has the Creator made humans good if they are destined for non-being? Of what value is a concrete history if that history is *dead*? In §47.4 "Beginning Time" and §47.5 "Ending Time" Barth further explains his anthropological limitation with an eye to answering this sticky issue. He first makes the basic point that the creature has a beginning in time. One is conceived, and only then has being. Christian belief permits no speculation about emanationism, or the possibility of pre-existent souls as held by Origen (III/2, 573). Nothing precedes the human self but the eternal God.

vs. pre-existence

Then comes death. To the psyche the ending of existence feels more threatening than its beginning. Barth does not soften the initial blow, since he makes no allowance for a continuation of the person through a disembodied soul. A person dies, then is no more; no natural life remains in body or soul; one is temporally, historically, truly extinguished at this final boundary. As far as creaturely life is concerned, one suffers *Ganztod*.[62] No one likes the fact of death, admits Barth. Death claims all. It ends existence. It threatens the creature by placing it under the weight of its sentence even while it lives. For the human consciousness it presents a terrifying, inscrutable riddle.

Even so, death's moral status should not be decided too hastily, chimes Barth. Non-being need not mean something evil. In God's providence, death can be good. The end of the human means the termination of all one's own possibilities and potentiality—but only the termination of those possibilities and powers coming from *oneself*. The eternal God is still there: He was there before one's life and He will be there after it. Temporal

---

61. Barth rarely ventures into matters of psychological motivation (which often draw upon natural theology for force), but, reading between the lines of §47, he clearly sees death as a stimulus for the crisis of faith. I have already noted how for the early Barth the line of death is a (the?) chief signpost of one's dependency upon the Primal Origin (e.g. *ER*, 156, 168).

62. Cf. IV/3, 310. Karl Barth joins Paul Althaus, Helmut Thielicke, Gerhard Ebeling, Jörg Baur, and Wilfried Joest, along with Eberhard Jüngel and Wolfhart Pannenberg in rejecting the soul as a pivot-point of personal existence, thus leaving the human as such to total obliteration after death (Henning, "Wirklich ganz tot?," 238).

being returns to the One who called it out of non-being, says Barth, and one's apparent end is hardly a tragedy if it ends "in God." In fact, death "signifies something supremely positive if it is the case, as we have seen, that we come from God. It can be negative and evil only if our end means passing not only into non-being [*Nichtsein*] but into the negation [*Nichts*] of being" (III/2, 595 = *KD*, 724). For Barth there is a distinction within death: "It is really our nothingness [*Nichtigkeit*] in His sight which is revealed in the destructive work of death" (III/2, 608 = *KD*, 740). Death can only finish off our temporal journeys, not the *relational position* of our histories vis-à-vis God. Only He may judge that position. It is appointed for us to die and then face judgment (Heb 9:27), for then and there we are sequestered into God's hands. Can it be that God will vouchsafe our ended histories? Indeed. We shall be alive no more, and yet, "We shall not be alone in death. We shall be with God who is the Lord of death" (III/2, 609).

That is, Barth makes a pronounced distinction between death and judgment. He refuses to see death *per se* as a curse, for in Jesus Christ's death and resurrection the real enemy is revealed: our guilty alienation from God. Cursedness would be established fully at death were it not for the crucified and risen Lord escorting us into God's own eternal life. But as it is, *this* sting of death—the nothingness of "hell"—has already and conclusively been removed, "so that we can now contemplate the prospect of death as something which is really behind and beneath us" (III/2, 614). After Christ death no longer has the meaning of perdition and negation. The Victor has dissolved all guilt, "making death irrelevant as its consequence" (III/2, 621). Death comes, but without the connotation of dire judgment from God, for that He has already taken on His own shoulders. The "first death" is not the "second death."[63] Therefore Barth would have his readers see physical death as a harmless sign of judgment, not the negating judgment itself.[64]

Death is a creational good, then? Yes. Having had its meaning liberated by Jesus Christ, death may be understood as something free from every harmful association of judgment, an occurrence "belong[ing] to the life of the creature" and thus "necessary to it" (III/2, 639). Death is revealed as negation, but as a negation negated by the Savior.[65] For the Christian

---

63. This terminology stems from Barth's exegesis of Rev 20:4–6 (e.g. III/2, 628, 634).

64. E.g. III/2, 626; IV/1, 349f.; Barth, *Against the Stream*, 238f.

65. This is not to say, however, that death can be identified with Christ or "resolved in a play of harmonies," as in the "romanticizing principle" of Novalis (*PTNC*, 366–67). Consider Barth's parallel discourse on the void in the creation account (III/1, 372ff.),

death remains a sign of God's judgment only as a hollow phenomenon disarmed by the greater sign of the cross. All that is really left operative is the good and proper order of the creation. Stripped of its damning significance, death meets the human as a natural terminus.

Barth entertains an objection to the division of death and guilt: How can we vindicate death, since we know of no example of death that does not involve guilt? Barth refuses to comment on the question of a death of a sinless prelapsarian Adam, but he does offer a tortured deduction about the death of Christ (III/2, 628ff.).[66] Jesus Christ, because He took on this burden *voluntarily* and lived it *sinlessly*, did not have to die the death of judgment. Nevertheless, Jesus did die. Therefore He had to be capable of dying, and since His death was not *out of necessity* a death of judgment, the only death fitting to Him would have been a natural death. He did not die *just* this natural death, of course, but, hypothetically speaking, this was the only death required of Him. In His innocence Christ could have died a "different" death, such as that of Enoch, Moses, or Elijah (III/2, 635ff.), though to fulfill His role as Mediator He experienced death *qua* judgment, so as to overstep this accursed boundary. The remaining arguments Barth makes for a blessed death are piecemeal and rhetorical, reiterating earlier contentions.[67]

It makes sense for Barth to want to domesticate death for his actualistic ontology, but—and I say this in direct contraposition to the exegetical portions of §47.5—his interpretations are simply misguided. For example, he passes over the cacophony of cries to God for deliverance from death and attends to the few examples of holy resignation in the Bible, such as Jacob and David, who are content to "go the way of all flesh . . . full of years" (III/2, 634). Or again, instead of seeing the assumptions of Enoch and Elijah as a blessing from God in which they are spared death altogether, Barth interprets their termini as equivalent to divine euthanasia, God putting them to a penalty-less death (III/2, 635ff.), which in turn suggests

---

that darkness is in no way the counterpart of light or the secret eternal wellspring, but that which exists only by not being that which is posited by God.

66. For the following cf. Berkouwer, *The Triumph of Grace in the Theology of Karl Barth*, who calls the following argument "a piece of abstract reasoning," insufficiently christological (p. 336).

67. We may extract two of them. One, death brought salvation, so it cannot be entirely bad: "And if His dying—in virtue of what it was as His—is the sum total of the good which God has shown to the world, how can we dare to understand man's mortality as something intrinsically negative and evil?" (III/2, 630). Two, death ends our sinning: endless life "could only mean in fact that we should be able to sin infinitely and even qualitatively multiply our guilt on an infinite scale" (III/2, 631).

to him that biological death is "general and neutral" (III/2, 637). Or, as a third instance, Barth makes much out of the New Testament's talk of death as "sleep," postulating that the early Christians reinterpreted the cold reality of death as nothing more than a somnolent slipping away, seeing in a person's external death-throes "the last conclusive symptom of a life surrounded by the peace of God" (III/2, 639). These comfortable sentiments call out for challenge. Biblical euphemisms about a person's death do not commend death any more than the biblical confidence about a believer's justification before the throne of God commends sin. Scriptural consolations to the believer facing death do nothing to exonerate the latter. None of the biblical texts mentioned by Barth says anything about the inherent goodness of death, though every last one says something about the righteous power of God *over* death.

To be fair, Barth claims that God should be justified and not death as such.[68] Yet for its service in handing humans over to God, Barth cannot help but name death "a servant commissioned by God" (III/2, 608), and its ministry of termination "an unequivocally welcome, because gracious, event" (IV/3, 927). Much like Jesus' shrouded victory on the cross, our own deaths are but the shadowy flip-side of God's gracious resurrection.[69] Death, while not salvation *per se*, is salvific insofar as lays out the boundary between time and eternity.

Are we to believe Barth when he says that the torturous spiral into oblivion is in fact only a toothless oarsman rowing us over to glory? *This* is the final foe of God (1 Cor 15:26), the great enemy about to be hurled into the lake of fire (Rev 20:14)? Barth's exoneration of creaturely death strikes me as both unconvincing and dangerous. His arguments are insufficiently Christological, appealing to the same sense of crisis that informs existentialism, i.e., the awareness of mortal limitation invites us to decide for that which is limitless. My only conclusion is that, behind the doctrinal and exegetical gymnastics, Barth's thanatology is an embarrassing remnant of natural theology.

Still, as much as I cannot accept his theology of limit, I have not entirely dismantled his more basic point, that human time's main weakness is that it lacks duration, that it needs a mode of perception that binds every moment into a life "secured firmly, properly held together, arranged and

68. God is the frontier of the frontier, after all (III/2, 609ff.). Cf. II/2, 265, 362; IV/2, 462f.; IV/3, 924ff.; IV/4, 15. Barth also includes, though far too late in the *Dogmatics*, the point that some will not die, being alive at Christ's return (IV/3, 924–26). E.g. II/2, 265, 362; IV/2, 462f.; IV/3, 924ff.; IV/4, 15.

69. Cf. Gorringe, *Karl Barth*, 60.

refined."[70] Let us then move on to discuss the general resurrection as a solution to human fragmentation.

THE ETERNALIZATION OF THE RISEN HUMAN

Nowhere in Barth's writings do we find a lengthy discourse on the after-life of the human. In fact, he discourages too much curiosity or longing for redemption as such. One is supposed to pine for the Savior in whom glorification lies.

> This all-embracing glorification includes that of the Church and of every individual Christian. This does not mean, however, that the Church, or the individual Christians within it, can or should live with a view to their own future glorification. This, too, would be treachery against their living hope. (IV/4, 199)[71]

Barth is particularly stubborn about cashing out Christ for the *beneficia Christi*, yet it should be transparent by now that he *has* given us some-thing of a doctrine of glorification by describing Jesus' own glorification. Biblically speaking, since Jesus Christ is the firstfruits from the dead (1 Cor 15:20–23), all eschatological assertions follow after Christologi-cal guidelines. This is certainly the case with Barth, whose Christological actualism (God's eternal being is freely identified with the act of Jesus' own finite history) points to anthropological actualism (the human's temporal being is by grace lifted into God's eternal being).[72] As sharers of Christ's risen life, humans too can enjoy the freedom of the simultaneity of God. Plainly: *the resurrection of the flesh means eternalization of this delimited life.*

The hope of the Christian has not to do with an individual's awaken-ing to a fresh, improved episode of time, says Barth.

> There is no question of the continuation into an indefinite fu-ture of a somewhat altered life. The New Testament hope for the other side of death is very different from that. What it looks

70. Barth, "What Is Enough," sermon on 31 Dec 1962, in Barth, *Call for God*, 82.

71. Thus saith the Logos: "I am not inviting you to speculate about your being in eternity, but to receive and ponder the news that here and now you begin to be the new man, and are already that which you will be eternally" (IV/3, 250).

72. Something Athanasian is detectable here in that the former actualism is rooted in God's nature and decision; the latter actualism is true only by God's gift. Just as God's eternity is capacious enough to embrace time, so each human's finite existence may enjoy God's eternal embrace by grace through faith.

forward to is the "eternalizing" of this ending life [*die «Verewi-gung» gerade dieses unseres endenden Lebens*]. (III/2, 624 = KD, 760)

The "eternalized" human has had his or her time sublated and fulfilled, transformed into a pure perception, a total duration, a simultaneity of all times. One is elevated into a totally other way of life: thus the resurrection is radical discontinuity. Yet one is elevated with the historical texture of "this ending life": thus the resurrection is radical continuity. In this future one becomes an eternal version of what one was. Observe how the resurrection does not undo human limitation so much as translate one's bodily existence to "the other side of death." (Not even death is reversed, unless one understands death to mean human limitation *per se*.) Through eternalization one's fleshly existence enters the overarching unity of past, present, and future. The eternal mode is never the human's as an independent quality but as something communicated by God. At this Day of days, "all the dead will live through [God] as that which they have been through Him and in relation to Him in their time" (II/2, 283). On that Day the creature will see "the investing of its corruptible with incorruption, the clothing of its humanity in divine glory, the perfecting of its creation by the new creation of its form in peace with God and therefore in and with itself" (IV/3, 315).

Instead of tasting destruction by the fragmentation and dissolution characteristic of the flux of temporal becoming, humans have their lives given to them whole and free. *Whole*, in the sense that their lives are made truly composite, knit into a durable tapestry by the weft of eternity. They possess "life in the unity and continuity of times; in unbroken rest and movement" (IV/2, 317). *Free*, in that they with God may transcend a point of space-time in order to access other times. They become contemporaries with Abraham, Isaac and Jacob, with Jesus and the disciples and all of God's redemptive history. They accompany God in His divine omnipresence, having been "assimilated" and "transposed" into the full scope of the Kingdom (I/2, 66).[73] Their encounter with eternity, given in part in this life through the Spirit's revelation, will one day open up into the uncontradicted experience of fulfilled time, covenant time, the great Sabbath, the totality of the world's moments caught up into God's time. The resur-

73. Pannenberg follows suit, subscribing to the end of the process of time as "the lifting up of temporal histories into the form of an eternal presence . . . dissolving all the differences between particular processes and instants" (Pannenberg, "Constructive and Critical Functions of Christian Eschatology," 138).

rection of the flesh, therefore, means the accessibility of one's life-act to all times, and the accessibility of all times to one's life-act. Temporal men and women will live again, not in the same flow of space-time, but in the divine mode of Jesus Christ.

Amazingly, to Barth none of this implies any sort of surrender of the body. Since body is a *sine qua non* of human identity,[74] God's eternalization of the human identity reproduces a fleshy existence. Barth makes no provision for an abstracted essence and disembodied eternity. The Christian faith is ineluctably about concretions, and so "when we confess *credo resurrectionem carnis* we cannot overlook the real and whole man who is a soul and yet also a body, we cannot overlook his hope as though the resurrection was not also promised to him" (IV/1, 653). Barth will not say much more than this, only that eternity does not abolish flesh without reconstituting it on a higher, truer, pan-temporal plane.

Others have picked up where Barth leaves off. Torrance surmises along the same lines when he says that our "eternity will not be a timeless monotone but an eternity with time in the heart of it."[75] More explicitly, Jürgen Moltmann has suggested that theologians begin talking not so much about the resurrection of the dead as "the resurrection of life," the resurrection of one's selfsame life, the divine embrace of our bodily histories. Since bodies are what people are, eternal life can only mean bodies in "the transmutation into the beauty of the divine life."[76] Moltmann notes Barth's dependence upon the Boethian tradition in which, "[A]pplied to human beings, eternal life means unrestricted livingness, perfect fullness of life in unrestricted participation in the life of God."[77] We are designated by the Father as those who may live in eternity even as our finite, concrete selves.

Before I return to my critique, let me acknowledge the strengths of Barth's creative proposal about human glorification through eternalization. For one, the idea of duration allows for a profound sense of ethical urgency. If *this* life, this bodily life, is the life slated for eternalization, then one must invest in the here and now, knowing it to be eternally significant.[78] Christians have a living hope (that is, a hope for living) because

74. Barth, *The Faith of the Church*, 91.

75. Torrance, *The Apocalypse Today*, 145. Since human identity is the actual existence of a body lived in time, any resurrection that is not a bodily resurrection "is surely a contradiction in terms" (Torrance, *Space, Time and Resurrection*, 82).

76. Moltmann, *Son of Righteousness, Arise!*, 60–62.

77. Ibid., 63.

78. "Real created time acquires in Jesus Christ and in every act of faith in Him

their earthly lives are the lives destined for eternity. John McDowell rightly praises Barth for a "non-escapist, eschatologically contoured ethic," one which encourages responsible and even radical living in the present life.[79] Crafted in this way, actualism means a rejection of the opiate of heaven offered in so much of the Christian tradition, substituting in its place a most praiseworthy existentialism of sorts.

Second, no matter how confusingly he presents it, Barth's stubborn commitment to the flesh is praiseworthy.

> [One] does not hope for redemption from the this-sidedness, finitude and mortality of His existence. He hopes positively for the revelation of its redemption as completed in Jesus Christ, namely, the redemption of his this-sided, finite and mortal existence. This psycho-physical being in its time is he himself. (III/2, 633)[80]

The durationalizing of humanity does not, in Barth's mind, detract from belief in the resurrection of the body. According to his logic the resurrection cannot be anything less than psychosomatic, for what is raised is the life of the whole person, the soul of a body, the body-soul. God saves humans' indelible temporal texture. Time is not eternity, of course, but the contours of temporal life are preserved within the ontological pleroma of eternity. In such a way Barth's actualistic formulation presents itself as a fresh affirmation of the Apostles Creed's teaching on the resurrection.

Still, something feels strained about Barth's reconfigured doctrine. As I warned from the outset, there are significant consequences to his equation of the resurrection with revelation, and here we detect a first set of problems. First, the reconstitution of time in eternity turns time into something that, for all its purported superiority, is only time-*like*. Barth interprets corporeality as a kind of quality that can be transferred from history into eternity. Instead of God raising the human body into renewed time, God raises a meta-body-existence, a conglomerated life. Barth's conviction is that the eternal constancy of Jesus Christ counts as newness of future.[81] I struggle to see how it qualifies as such. Barth's conviction is that

the character and stamp of eternity," says Barth, "and life in it acquires the special characteristics of eternal life" (II/1, 617).

79. McDowell, "Barth's Having No-Thing to Hope For," 39; cf. McDowell, *Hope in Barth's Eschatology*, 56, 134. This is certainly what Barth aims at when he says, "Eschatology, rightly understood, is the most practical thing that can be thought" (*DO*, 154).

80. Cf. IV/2, 316f.

81. "I fail to see to what extent this rules out a futurist eschatology" (Barth, *Karl Barth Letters, 1961–1968*, 236).

the retention of the corporeal *texture* of that history counts as the flesh. I do not deem it so. The compounding of time means the compounding of flesh, not a bodily way of life that is resumed and continued.[82] Barth's insistence that the movement of space and time are permanently ended suggests a human both more complete and less alive. Humans in risen flesh exceed their boundaries, but at the expense of entering a kind of memorialized stasis; humans "stand" in God's eternal presence. Farrow's objection to the "refracted" life-act of Jesus can be applied to Barth's concept of the general resurrection: "Is this not the raising of a history rather than a person?"[83] That is, either with Jesus or with ourselves, the resurrection does not reconstitute the kind of vital, forward-moving self we are in this life. In the eschaton we are collected—but are we living agents?[84] We have time—but do we have a dynamic future? We have the fullness of our corporeal history—but are we animated? Barth's presentation yields bodies weirdly lighter *and* denser than flesh. Consequently, even after all Barth does to wed act with being, his doctrine of the resurrection of the flesh has a strange odor of timelessness, the very objection Cullmann and Roberts, Gunton and Jenson each posed in their own way.

Furthermore, as I argued before, Barth's actualistic anthropology is forced to reverence death as the noble servant of God. Ethically, the death-limit spurs humans to faith in the transcendent Lord of Life. Ontologically, death is the finalization of the creaturely life, the provider of the terminus. Death gives final definition to a human history so that the anthropic texture might be raised to the eternal level. (Should it be any surprise that Barth comes around to saying that personal death is interchangeable with the return of Christ?[85]) Death offers the point of translation of first-order time to second-order duration, and therefore must be considered necessary and even holy. Here, aside from possible influence from Plato and Feuerbach, Barth has drunk too deeply from the well of existentialism. His grudging respect for physical death as the transportation to the realm

---

82. Cf. Berkouwer, *The Triumph of Grace in Karl Barth*, 163f., 344.

83. Farrow, *Ascension and Ecclesia*, 234, 249.

84. It is almost as if Barth feels that death sanitizes our creaturely rebellion for God's presence, for "God and man, despite fine passages to the contrary, are still defined by their opposition to one another, an opposition which can only be resolved by the death of man (which belongs already to the determination of his finitude) and by his reconstitution as a moment in God's eternity" (Farrow, *Ascension and Ecclesia*, 246).

85. End-by-death and end-by-Return are "the same transition to the same participation in the same glory" (IV/3, 925).

of eternalization sounds very much like other twentieth-century theologians influenced by existentialist philosophy.[86] For all its usefulness, this position cannot be squared with the violent hatred God has for death in the Scriptures. Barth cannot say unequivocally, "The last enemy to be destroyed is death" (1 Cor 15:26). Barth cannot join Jesus in weeping at the tomb of Lazarus (John 11:33–38). This is simply unacceptable. Any worthwhile eschatology must do more than neutralize or reinterpret or repristinate death. Death must be reversed and eliminated from the field.

Perhaps it is best to say that Barth's weakness lies at his very point of strength. He finds human life not simply *from* God but *in* God. This paradigm forbids the vagaries of a deistic theism in which humans rely upon their own autonomous intellect and constitutional immortality. Barth's approach is something participationist to the core: only in God may one find real being, only in Him the fount of creaturely life and source of final glorification. Time and flesh and even death become good in the hand of the Eternal One. For Barth the Christian afterlife is an anthropological doctrine couched in the doctrine of God. Since *He* alone is immortal, what more can one say besides, "God is my Beyond" (III/2, 632, 640)?

I have suggested, however, that a theology that sublates the earthly into the heavenly has not necessarily saved the earthly. Totalizing the earthly condition by raising it into the divine has been presented by Barth as a fulfillment. But it could also be construed as a quarantine. Barth too often portrays human continuity as a matter of closure rather than a matter of perpetuation. The perceived messiness of the dimensions of time and space, change and flesh, seems to cry out for *resolution*—but, as I have tried to argue, resolution does not necessarily mean *redemption*, even if that resolution happens in God Himself. We will have to follow a second line of thought from Barth to see if human continuity remains intact after being raised into the divine.

---

86. Pannenberg (*Systematic Theology*, vol. 3, 602) sees an analogy between Barth's view and that of Tillich and Schelling with their idea of "essentialization." A similar interpretation has cropped up in a surprising number of places in recent decades, including Jüngel, *Death*, 115–36; Rahner, *On the Theology of Death*, 26–31; Lash, "Eternal Life," 271–84; Tanner, *Jesus, Humanity and the Trinity*, 79–119; Sonderegger, "The Doctrine of Providence," 152ff.

4

The Resurrection of the Flesh
as Manifestation

ANY ACCOUNT OF THE resurrection of the flesh must address it as some sort of manifestation. Jesus Christ "appeared" to His disciples (e.g., Mark 16:12–14; Luke 24:34; John 21:14), and believers too will "appear" with Him in glory (e.g., Col 3:4; 1 John 3:2). The Scriptures thereby suggest an active disclosure in which resurrection displays the truth of redeemed persons, showing forth their glory. But what is involved in this display?

With the last chapter I risked misleading the reader by portraying Barth's view of the resurrection so much in terms of an ontological shift, a superaddition of eternal duration to the hitherto temporal human. Barth's has a second line of thought: resurrection is the manifestation of one's true, already-established identity. For him, eternalization and manifestation are both true Christologically. From the position of the condescending Son of God, obedient and helpless before the Father, resurrection is the eternalization of His being; from the position of the exalted Son of Man, glorious and empowering to other humans, resurrection is the manifestation of His being. The former underscores the Father's livening verdict, the latter the Son's own living declaration. The former suggests retroactivity, the second retrospectivity. The former leans toward the ontological, the second the epistemological. Both former and latter are true for Barth, but I think it safe to say that the resurrection as manifestation is his preferred theological statement. Therefore, we do well to grant what was said in the last chapter and, as it were, begin again from the beginning.

Our second approach involves a discussion of the integrity of Jesus Christ. As the God who takes flesh, the Son is the perfect union of deity and humanity. The unity of the human essence with the divine essence is salvation for the former. Barth says that Christ's two natures, fully communicative, operate simultaneously, actualizing themselves fully in His incarnate life. Jesus Christ wrought salvation, became salvation, even was saved—*before and without the resurrection*. The integrity of His being-with-God secured everything.

Jesus' resurrection revelation to others in the subjective sphere, then, has nothing to do with the perfection already accomplished in the incarnation's exchange of natures. This is Barth's way of standing firm on the finality of Jesus Christ. What, then, is the resurrection? Barth asserts that it can only be the active manifestation of Jesus Christ's own life as He opens it publicly to the world. It can only be the public power of His integrated being as it goes out to vivify others and win them to Him. It can only be a making-known, a "noetic" moment which displays the power of a fixed reality. In what follows, I acknowledge that Barth successfully guards the objectivistic *solus Christus* against subjective elements which Neoprotestants, Roman Catholics, and pietists would try to add to the one work of salvation, though I also point out that Barth's Christology (and therefore his soteriology) operates with an internal framework similar to early Lutheranism, and is clearly partial to an Alexandrian logic.

In contrast to Jesus Christ, other humans dwell in the hiddenness of earthly existence. They show no integrity; they do not reflect the *imago Dei*. While Jesus Christ's atonement has healed the disjuncture between God and humanity, no one, not even the saintliest saint, reflects this perfect wholeness. Everyone lives as a walking contradiction: saint and sinner, enlightened and darkened, a person caught between life and death. A person's creaturely condition as such does not display its appointed glory, for obscurity is the condition of mere flesh. Only the resurrection of the flesh will disclose one's true identity in Jesus Christ. The raising of the dead makes public the truth of one's identity as a child of God. At Christ's appearing the saints will appear with Him, purified and overjoyed at the vision of His glory. Each believer will be "present" in His presence.

Barth hopes to avoid spiritualization in the concept of manifestation. Human flesh is caught up in the moment of manifestation. Because salvation concerns a person's whole identity in union with Christ, a person in the resurrection retains his or her whole nature in the manifestation, including the bodily flesh. Barth's logic goes deeper: Because God reveals Himself to those in the flesh in this life, those in the flesh must be revealed in the coming life. Just as the Son revealed Himself to others in the fleshly quality of His whole self, so humans will be conclusively revealed with their fleshly character.

My critique of Barth intensifies in this chapter. I will argue that the resurrection-as-manifestation line of thought suffers from a certain implausibility, as Barth has not made it so that our coming disclosure can carry all the same meanings as Christ's. More seriously, Barth's strongly noetic function of the resurrection diminishes the bodily character of redemption, relegating the salvation of the flesh to a footnote. Since eternal life is put in terms of knowledge of God and knowledge of self in the moment of "manifest presence" (an idea sibling to the beatific vision), the ultimate meaning of resurrection sounds more like a "going to heaven" than a public re-identification of the bodily person in the world. Somewhat unexpectedly, Barth's link between glorification and the internal relations of Christ's communication of natures has the effect of turning the doctrine of the resurrection into something of a doctrine of deification. Concealed and revealed in God, the flesh gets harder and harder to find.

THE INTEGRITY OF THE SON

To Barth's credit, every construction in his *Church Dogmatics* is done under the auspices of the Mediator, working out of the great truth that all Christian doctrine is an unpacking of the theme of Christ. As George Hunsinger puts it, "That there is only one work of salvation, that it has been accomplished by Jesus Christ, that it is identical with his person, and that being perfect it needs no supplementation but only acknowledgement, reception, participation, anticipation and proclamation for what it is—these are the great themes of Barth's soteriology."[1] If the Christian understanding of salvation really banks on Christ, if it indeed holds to a *solus Christus*, then there can be no talk of addition. The great temptation of soteriology is, at some point or another, to leave the domain of Christology and perform an independent inquiry about salvation. Anthropocentric approaches take different forms: Neoprotestant theology looking for salvation behind the historical Jesus; Roman Catholicism's exercise of the infused grace of Jesus Christ under the guidance of the institutional clergy; or the way "positive," evangelical Christianity wants to add an experiential or volitional appropriation in order to make salvation real.

---

1. Hunsinger, Review of *Barth's Moral Theology* by John Webster.

CD IV/2 can read as an extended response to these three groups.[2] Barth places against these anthropocentric options the finality of Jesus Christ.

The way he guarantees the finality of Jesus Christ is to speak of the Son's own integrity of being, a prominent theme in §64.2 "The Homecoming of the Son of Man" and §64.3 "The Royal Man." It would be hard to say too much about Barth's Christology, to which he devotes extended attention and achieves profound comprehensiveness. His own treatment portrays Jesus Christ as the fulfillment of the covenant between God and humanity. To accomplish this Barth takes up the terminology of Christian orthodoxy—nature, person, union.[3] But it is important to understand that he is working hard to restructure classical metaphysical categories into something more dynamic: the great exchange of the incarnation happens as a historical act. Barth creatively inhabits the legacy of the fourth ecumenical council, at which the Church at Chalcedon (451) laid the general parameters for discourse about the incarnation of the Son of God.[4] According to the council's definition, Christ's two natures must be interpreted as "without confusion" (*asugchutōs*) and "without mutation" (*atreptōs*), guarding the distinction between deity and humanity, yet also "without division" (*adiairetōs*) and "without separation" (*achoristōs*), guarding the unity of the person. Historically, theologians have labored to work within the Chalcedonian boundaries. Barth strains to do the same, and in the end offers a daring interpretation of two-natures-united-in-one-person, performing the deceptively simple move of "actualizing" Jesus Christ's deity and humanity in one "history." Each nature is specific and distinguished, yet together unified and integrated, in the one personal act of Jesus of Nazareth, who is the Logos become flesh. "We accept [Chalcedon's] insight, even if we have to give it another form," Barth says optimistically. "But the whole point is that we do have to give it another form" (IV/2, 109).

Rather than metaphysical discourse, Barth's narrative structure of the incarnation plays out as a double story-line, God's and humanity's, played out simultaneously. Jesus Christ is the Son of God in the state of humiliation (*status exinanitionis*), humbling Himself and pouring out His

---

2. Barth explicitly mentions the three at the head of the part-volume (IV/2, ix–xi). While he comes to new agreement with pietism and extends a fresh response to Roman Catholicism's claims about sanctifying grace, Barth refers readers back to his early work for a repudiation of Neoprotestantism.

3. Barth comes to prefer the more dynamic term, "essences." I will use it and "natures" interchangeably.

4. For the following, cf. Hunsinger, *Disruptive Grace*, 131–47. A good summary of volume IV can be found in Mangina, *Karl Barth*, 115ff.

divine glory by taking up a human existence. Yet He is at the same time the Son of Man in the state of exaltation (*status exaltationis*), being brought under the auspices of the divine life. These aspects are fully concurrent, being "two opposed but strictly related moments in that history which operate together and mutually interpret one another" (IV/2, 106). To tell one side of the story is not to tell the other exactly, just as the condescending divine nature cannot be confused with the elevating human nature. Still, the totality of Jesus Christ's one incarnate life is a marriage of operations: the two "movements" or "aspects" happen simultaneously in the one person of Jesus Christ as He lives out His incarnational mission.[5] Here is where Barth reconfigures the communication of natures to say something novel about the Jesus-narrative itself: just as there can be no chronological succession of the natures (in which Jesus Christ was a man for a while, then God), there can be no chronological succession of states (in which He was humiliated for a while, then exalted). Barth rejects the traditional teaching that Jesus Christ as God and man was humiliated through the incarnation, suffering, death and burial, but exalted through resurrection, ascension, session and return. Rather, the humiliation and exaltation of Jesus Christ happen *simultaneously*. Instead of the typical "V" adumbrated in the ecumenical creeds and developed in Reformation theology, Barth fuses together the states hypostatically, overlapping humiliation and exaltation into an "X."

We recall that *Church Dogmatics* IV reflects this schema. The Christology of IV/1 tells the story from the aspect of the divine nature: the Son of God's obedient "going into the far country," His display of power through the powerlessness of sinful human existence, His humble exercise of freedom as the Judge judged in our place. The Christology of IV/2 brings forward the human nature: the Son of Man's acquired splendor, His restoration of humanity's place as the covenant partner of God, and in Him the "homecoming" of humanity as it is lifted up to a royal place. After telling Christ's story these two ways, all that is left for Barth in IV/3 is to speak of these two aspects synthetically, in the unity of the "descent" and "ascent" of Jesus Christ's single being-in-act. Thus, Barth's Christology speaks to the complete integrity (that is, integration) of Jesus Christ's person acted out in His incarnate life and completed in His death.

Why integrate the natures of Christ in this actualistic manner? At the center of his various purposes, Barth sees in his program a way to

---

5. The two movements are "the inner dialectic of the Christian doctrine of reconciliation" (IV/3, 5).

assert the finality of Christ. In Christ's divine condescension He actually and finally procured justification for humankind; in His human exaltation He actually and finally procured sanctification. This one Jesus Christ, the Son of God and Son of Man, is complete and glorious in Himself. The salvation He bestows comes without development or requirement for augmentation. No divine development or human evolution need build on top of Jesus' work. His divine-human integrity is established. Salvation is complete in Him. *It is finished.* Finality is Barth's chief point after all is said and done.

Barth's move to absolutize the work of salvation in Christ's cross-culminating history comes with a serious reinterpretation of the gospel story. In making salvation wholly independent of human appropriation, Barth also accepts that salvation is *independent of Christ's own resurrection, ascension, session and return.* Christ's whole atoning performance has been compressed into His pre-resurrected earthly life. Reconciliation proper is perfected in Jesus' terminal history, without reference to His risen life. There is nothing that needs to be "turned around" in His story, for Barth's incarnational grammar conditions Jesus' movement to the cross. Jesus Christ's condescension, suffering, and death are not humiliation *per se,* but the divine humiliation which is in fact humanity's exaltation, resulting in the double boon of justification and sanctification. Resurrection adds nothing to reconciliation as such.

When from the cross Jesus utters "It is finished (*tetelestai*)" in John 19:30, Barth hears total closure of Christ's saving history. Because "any limitations of the *tetelestai* are quite alien to the New Testament," there can be no talk of a continuation of the atonement or further actualization of a latent possibility (IV/1, 306). His death achieved "absolute fulfilment" (IV/2, 256).[6] His history achieved its telos at Golgotha, for there God's Son achieved His mission by subjecting Himself to the depths of human misery and raising the human essence to the pinnacle of divine fellowship. The whole of Jesus' incarnate ministry is at work here, but the death of Christ is *"in nuce* the redemptive act and actuality of His existence" (IV/2, 257), "the secret of the incarnation in all its fulness" (IV/2, 293). Instead of resurrection being the decisive moment for Jesus, now the attention goes to Christmas and, even more, the cross. If the grand reunion of God and

---

6. Barth's reconfiguration of the Reformational *solus Christus* has led commentators to wonder if the force of Barth's "Christological perfect" leaves room for anthropological and eschatological unfolding. E.g. Sauter, *What Dare We Hope?*, 76, 102ff.; Bayer, *Martin Luther's Theology*, 208f.; Bloesch, *Jesus Is Victor!*, 32–42; Forde, *The Preached God*, 82.

humanity culminates with Jesus' death, no need remains for the resurrection to "save" Jesus or ourselves, strictly speaking.

Before further examining the significant disruption Barth's crucicentrism brings to the concept of resurrection, I want to show that it is possible to classify historically his Christology. Barth's own preference for Reformed nomenclature has led many readers to overlook the extent to which he orders his Christology along Lutheran lines. There we find a similar tendency to compress salvation into Jesus' pre-resurrection existence.

To make my claim it is helpful for us to revisit the debate in Lutheran and Reformed scholasticism.[7] The Christian Church has always held to some sort of conception of the state of humiliation and state of exaltation of Christ, but it was only after the Reformation that competing interpretations surfaced. Following a certain line of thought through Augustine, Lombard and Aquinas, a Königsberg professor by the name of Stancarus promoted the idea that Jesus Christ was mediator according to His human nature alone. This was initially opposed by sixteenth-century Lutheran and Reformed theologians alike, though their positions on the states diverged in the following years. Luther had promoted, for the sake of divine immutability, the traditional view that Christ's human nature alone underwent the change inherent in humiliation and exaltation, emphasizing that His divinity was merely concealed. More important to Luther, however, was the unity of the natures in the incarnation, the deep transfer of predicates which secured not only salvation but also underwrote a consubstantial view of the sacraments. The deity of Christ, hidden with, in and under His humanity, lifted up His humanity. In the hands of Lutheran theologians Martin Chemnitz and Johann Brenz, Christ's hiddenness involved not only the glory of the divine Son but also the concealment of already-glorified humanity. Even with the concession to the Giessen faction (which held the divine attributes were temporarily unexpressed in Christ's humanity during His lifetime), Lutheranism continued to teach the communication of properties as the source and content of glorification. The *status exaltationis*, then, referred to the degree to which the already-present exaltation of Christ's humanity was permitted to shine through.

Calvinist theologians of the time, ever on guard against idolatry, opposed the Lutherans' direct exchange of attributes between the natures. In their minds, failure to guard the distinction of the natures at every point

---

7. For the following historical points, see Gritsch and Jenson, *Lutheranism*, 97–101; Pannenberg, *Jesus*, 307ff.; Thompson, *Christ in Perspective*, 20ff.; Bavinck, *Reformed Dogmatics, Vol. 3*, 364ff.; Heppe, *Reformed Dogmatics*, 410–509; cf. IV/1, 180ff.

would surely lead to the apotheosis of the human. They therefore emphasized more strenuously the need for distinction by couching the unity of Christ, His common idioms and operations, in the one *person* of Christ. The divine nature retained its unblemished power, and the human nature had to be guarded against absorption into deity. That is, on one side, the Reformed preserved a sense in which the deity of Jesus Christ exceeded the activity of His human nature, even during His earthly ministry;[8] on the other side they promoted the sense in which the human nature was always thoroughly human during Jesus' earthly life and death, resurrection, and ascension. Even during His heavenly session He lives in human flesh, so as to be our High Priest. This meant that the *communicatio idiomatum*, however important to the Reformed, never included the *genus maiestaticum*, that is, the human nature's exercise of divine predicates like omnipotence, omnipresence, etc. So as not to be outstripped by the Lutheran emphasis on the unity of Christ, Reformed scholastics highlighted the state of humiliation and state of exaltation as two distinct chronological movements undergone by *both natures together* in the same Person's condescension or exaltation.[9] Each historical occurrence affected the Son's natures differently, according to the character of that nature (for instance, Jesus' death meant concealment for the divine nature, physical death for the human nature), but—and this "but" is the point here—the humiliation or exaltation of the divine nature runs parallel to, and in utter solidarity with, the human path of mortal abasement and new glory. Each nature goes in the same "direction." The double effects upon Jesus in His history are analogous in the Spirit. Lutheran theologians did not interpret the Jesus-narrative so straightforwardly, instead holding that the human nature was secretly exalted while the divine nature condescended to hiddenness during Jesus' life.

Therefore, Barth's self-assessment is misleading on this point. He claims to be in closer agreement with the Reformed perspective when it comes to Christology,[10] and this is accurate to the extent that Barth rejects

---

8. Lutherans applied to this view a pejorative title, *extra Calvinisticum*, "the Calvinistic extra," suggesting that the Reformed had succumbed to the Nestorian heresy which taught that Christ was actually two persons, His divinity operating independently of His humanity.

9. See Heppe, *Reformed Dogmatics*, 488ff. Also observe, e.g., how Francis Turretin in his *Institutes of Elenctic Theology* follows a rejection of the Lutherans' formal communication of attributes (XIII, q.7) with a discussion of the states of exinanition and exaltation (XIII, q.8).

10. IV/2, 52, 68f., 79ff.

any interpenetration of the natures and positions the unity of Christ in the context of His single "person" or "history." However, in the end his Christology bears more in common with the Lutheran blueprint.[11] I see this happening in three ways: his primary interest in the unity of the two natures, his conflation of the states as aspectual trajectories, and his concept of human glorification.

First, Barth's emphasis falls most heavily on the unity of the two essences. Barth's ongoing war against abstraction impels him toward this intense connection of the natures in order that he might cut off speculation about the divine nature apart from the flesh of Jesus Christ. The divine nature is to be found at no other place than the humanity of Christ, and the humanity of Christ at no other place than His deity. There is no Logos apart from His humanity, and no humanity apart from Logos. Accordingly, Barth presses for a robust sense of the divine-human exchange through full communication: the *communicatio idiomatum* (the mutual impartation of the two essences), the *communicatio gratiarum* (the address of the divine essence to the human essence), and the *communicatio operationum* (the shared operations of the essences).[12] To my mind, Barth privileges the third communication as a holding category for the first two. This would seem to be a Reformed move until one considers that he has reinterpreted the shared operations of the natures in one person as the common actualization of the natures in the one history of Jesus. The actualistic approach is neither Reformed nor Lutheran exactly, but in the end it serves to underline the intimacy of the union of the natures as they shape each other. Therefore, Barth's repeated warning in §64.2 that unity cannot mean a union in which the two natures are blended or confused is proof not of his Reformed leanings so much as an awareness of his own commitment to the deep exchange of predicates between the natures. Note how he returns to unity (not to differentiation) as the fundamental fact about the person of Christ: "If the word union were not strictly understood, we should completely miss the actuality of Jesus Christ, and speak this time of two arbitrary figments of the imagination" (IV/2, 64). Indeed, "all that

---

11. Barth confesses that his actualistic, chiastic model of Christ's unity, full of "decisive innovations" (IV/1, 133), can hardly be called a theory of the "states" at all (IV/2, 110). Is this not, I wonder, his way to "appreciate the attraction of the particular Lutheran interest in the *communio naturarum*" (IV/2, 69), by suggesting an even better innovation? Thus Barth's admission that "we have left even Reformed Christology far behind. We cannot expect to be praised for our 'orthodoxy' from any quarter" (IV/2, 106).

12. IV/2, 73ff.

we have seen concerning this union—the two-sided participation of the divine and human essence, the genuineness of both even in their conjunction, but also the reality of the union as such—in short, *the whole doctrine of the two natures in the strict sense depends on this primary and proper union and unity"* (IV/2, 65–6, emphasis added)." Unity is the fundamental thing at stake for Barth, a strange feature for a Reformed theologian.[13]

Second, in the same vein, his program conflates Christ's states of humiliation and exaltation. Instead of reading (with the Reformed) the two natures' parallel paths and meanings in their common operations, Barth relativizes the natures by compressing them into an inner hypostatic exchange: "[I]t is the act of the humiliation of the Son of God as such which is the exaltation of the Son of Man, and in Him of human essence" (IV/2, 100). The old Reformed view saw the occurrences of the Jesus narrative as having a concurrent "path" for each respective nature: both condescend together, both rise together. The natures play out their distinct actions *together*, natures worked out towards the same ends and undergoing the same circumstances, harmonized in the one subject. As it is, Barth's making the states simultaneous has the effect of "bringing down" the divine essence as it "lifts up" the human essence, a counter-directional set of relations between the two natures. In Barth's view, deity and humanity do more than communicate in Christ. Rather, they become inverted movements or inner counterparts within the one hypostatic narrative. While I know of no Lutheran who made the states operate counter-directionally, Barth's view comports better with the classical Lutheran theologian willingness to reconfigure the states of humiliation and exaltation, to read them not at historical face-value but paradoxically, even as coincidental states during Christ's life.[14]

Third—and here is Barth's most overt lean toward Lutheranism—glorification is a fruit of the incarnational unity as such. The assumed human nature gains its nobility not from the resurrection but its proximity to God. The human future not only comes from God: it is the life *of* God *in* God. Glorification comes not from restorative vivification but from the unveiling of the hidden, divine glory previously imparted to the whole

---

13. Among Calvinists Barth is alone in stressing unity rather than distinction, says Colin Gunton (*Father, Son and Holy Spirit*, 99).

14. E.g., Luther's idea that the state of exaltation begins with Christ's descent into hell in Jesus' secretly glorified humanity (Luther, Small Catechism, q.184, an idea parroted by Koehler, *A Summary of Christian Doctrine*, 100f.). Coincidental states of humiliation and exaltation appear in the work of Brenz (Berkhof, *Systematic Theology*, 326).

self. Christ's glory has only gone undercover in death, so that the communication of the covenanted natures appears inactive. While the Reformed have not been without their crucicentricism, the resurrection, ascension, and session of the bodily Christ have been understood as determinative for Christ's glorification. That has not been the case for classical Lutheran dogmaticians, who to a much greater extent have frontloaded the glorification of Jesus' humanity into the history between Christmas and cross, making salvation a matter of divine properties shared with the human nature.[15]

To summarize, Barth allies himself with Reformed Christology in his terminology, especially through his distinction of the natures and the unipersonality of Christ. Yet so far as he places the emphasis on unity, so far as he abandons the chronological presentation of the states, so far as the communicative concept of glorification is underscored, Barth should be numbered with the Lutheran Christologists—a classification at which others have already gestured.[16] This is not to say that Barth's Christology has been readily assimilated by Lutherans, or that non-Lutherans have spurned it; neither is it to say that Calvin or the Reformed scholastic theologians never ventured into communication. My report certainly does not agree with Barth's own self-analysis.[17] I simply want to point out that

15. E.g., Formula of Concord (Solid Declaration), VIII.7–9; Elert, *The Structure of Lutheranism*, Vol. I, 248.

16. George Hunsinger notes Barth's reliance on Luther for an "eminently substantive" Christology with its attendant *theologia crucis* (*Disruptive Grace*, 283–90). Amy Ellen Marga points out that Barth's retrieval of Luther's Christo-logic freed him from the gravity of Enlightenment subjectivism ("Jesus Christ and the Modern Sinner," 260–70). David Ford states things more clearly: "As in the similar dispute over Christ's divinity and humanity the bias of Barth's method is Lutheran and he makes up for this by all the stronger assertions of the hierarchy [of the divine over the human]" (*Barth and God's Story*, 140). One might even conclude that Barth re-opens the door to an even stronger version of the *genus maiestaticum* (Malysz, "Storming Heaven with Karl Barth, 73–92)! Therefore, to conclude that "Barth has done as much as he can—on Reformed soil—to honor the Lutheran concern" (McCormack, *Orthodox and Modern*, 243) grants too much credibility to Barth's self-analysis. In my estimation, Barth has done as much as he can to shore up Reformed concerns before operating in the Lutheran idiom, having "left Reformed Christology far behind" (IV/2, 106).

17. Barth publicly identifies with Reformed theology over Lutheran, including in matters of Christology (e.g., I/2, 70, 830ff.; IV/2, 52, 66; Barth, *Letters, 1961–1968*, 255), but his intention to find middle ground between the two camps is vocalized when he classifies seventeenth-century wrangling as "useless controversy" (II/1, 487). Indeed, his most basic attitude may actually be found from a lecture at Göttingen: "There is enough Lutheranism in Calvinism, and for good or ill Lutheranism has had to take enough Calvinism into its system, to prevent us from talking about a fork in the road" (*GD* I, 173).

Barth's cluster of concerns and strategies regarding the communion of natures caters to one side of the Reformation debate.

If we consider the matter more foundationally, Barth's position can be classified within the original opinions surrounding the controversy surrounding the fourth ecumenical council, at Chalcedon. Alexandrian and Antiochene schools competed for the exact meaning of the *vere Deus vere homo*. Where Alexandrian theologians sought to underscore the unity of Christ, Antiochenes hoped to preserve the distinction of natures. Where Alexandrian theologians held that salvation depended on the flow of the divine nature to the human flesh in Christ (and so removed theoretical impediments to the communion of the natures), Antiochenes were more concerned that the divine benefits conferred to Christ's humanity never come at the expense of His humanity (and so drew a thicker line of definition between the natures). Where the school of Alexandria emphasized the one divine Subject who assumes the additional human existence, the Antiochenes thought it better to err on the side of the distinction of God and humanity in the person of Christ. My conclusion is that while Barth honors the Chalcedonian compromise, he bears more in common with the Alexandrian project.[18]

Since theologians lean (often subconsciously) toward either Alexandrian or Antiochene camps to this very day, it should come as no surprise that Barth's Christology has received mixed evaluation. For example, in the Alexandrian vein Thomas Torrance praises Barth's reclamation of the Eastern resources in order to undo "a damaging disintegration of the wholeness of God's reconciling work in the incarnate life and passion of our Lord,"[19] and Andrew Burgess unflinchingly describes Barth as teaching that "it belongs to the true *divinity* of Jesus Christ that He is also truly human."[20] Similarly, others have found in Barth's actualistic syntax the chance to eradicate dangers of a *deus absconditus* associated with the immanent Trinity.[21] On the other side, when G. C. Berkouwer complains that Barth's doctrine of the simultaneous states leads to "an obscuring of

---

18. Barth's attempt at balance has elicited the praise that it is fully Chalcedonian (Hunsinger, "Karl Barth's Chalcedonian Christology," 127–42), or, in one case, the accusation that it is doubly heretical, both docetic *and* Nestorian (Prenter, "Karl Barths Umbildung der traditionellen Zweinaturlehre in lutherischer Beleuchtung"). But here I am in basic agreement with Charles T. Waldrop's assessment (Waldrop, *Karl Barth's Christology*; Waldrop, "Karl Barth's Concept of the Divinity of Jesus Christ," 241–63).

19. Torrance, *Karl Barth, Biblical and Evangelical Theologian*, 234.

20. Burgess, *The Ascension in Karl Barth*, 30.

21. E.g., Jüngel, *Barth-Studien*, 51–53; McCormack, *Orthodox and Modern*, 192–96.

the decisive [temporal] transition from humiliation to exaltation which took place at the resurrection,"[22] or when Douglas Farrow concludes that the fusing of the natures with the states results in a "thinning" of Jesus' post-mortem history, in which the human nature "remains trapped in the circle" of an already-actualized life,"[23] the red flag of the Antiochene school is raised. Those of an Alexandrian persuasion will praise the actualized nature-states as "dynamic," even "time-affirming."[24] Those sensitive to the Antiochene concerns will fear that this incarnational dynamic "undermines the claim that Jesus Christ is fully human."[25]

In chapter 5 I explore and criticize Barth's Alexandrianism in greater depth. At this point it is simply helpful to recognize that Barth dons Reformed armor even as he wields Lutheran weaponry, and visits Antioch even as he establishes citizenship in Alexandria. For now it is better to move on, acknowledging that Barth does all this to preserve the finality of Christ and His work. The glory of Christ—the glory of the whole *theanthropos*—is complete in the determinative drama of the incarnate life. All that remains is the lifting of the curtain.

THE MANIFESTATION OF JESUS CHRIST

The startling consequence of Barth's understanding of the incarnation is that Christ's resurrection, ascension, heavenly session, and return are not exaltation for Him. In fact, they do not add a single iota to His person or reconciling work. The "afterlife" of Jesus generates nothing new on the ontological level, since the history between conception and cross constitutes His full identity. "His work, His being and action, were not augmented by the resurrection," Barth says matter-of-factly. "How could they be? His work was finished" (IV/3, 282). Christ by definition was (and is and ever more shall be) the Living One, so His death does not need to be "undone." What is more, since reconciliation has been absolutely completed between the two termini of His earthly arrival and His earthly death, nothing salvific needs to be added to His one sacrifice. He was (and is and ever more shall be) the absolute salvation of His people in His death. How, then, should one classify resurrection?

22. Berkouwer, *The Triumph of Grace in the Theology of Karl Barth*, 315.

23. Farrow, *Ascension and Ecclesia*, 247–49.

24. Lewis, *Between Cross and Resurrection*, 192; cf. Mangina, *Karl Barth*, 121.

25. Waldrop, "Karl Barth's Concept of the Divinity of Jesus Christ," 263.

The resurrection is the *manifestation* of that which has already been accomplished, says Barth. By expressing it this way, he reframes the problem of objective and subjective elements of salvation as the problem of promulgation, that is, the question of how the objective reality in Christ becomes ours as He shines forth and illuminates other subjects. Barth therefore poses a new set of questions with the resurrection: How does "reconciliation" also become "redemption" for us? How has His finished act extended its reach so as to awaken us to God? Or, as Barth comes to put it, "How can that which He was and did *extra nos* become an event *in nobis*?" (IV/4, 18). The answer to each question is the resurrection of Jesus Christ.

We may observe that throughout *CD* IV Barth retains his early dialectic of veiling and unveiling with regard to Christ's death and resurrection. In 1935 he says,

> The *secret* of Easter . . . can in its substance be none other than that of Good Friday—which again is that of Christmas. There is only *one* secret of the Christian faith: God and man in their community through God's free grace. What in particular makes, in this instance, this one secret the mystery of Easter is, to put it in the simplest way, this: that all that we have recognised as the mystery of Good Friday is, as God's decree, will and deed, *true* and *valid*. . . . All that in the crucifixion of Christ was done by God in a hidden way is by the resurrection set in the *light* and put into *force*.[26]

The resurrection is the most potent of all signs since it makes God's incarnation in its totality "active and knowable" (I/2, 183). The resurrection of the Son discloses His inner life. That which was veiled at Christmas and the cross was unveiled at Easter. An older Barth affirms the same in greater detail, saying,

> As His *self-revelation,* His resurrection and ascension were simply *a lifting of the veil.* They were a step out of the hiddenness of His perfect being as Son of God and Son of Man, as Mediator and Reconciler, into the publicity of the world for the sake of those for whose reconciliation He was who He was and is who He is. His resurrection and ascension were simply *the authentic communication and proclamation of the perfect act* of redemption once for all accomplished in His previous existence and history. (IV/2, 133, emphasis added)

26. Barth, *Credo*, 102.

This last passage is especially characteristic of Barth's doctrine of revelation. Note how the resurrection is the *personal* disclosure of Jesus Christ, God Himself revealing Himself by Himself. Yet resurrection fills out the epistemological dynamic of revelation, something *dialectical*, resurrection being the positive expression of revelation's "lifting of the veil." And in this quote Barth explains resurrection as the *declarative* phase of a previously perfected act. Nothing new comes to Jesus' own identity through His resurrection. Neither must anything new come to Him, since He always had life in Himself. Easter merely opens up an aperture though which Christ's eternal majesty illuminates and conforms others to the theanthropic reality perfected in Him. Jesus' forty days of appearance mark the primary demonstration of the mystery of the Incarnate One. Jesus, in the newness of His resurrection mission, appears again so that He might decrypt the mystery of that which He was and did before. The light concentrated in the life and death of the Savior is transcendentally unleashed in this "interspersed history [*Zwischengeschichte*]," this "transposed report [*Zwischenberichte*]" (IV/2, 132 = *KD*, 148).

While Barth's paradigm is not without its perils, let us acknowledge that his construal of the resurrection as manifestation has some sort of biblical basis. Nine times in Scripture the phrase "He was seen/ He appeared" (*ōphthē*) is used to describe the post-Easter event of Jesus Christ. Similarly, deutero-Mark and the gospel of John claim that "He was revealed" (*ephanerōthē*) or "He revealed Himself" (*ephanerōsen*). In a unique construction, Peter preaches that "God raised him on the third day and made him manifest (*edōken auton emphanē genesthai*); not to all the people but to us who were chosen by God as witnesses, who ate and drank with him after he rose from the dead" (Acts 10:40–41 [RSV]). Barth reads this manifestation as a kind of supernatural Christ-display; not Jesus in a second, regenerated life, but Jesus as He once was, now presented in the mode of God, *present* to the disciples in all openness. While scriptural words like "appear" and "reveal" and "manifest" do not strike me as technical designations, Barth does, and on that basis he assigns the resurrection the task of illumination. Where Jesus Christ's earthly life-to-death history accomplishes, achieves, enacts, and completes reconciliation, the resurrection manifests, declares, reveals, communicates, confirms, and makes known that work.

At regular intervals Barth refers to the former as "ontic," the latter as "noetic."[27] The ontic side of things concerns the Son's *esse*, His being,

---

27. To my knowledge no one has traced Barth's usage of the ontic-noetic to its

the matter-of-fact life He led and the reconciliation won through it. The noetic side is the *nosse*, the knowledge of Him and His work, the "movement" of revelation as it enlightens and seizes others. The former concerns the objective, the latter the subjective (or, more accurately, the objective-crossing-over-to-the-subjective). The objective reality of Christ at the cross has a beyond, an "also." Again, the actuality of the finished incarnational history comes with an intellectual *possibility*,

> the possibility of a special perception to meet it, a perception which is controlled and mastered by it, attaching itself to it, following and accompanying it, imitating and repeating it. . . . In short, we have to reckon with the fact that the same divine act of majesty with which we have to do in the incarnation of the Word has not merely the character of objective being and occurrence, but also, as an event within the world and therefore in the sphere of human cognition, a subjective character as well. (IV/2, 120)

The subjective event of the one "divine act of majesty" is Jesus' resurrection. In this move the Lord offers those in the world a seeing, knowing, and doing which corresponds to the fact of His own life-act. Christ's being and work are finished, yet there remains a subsequent movement of the Son to others, the *Heilsgeschichte* of His person as it blossoms into an *Offenbarungsgeschichte*. Rather than the crucifixion of Jesus becoming a

---

fountainhead. Certainly the terms existed in philosophical literature, and around the same time as the writing of the *Church Dogmatics* Martin Heidegger employed the terminology (albeit very differently). Barth's language here is undoubtedly "idiosyncratic" (Dawson, *The Resurrection in Karl Barth*, 214). The apparent entrance of ontic-noetic nomenclature comes into play during Barth's (second) class lectures on Anselm, written in 1930 and published the following year. In this study he notices, contrary to general consensus, that for Anselm knowledge of God is not something worked toward, speculated about or deduced. God's givenness starts theological inquiry. God speaks objectively and is thus subjectively heard, for "when we speak of the gift of this Word, the effect of the Word is, invariably, that both the Word and the event of the hearing of the Word are understood together" (Barth, *Anselm*, 34). God's Word facilitates the *intellegere*: from His side the ontic has a noetic movement, and from our side the noetic has its sure, ontic basis. To be clear, "Ontic rationality precedes noetic" (ibid., 50). But God stands behind the ontic *ratio* and noetic *ratio* alike, assuring their unity. Since Barth's work on Anselm represents the coming of age for Barth's dogmatic method, it comes as no surprise that he carries over this terminology into the doctrine of revelation in *CD* I (e.g., I/1, 22, 307; I/2, 170ff., 181) and, ultimately, into the treatment of the resurrection in *CD* IV. For the latter theology it was only a matter of replacing *Anselm's* ontic *ratio* with "the incarnational history," the noetic *ratio* with "the resurrection," and the God of the *rationes* with "the Mediator."

great star collapsing into itself, the finalization precipitates a noetic super-nova. Christ makes Himself known.

Ontic and noetic—yet just when the reader purchases this conceptual distinction, Barth refuses to let the two terms divide: "What we have is a divine noetic which has all the force of a divine ontic" (IV/3, 297). The resurrection as such may not be determinative for the being of Jesus Himself, but that does not preclude it from having an abiding ontic character. Barth never catalogues the ways in which this is true, but, in loose correspondence with Barth's five points about the "Beyond" of the cross in IV/1, I propose the following lines of reason: 1) The resurrection is a noetic with the force of an ontic in that *knowledge of God comes about through God's free act.* He is the Subject overseeing this subjective echo of reconciliation. More specifically, in the resurrection it is the transcendent Jesus Christ who acts and effects such knowledge. He who is in the mode of God raises others' consciousness to His perfect perception.[28] 2) The resurrection is ontic in that *its knowledge is a distinct movement*[29] *beyond the cross.* For as much as reconciliation precedes cognition, Jesus' manifestation comes as new shedding of light beyond the old boundaries. Jesus reaches out to establish new relationships, and "for Barth relation is an ontological category."[30] 3) *Resurrection knowledge was already implicit in the cross's ontic.* Barth is not entirely consistent on this score, but he says one thing clearly enough, that even when God's Yes was concealed by Jesus' suffering and death, it was still a Yes. Resurrection inhabited Golgotha as its hidden glory, an intention ready to be vocalized.[31] Revelation has its basis in the ontic act of dying, but the ontic has its goal in revelation. 4) *This knowledge allows humans to step into a fresh historical reality.* Christ's revelation in the resurrection imparts a transformational kind of

---

28. Christ is not transformed in His self-revelation—though He does become the trans-former, the one who through His manifest presence brings change from God's eternal vantage point.

29. I detect in Barth's terminology a growing willingness to speak of the "movement" of revelation rather than the "event" of revelation. Salvifically, the movement concerns that of Jesus to others in the range of His open effect. Dogmatically, Barth deploys the resurrection as the transition of Barth's Christology to discussions of soteriology, hamartiology, ecclesiology, and the Christian life.

30. Gunton, "Salvation," 144.

31. "Reconciliation is not a dark or dumb event, but [one] perspicuous and vocal. It is not closed in upon itself, but moves out and communicates itself" (IV/3, 8). Yet this connectedness privileges a kind of ontic core secured on Good Friday, for "[w]hat happened on Easter Day was nothing new: it was simply the flaring up of the light already lit in that darkness and at first shrouded by it" (Barth, *Call for God*, 53).

knowledge that actively conforms human lives into Christ's likeness even while in this world. By this knowledge they actually come to reflect, however provisionally, the new life belonging to the children of God. Those in the Church are illuminated, transformed, changed. The cross alone did not do this; it required the resurrection. He arose, He appeared, He interacted with those in history. Even now through the resurrection, the kingdom comes on earth as in heaven.[32] 5) *Resurrection knowledge is ontic insofar as it is the coming presence of the selfsame Jesus Christ.* The very same Savior is at work in the noetic task. He Himself shows up in this knowledge, and He Himself is the real. What is at the heart of this movement is Jesus' own concrete person. If He acts as the personal agent of this impartation of personal self-giving, how can one possibly categorize the resurrection as mere knowing? In sum, we see in Barth's arguments a relentless unity of the ontic and noetic.

Why then does he return so often to the differentiation between the cross' ontic and the resurrection's noetic? Barth's insistence on this point makes more sense when it is understood as a response to three competing nineteenth-century theological systems: liberal Neo-Protestantism, Roman Catholicism, and "positive" evangelicalism. *Church Dogmatics* IV can be understood as a lengthy response to these three groups.[33] The great temptation of soteriology is, at some point or another, to leave the domain of Christology and center oneself in anthropology. It is to cast an independent inquiry about what salvation is, rather than persist in the person and work of the Son. Barth sensed that each of these enterprises had violated the finality of Christ, since each called for a salvific component to be added or appropriated by the believer, a component which went above and beyond the work of Christ so as to complete it. In the liberal theology of Neo-Protestantism the vitality of religious consciousness through reason and romantic awareness replaced Jesus' atoning work. Roman Catholicism compromised the finality of salvation by continuing to teach a necessary supplementation of Jesus' saving ministry through the institutional mediation of grace. Evangelicals fared little better, trying to augment the death of Christ with a pietistic religious experience (or epistemological

---

32. Katherine Sonderegger supports the view that Barth's divine noetic category does not compromise the historicity of the event, if by historical one means that happenings of the resurrection "will be historical in the proper and exalted sense: the unfolding of the life, death and victory of God with his creatures, the unfolding of God's own time" ("Et Resurrexit Tertia Die," 201). Cf. Lorenzen, *Resurrection and Discipleship*, 66–71.

33. Cf. IV/1, ix; IV/2, ix.

certainty through apologetical evidences) which would evoke faith, which in turn would appropriate salvation's otherwise impotent reality. Each of these religious additions, felt Barth, betrayed a lack of trust in the objective reality established in Jesus Christ, the one Mediator crucified once for all.

By anchoring the ontic so much in the death of Christ, Barth concedes a major point to modern Christian expressions: Jesus' resurrection manifestation is a subjective event. It takes place at the anthropological realm. Barth's concession looks very modernist at first glance. For liberal theology, after all, the resurrection was reinterpreted as one's own attainment of spiritual enlightenment and performance of moral deeds somehow prompted by the love and teachings of Jesus; namely, "the power of Christ rising up in our hearts." To a lesser extent, even Roman Catholics and evangelicals could transmute the idea of resurrection into an inner, spiritual-moral awakening within the person; a mere "He lives within my heart." Barth also affirms the resurrection as a subjective reality to the extent that the Jesus-event of resurrection happens in the subjective, personal, noetic field.

Yet Barth will not make resurrection the *property* of the human consciousness. It is still *Jesus*, Jesus manifesting Himself. Thus, the resurrection is a noetic with the "force" of an ontic. It is intimate knowledge of the One who is actually risen, living, and active. The resurrection continues to be primarily a statement about Jesus' own manifestation, and only secondarily a statement about the believer's illumination and coming to life spiritually.

To remain on the subject of Jesus Christ when speaking of His resurrection, then, means to ask further about Him in this manifestation. Christ is manifested to other humans, of course, but it should be apparent by now that Barth is going after something more. Jesus Christ's *integrated identity* as the God-man is showing forth.

Which nature is manifested in Jesus Christ's resurrection? Both: "Each is to be recognized in the other" (III/2, 216). In chapter 3 I examined how the resurrection for Barth presents Jesus Christ in divine freedom. The disciples "came to see that He had always been present among them in His deity, though hitherto this deity had been veiled" (III/2, 448). For all His condescension unto flesh and suffering and death, Jesus is shown by the Father to be the Son of God, contemporaneous with all times, fully durable, having access to all moments. From Easter on, but especially during the forty days of appearance, Jesus became present to others "in the mode of God."

The shining forth of Christ's deity is a key idea in IV/1, written from the perspective of the Son of God. Interestingly, however, the revelation of the divine essence comes out even more strongly in IV/2, from the perspective of the Son of Man in exaltation. In that part-volume Christ's deity is shown to be deity *expressed through* the exalted human nature of Christ, for "if He was and is revealed as the Son of God in His resurrection and ascension, it is in the power and glory of His unity with the man Jesus of Nazareth" (IV/2, 150). In His human existence Jesus Christ's deity is manifested, intermittently through His incarnate ministry and fully in His resurrection and ascension. In IV/2 He is "the royal man," the human essence raised to majestic fellowship with God in the incarnation. Before the resurrection human essence has been brought to the heights of heaven, made holy, welcomed into the kingdom of God. But for Barth the exaltation of Jesus' humanity is shrouded in the divine concealment of the incarnation. Humanity is already "risen" in Jesus' death, but that risen-ness becomes apparent in the resurrection. On the wings of His now-apparent deity rides Jesus Christ's humanity, displayed for others to behold.

Has Christ's humanity really been sustained in the resurrection? Barth certainly desires this. The resurrection is "aimed at the establishment of genuine human life," he claims, though he also admits that the means to genuine humanity is a "divine predicate . . . ascribed to this life" (IV/2, 316f.). Jesus Christ's humanity is manifested only with the manifestation of His deity; Jesus' divinity expresses both itself and its claimed humanity. If the raised human essence does not stand on its own two feet, so to speak, but is totally reliant on the divine essence to elevate it and manifest it, do we at least find some markers of humanness in the resurrection?

Like the early Church, Barth recognizes that the litmus test for the preservation of Jesus' human essence in the resurrection has to do with His bodiliness. Statements about Christ's corporeal resurrection pepper the *Church Dogmatics* in answer to this very test. At regular intervals, Barth argues that Jesus' resurrection was undeniably bodily because the incarnation involved the *unity* of God's essence with human essence; therefore the *whole* Christ died and was raised, and therefore the *whole* man died and was raised. Barth spurns any division between body and soul or divine and human. How can we say it is the risen Christ if He comes to us without His full self?

> It is impossible to erase the bodily character of the resurrection
> of Jesus and His existence as the Resurrected. Nor may we gloss
> over this element in the New Testament record of the forty days,

as a false dualism between spirit and body has repeatedly tried to do. For unless Christ's resurrection was a resurrection of the body, we have no guarantee that it was the decisively acting Subject Jesus Christ Himself, the *man* Jesus, who rose from the dead. (III/2, 448)

Risen—but risen *flesh*. For all the dominance of the divine essence in the incarnational union and the manifestation thereof, the human essence abides.

The power of the resurrection of Jesus Christ may be known by the fact that it snatches man upwards. But again we must make a careful differentiation. The higher level to which it snatches him is not the dubious height of an abstractly spiritual life, of pure inwardness. It is a matter of man's life in its totality, of man as the soul of his body, . . . *He is flesh and blood in His being and therefore in its revelation.* It is inevitable, then, that the power which proceeds from His resurrection, and He Himself as the Resurrected, should sow a seed which is not only psychical but physical, and give nourishment which is not only spiritual but material—a whole preservation of the whole man. Eternal life as it is applied to man by this power is the declaration and pledge of *his total life-exaltation*, from which not a hair of his head or a breath that he draws can be excluded. . . . The power of the resurrection of Jesus Christ will be seen in *the totality of the upward movement* which is its work." (IV/2, 316–17, emphasis added)

If Christ rises, revealing Himself, then the divine nature and the human nature alike are manifested. Who comes to us in the resurrection movement? The selfsame Jesus of Nazareth, body and all.

Barth's determination to equate the crucified Jesus and the risen Jesus leads him to the classical profession of the resurrection of the flesh: Jesus' *original body* is raised. The physical, flesh and bone history of His earlier earthly ministry is what is raised by God on Easter. No separation exists between the Jesus of history and the Christ of faith. He is in the resurrection what He was in the incarnation, says Barth. That is not to say, however, that the body Jesus once lived in is repaired, recalibrated, or changed in any way through the resurrection so as to be reintroduced into time. Instead, the resurrected body of Jesus is the visible fullness of who He was in His bodily history, an eschatological revelation of the One who earlier took up existence bodily. The incarnate Christ returns with and as the same bodily substance, albeit a substance transformed, transfigured, turned "inside-out" so as to display publicly its godly predicates. Put another way, in the resurrection the old body of Jesus "appears" clothed in its divine raiment, "being seen" as the same bodily person exhibited in a heavenly matrix. In Barth's perspective the body of Jesus is not a new body, therefore, but the old flesh caught up in the manifestation of the divine glory. Not so much "in" but "with" this exact body does Christ return for His Paschal sequel.

Corporeality of this quality falls short of the redemption of the flesh, in my judgment. The "stuff" of Jesus' risen body may remain the same, but the abandonment of the human mode results in something less than redeemed humanness. The risen Jesus Christ may have flesh, but He *lives* quite uniformly "in the mode of God" (III/2, 448), not in the mode of humanity. Nevertheless, let us examine what Barth is able to do anthropologically with the conceptual dynamics of integrity and manifestation.

THE AMBIGUITY OF THE HUMAN

Barth claims to be able to derive a doctrine of the human from the glorified God-man. The human in his or her created and sinful state cannot be ascertained directly, but the manifestation of the Lord Jesus supplies us with an anthropology (and hamartiology) largely through contrast with what He is in His manifested integrity. In the last chapter we found Barth teaching that humans are limited. In the present context he adds that they are *ambiguous*. The ambiguity of the human creature in the first place (being a thing needing God but different than God) becomes real contradiction through rebellion against God. Even after the fact of reconciliation by Christ, believers are caught in a new ambiguity, swinging between their competing identities as saint and sinner in the present age. Registering Barth's thoughts on the ambiguity of the human helps to clarify what he means by the resurrection of the flesh for humanity in general. Our coming manifestation is the resolution of our existential ambiguity.

Though he rarely develops it in any one spot, the idea of contradiction is important for Barth. Contradiction, viz., the lack of consistency and integrity, is the "ultimate fact" of human existence (III/2, 47). On a certain level, he says, this possibility of being at odds with God, self, and the world is built into the very fabric of humanity. Humans are created good by God, but good only in unity with Him: "Man exists only in his relation with God. . . . [only] to the extent that not he himself but God is His sovereign Lord, and his own sovereignty flows from God" (III/2, 123).

The human *qua* human loses his or her goodness when independent from God in any way. From the beginning humanity received its integrity from fellowship with God, not a self-possessed dignity. Because humanity is not God, because it exists only by and with and for its divine counterpart, seemingly by definition the covenantal life of the human creature contains a kind of built-in temptation. God calls the creation good, but goodness does not denote self-contained goodness.

Will Adam see his "impairment," his necessary dependence on the Uncreated One, as an invitation to rebel? Will he turn to a religion of self-reliance and become *homo incurvatus in se*? The shadowy possibilities cast by creation do not have to fructify into evil contradiction, says Barth: "In the knowledge of Jesus Christ we must abandon the obvious prejudice against the negative aspect of creation and confess that God has planned and made all things well, even on the negative side" (III/3, 301). Like limitation through earthly death, the ambiguous status of the creature does not have to result in immolation. Life in the covenant addresses the potential human disjuncture between "self-ness" and "selfed-ness." Life in the covenant means being whole in God.

Sadly, humans have plunged headlong into chaos, says Barth. Rebelling against our Maker, we lack the integrity achievable only in Him. Pridefully denying our divine judgment by and in Jesus Christ, we pursue an insane identity, pretending to be judge of God and others. We grow slothful and stupid. We attempt to rule ourselves rather than accept our true definition in Christ. We ignore the Spirit of God and lie to ourselves about our own autonomous spirit. By doing so we rend ourselves in two. Sin creates fissures between the self and God, the self and neighbor, even the self and self. We continually take our creatureliness, meant to be God's good gift in the covenant, and pervert it into a contradiction of the highest order.

Sometimes Barth speaks of the false identity ontologically, in terms of "nothingness." Sin, technically speaking, does not have being: "It 'is,' not as God and His creation are, but only in its own improper way, as inherent contradiction, as impossible possibility" (III/3, 351). By extension, when humans enter into sin they enter into a bizarre double status, a something trying to become nothing, the covenanted creature behaving as if uncovenanted, the children of God pretending to be strangers; in short, the living identifying themselves as dead. Likewise, Barth can call attention to this quandary in epistemological terms.

> Human nature as it is and in ourselves is always a debatable
> quantity; the human situation as we know and experience it is
> dialectical. We exist in antitheses which we cannot escape or
> see beyond. We bear various aspects none of which can be dis-
> owned. Our life has no unity. We seek it, as the various theories
> of man bear witness. But we only seek it. All theories of man are
> one-sided, and must contradict other theories and be contra-
> dicted by them. There is no undisputed and ultimately certain
> theory of man. At bottom there is only a theoretical search for
> the real man, as in practice there is only a striving to attain real
> humanity. The final thing is always unrest. . . . The ultimate fact
> about our human nature, as we shall constantly see in detail, is
> the self-contradiction of man, and the conscious or unconscious
> self-deception in which he refuses to recognise this truth. (III/2,
> 47)

Disregard for God's Word leaves humans in the dark. We lack clarity about
our identity because we will not hear the truth. Caught in our own delu-
sions, we lack the kind of integrity handed to us in Jesus Christ.

"What a wretch I am! Who will save me from this body of death?
Thank God—through Jesus Christ our Lord!" (Rom 7:24–25). The only
way out of the contradiction is by returning to the One who unequivocally
defines humanity as God's own. Repentance involves faith in the Savior
who alone can extract others from schismatic identity.

> In Him are the peace and clarity which are not in ourselves. In
> Him is the human nature created by God without the self-con-
> tradiction which afflicts us and without the self-deception by
> which we seek to escape from this our shame. In Him is human
> nature without human sin. (III/2, 48)

The dualistic human situation finds its remedy in the One who set the
boundaries for human identity in the first place. Therefore Christian
preaching calls the unconverted into the pure light of Christ, out of the
darkness of "abnormal, contradictory and impossible being in sin" (IV/3,
807).

A lingering condition remains for believers, too. In faith they understand themselves to be the people of God, the body of Christ, the temple
of the Holy Spirit. They know and act according to the truth of human
identity in Jesus Christ. But they are still perplexed by their sinful machinations. They too often teeter between righteousness and wickedness,
humility and pride, majesty and devilry, enlightenment and deceit. They
have heard the voice of Christ, for He has spoken it to them. However,

eternal life not another, 2nd life

"He has not yet spoken of it immediately [*unmittelbar*], i.e., in such a way that even those who are awakened by Him to faith and love can hear His voice in perfect purity [*vollkommenen Reinheit*] and to the exclusion of every conceivable contradiction and opposition and above all participation in human falsehood" (IV/3, 903 = *KD*, 1036). In short, Christians are caught between the already and not yet (in the kind of dialectical existence described in Barth's early work). Revelation has touched us and raised us to the divine—but somewhat tangentially: "Thus even at best our life is an indirect seeing, a seeing *in contrario*, and to this extent an improper seeing" (IV/2, 839). This indirectness, this contrariness, this double existence lingers for as long as the mortal has not yet been "swallowed up by life" (2 Cor 5:4). This present time can be lived by the Christian with confidence and hope, says Barth, for the future is sealed by the sure salvation of Him who died and rose again for us. Still, there is something indelibly painful about the contradictoriness of this life, since the dialectic of identities cannot be concluded by anything from our side. We are not able to resolve it by our own strength. Only Christ can accomplish that. Will He come and do that very thing?

THE MANIFESTATION OF THE HUMAN

In 1961 Barth writes a fascinating letter to a Swiss layman who had become distressed while listening to a radio program in which Barth made a cryptic remark about the afterlife. Barth's explanatory letter to Mr. Rüegg is an excellent summary of some concluding themes of *CD* IV, and offers a peek at his doctrine of redemption:

> Eternal life is not another and second life, beyond the present one. It is this life, but the reverse side which God sees although it is as yet hidden from us—this life in its relation to what He has done for the whole world, and therefore for us too, in Jesus Christ. We thus wait and hope, even in view of our death, for our manifestation with Him, with Jesus Christ who was raised again from the dead, in the glory of not only the judgment but also the grace of God. The new thing will be that the cover of tears, death, suffering, crying, and pain that now lies over our present life will be lifted, that the decree of God fulfilled in Jesus Christ will stand before our eyes, and that it will be the subject

> not only of our deepest shame but also of our joyful thanks and praise.[34]

I think it worthwhile to unpack this rich, dense paragraph in light of *CD*. In what follows I will focus on how Barth depicts the coming resurrection as the manifestation of our fleshly histories in Christ.

First and foremost, Barth states that the resurrection will be a manifestation of *this* life: "Eternal life is not another and second life, beyond the present one." Here we might revisit the actualistic ontology described in the previous chapter: one's life is the total history of temporal moments, a collection ultimately possible only by couching time in eternal duration. Eternal life fulfills human nature, for one's earthly life from conception to death is the "material" that is raised. Because the resurrection of the dead has its template in a person's collected history, it is not as if a different subject comes out of the nothingness of the grave. Nevertheless, the resurrection will spell out the hidden truth about that collected life, for on the Last Day "the veil will be taken away and everything that ever was and is and will be will be set in the light of God, divested of its dubiety and frailty and therefore redeemed" (IV/3, 916). Eternal life "is this life"—that is, life manifested.

At first glance it appears that Barth has not commented on the future of the body, but discriminating readers will hear in this statement his affirmation of the corporeal mode of this life. "This life" is irreducibly physical, body with soul, and if we have been physical here, our coming resurrection will be physical. Just as the risen person of Christ appeared with real historicity and tangibility, with all the human predicates of His earlier existence, so each individual will appear in the full breadth of his or her history, a history with corporeal dimensions. As Barth puts it, "[W]hen we confess *credo resurrectionem carnis* we cannot overlook the real and whole man who is a soul and yet also a body, we cannot overlook his hope as though the resurrection was not also promised to him" (IV/1, 653). The glory of salvation shall "one day be unveiled and revealed . . . as embracing the whole man, including his bodily nature" (II/1, 642). Something akin to the patristic sentiment is at work here: all of that which is assumed is saved; the whole human is assumed by Christ; thus the whole person is saved; the flesh is part of the person; therefore, the flesh too is saved. Barth's actualism prevents the earthly medium from being discarded—though whether it does more than that is open to question.

---

34. Karl Barth, letter to Werner Rüegg, 6 July 1961, in Barth, *Letters, 1961–1968*, 9.

Second, there is in the above letter an orientation to the manifestation of one's life *in Christ*. The Pauline *en Christō* is the fundamental pole for Barth, and it means for the resurrection that we are to be raised not simply as what we were but raised in the fullness of "this life in its relation to what He has done for the whole world." Christ's glory, even the glory communicated to the human nature, is to be revealed in others in an unsullied manner. Not simply what we are but what He is—*that* will be the substance of our risen life. His righteousness, beauty, love, and power will shine through us. That is our identity even now, but only at the resurrection-manifestation will we appear as such. I want to make clear that Barth does not speak of the general resurrection as a second thing apart from Jesus' own resurrection. Formally speaking, there is but one resurrection, Jesus', whose manifestation in the forty days awaits only a greater scope, namely, when the rest of humankind is revealed with Him in glory.

Third, the resurrection will mean *a purifying judgment*. Our manifestation with Christ necessarily reveals "the judgment but also the grace of God" upon our lives. How could it be otherwise, since we have sought for ourselves a rival identity, a pact with nothingness? As noted earlier, humanity has its one true identity secured in Christ's atonement, but this reconciliation is obfuscated in the present age. Only the final resurrection takes away this ambiguity. Behind the impossible paradoxes of human lives beats the one truth: we belong to God. In the penultimate age the chosen of God find themselves living in a half-light, caught between two kingdoms and two identities. But "when the saints will be revealed as such, the contradiction will be ended between what they still are and what they are already, and they will enter into the eternal life, the light, to which as the people of God they are now moving with the whole cosmos" (IV/2, 598). Barth does not have a well-shaped doctrine of the last judgment. In his mind, the separation of the goats from the sheep has been so radically conditioned by Jesus Christ's own damnation and predestination so as to relegate any future Great White Throne event to the realm of barely-thinkable speculation. He has, however, built the idea of judgment into his doctrine of the resurrection by speaking of the removal of the contradiction of human lives. God's grace is a purifying judgment. All along (but especially at the end of life) humans must encounter His terrifying, transfiguring power, walking "into the fire of a radical and incalculable testing" (IV/3, 922), purged of sin so as to find "pardon in the strict and final sense" (IV/3, 931). God's enlightening gift exposes every deed and misdeed. Certain excrescences and abscesses will be consumed, though one's life will hardly be fragmented or piecemeal, Barth seems to think. For those Christians who had tripped and plodded through the penultimate age, "their concluded existence, though it be only a torso or the fragment of a torso, will be seen as a ripe fruit of His atoning work, as the perfect manifestation of the will of God fulfilled in Him, being thus illuminated, having and maintaining its own light, and bearing witness to God in this renewed form in which it is conformed to the image of the Son of God" (IV/3, 928).[35] Our manifestation in Christ will be a judgment of grace (a kind redaction, so to speak)—and therefore the evocation of our joyful thanks and praise.

Lastly, Barth drives home the point that the resurrection means *the vision of God*. When Barth writes in the letter to Rüegg that resurrection life "is this life, but the reverse side which God sees," he is certainly alluding to a beatific vision in which the cosmos no longer obstructs "the direct vision of God" (III/1, 141). In his earliest venture into eschatology proper, Barth describes it in agreement with the Augustinian tradition,

> The *visio Dei, visio immediata, intuitiva, facialis, visio essentiae divinae*, the unbroken awareness of God in the totality of His personality and aseity. That's the thing which even now the angels do not see, and what the prophets have not yet seen. But the redeemed, enlightened by the *lumen gloriae*, shall see and comprehend it. (*UCR* III, 485–86)[36]

In *Church Dogmatics* Barth accentuates the *visio Dei*, viz., the ability, in God's presence, to see things from God's perspective. And so the aforementioned letter says, "The new thing will be that the cover of tears, death, suffering, crying, and pain that now lies over our present life will be lifted, that the decree of God fulfilled in Jesus Christ will stand before our eyes." We will see ourselves whole, entire, and simple. Far from being ashamed or disappointed, this kind of deific perspective will wipe away every tear. We will understand the beauty of the whole as our lives are wholly unveiled.

Again, the resurrection of the flesh is the manifestation of this life in Christ as a purifying judgment that allows direct vision of God and ourselves. Barth's eschatology stands on its strongest leg when he highlights manifestation, in large measure because he can appeal to strong biblical precedent. For instance, the glories of salvation will be brought to the elect "at the revelation of Christ" (1 Pet 1:5, 13); when Christ appears they also

35. Perhaps the holy remainder of the eschatological recension counts as the special reward given to the righteous, though Barth does not develop the idea.

36. Cf. *ER*, 308; II/1, 630.

"will appear with Him in glory" (Col 3:4), the "revealing of the sons of God" will be their adoption, *tēn apolutrōsin tou sōmatos hēmōn* (Rom 8:18, 23); at His appearance "we shall be like him [*homoioi*], for we shall see Him as He is" (1 John 3:2). Barth's reading of the Scriptures makes these verses the interpretive center of other eschatological concepts, so much so that full self-comprehension in Christ *is* what it means to be saved in the End. Christ's final appearance in glory triggers the lifting of the cover of darkness over our lives. In this way, Barth's *theologia crucis* bears fruit for the human too: the veil of dereliction is eradicated once the glory of the children of God is raised to the surface. At the resurrection we will behold "one continuous demonstration of the being of Jesus Christ and our being in Him," an age when God proves His love by "a steady, all-embracing and all-pervasive light," and in which we exist in "a complete and unbroken perception of His being and our being in Him, and therefore in a full and perennial response to His love" (IV/2, 286).

At this juncture I think it imperative to shift terminological gears, as Barth does, and concentrate on the concept of *presence*.[37] The Son's integrity (and, by grace, ours) has to do with relational proximity, a proximity of identity. God and humanity are wholly proximal in Jesus Christ in His own personal history, allowing His two natures to be fully communicative. This transfer in the Son opens up a corresponding transfer of predicates between humans and God, who have been reconciled (i.e., brought together) in Christ. The disclosure of this divine-human proximity is resurrection. The manifestation of the one Mediator leads to sub-manifestations as other persons have this determinative reality disclosed in them. Earlier I observed the importance of strains of thought in Barth's life, including romantic idealism (from Schleiermacher through Herrmann), which anchored thought in the irreducible primal knowledge of God in immediacy, and pietism (especially the Württemburg strain), which grounded Christianity in the personal encounter with God.[38] More might be said about Kierkegaard, who helped Barth articulate the moment of revelation

---

37. For various reasons (not least because of his criticism of Christian experience and his own late-breaking change in terminology) Barth scholars have missed the harvest around this key to his work, though on the doctrine of revelation see Richardson, "*Christus Praesens*," 136–48.

38. For all the vulnerability of the mindset, pietism recognized the closeness of God to humanity, the powerful and constant presence of God to the Christian. "Blumhardt always begins right away with God's presence, might, and purpose. He starts out from God; he does not begin by climbing upwards to Him by means of contemplation and deliberation. God is the end, and because we already know Him as the beginning, we may await his consummating acts" (Barth, "Afterword," 219).

as a co-existence with the risen Lord, becoming contemporary to Him by faith.[39] Likewise, in chapter 3 we discovered how Barth could speak of the resurrection as a pan-temporality in the divine presence. Through his entire career he crafts a sense of glorification dictated by the rubric of proximity.

Therefore we are ready to consider how Barth restructures the conception of parousia. By "parousia" Barth means not simply the final return of Christ, but "the effective presence of Jesus Christ" (IV/3, 292). In New Testament usage the term denotes the coming of Christ at the end of time, that is, His glorious return to earth. In Barth's hands, however, there is a *threefold* parousia: resurrection, revelation in the present age, and the final return. Any apocalyptic "coming" qualifies as Jesus' parousia. The triple expression of Christ's eschatological presence with humanity becomes a key structure to Barth's eschatology, coming through explicitly only at the end of *CD* IV/3 and the beginning of IV/4 (his part-volume on the ethics of reconciliation), although some foreshadowing can be detected in earlier works.[40] The manifestation of Christ is an event breaking through in three forms. These three have a certain order and bear certain distinctives, though they are really the one great act of revelation in something like perichoretic unity.[41] Easter, Pentecost, and the Day—commencement, continuation, and consummation—the Risen Christ who was and is and is to come: however one phrases it, the effective presence of Christ is triple. The three terms stem from the simple transcendence of Christ. The

---

39. See Farrow, *Ascension and Ecclesia*, 222ff.

40. Barth long considered the forty days of appearance and the return of Christ the same event (e.g., *WGWM*, 90; III/2, 490; IV/1, 333). Even before starting volume IV Barth speaks of resurrection, the outpouring of the Spirit, and the final appearance of Christ "to be understood as a unity, as a single fulfilment of this last predication of His future destiny" (III/2, 504). Note, however, how Barth is inconsistent along the way, at one point calling the parousia "the *immediate visible* presence and action of the living Jesus Christ Himself" (IV/1, 725, emphasis added), which would disqualify the Spirit's outpouring as a form. Sauter is probably right to call Barth's formulation of the three-fold parousia a "variation of a dominant theme 'discovered' *ad hoc*" ("Why Is Karl Barth's *Church Dogmatics* Not a 'Theology of Hope'?," 421).

41. IV/3, 296. Barth implements various Latin phrases to capture the triple immediacy of Christ, such as *a parte poteriori* (that each form of Christ's presence has the force of the whole) or *in parte pro toto* (that each form of Christ's presence points towards the whole). The unity of the threefold form of the parousia overwrites Barth's earlier claim that the threefold form of the Word of God (written, preached, revealed) is the only analogy of the Trinity (I/1, 121). Sauter asks if Barth here has not mistaken a triad for the divine triune ("Why Is Karl Barth's *Church Dogmatics* Not a 'Theology of Hope'?," 421).

contemporaneity of Jesus with all times makes the three quintessentially related. And in each of its three expressions, Christ's presence does more than bring salvation; it *is* salvation.

Lest all eschatological distinction become lost, Barth (a little anxiously?) tries to differentiate the threeness of Christ's effective presence. The first Eastertide was "the primal and basic form of His glory" (IV/3, 281), being "definitive" for all future revelation of Him (IV/3, 305). Easter was also a direct kind of manifestation in that the disciples could perceive Jesus face to face, interacting with Him in every concrete way. Yet Jesus was manifested "particularly and provisionally" (IV/2, 107) in this time, with limited scope and duration, His patent revelation being confined to the small band of disciples for forty days.

As for the second manifestation of the parousia, Christ continues to be available to the community in the age of Pentecost through a "middle [*mittler*]" form.[42] Barth is impelled by the (oft-quoted) verse, "Verily, I will be with you always, unto the end of the age" (Matt 28:20), a promise he interprets in the plain sense, that the Spirit *is* the Son's presence.[43] In this in-between time God patiently awaits others to respond to the covenant and reflect His grace, calling and edifying and sending others through the indwelling Holy Spirit of Christ. "This time is not, therefore, a vacuum between the other two," says Barth (IV/3, 794), though he admits that the middle form of the parousia lacks perfect, universal scope. More disorienting is Barth's claim that Christ's proximity in the pneumatic age is characterized by the paradox of immediacy in distance. In the penultimate era, Christians can get only "a look [*Blick*] at the risen and living Jesus Christ" (IV/4, 158), waiting for something utterly complete.

The eschatological presence of Christ has been and is being manifest, but Barth attempts to carve out room for one more form. The final return of Christ is the goal and end-point of the previous forms. Jesus "moves from the one Easter Day to the day of all days, to the last day, to the day of His final and conclusive return" (IV/3, 327). Nothing needs to be added to Jesus' presence, it simply needs to be made ultimate. This third and final form of the parousia is "the last definitive and universal revelation

---

42. IV/3, 350–51, 360, 481, 794. It is the "middle period and situation" (IV/3, 363). What would Barth, if pressed, make of the ten days between ascension and Pentecost?

43. For Christians, "the Holy Spirit, i.e., Jesus Christ Himself in the power of His resurrection, sets them on their way in this world which is not yet redeemed and perfected, and accompanies them on this way with His promise of the eternal kingdom and their eternal life" (IV/3, 352–53). In the next chapter I address the serious consequences of this conflation of the Spirit into the risen Son.

of Jesus Christ" (IV/4, 89). The distance between Jesus and ourselves, the distance between Him in fulfilled time and us in the imperfect, the distance between Him in the new world and us in the old, will end. His consummate presence will cast out any ambiguity about His identity or our own. Christ's immanence will be supreme, supplying an unimpeded knowledge of Him. He will speak to women and men immediately, "in such a way that even those who are awakened by Him to faith and love can hear His voice in perfect purity and to the exclusion of every conceivable contradiction and opposition and above all participation in human falsehood" (IV/3, 903). What is more, every knee will bow and every tongue will confess on that day, expressing an unlimited scope of revelation to the whole created world: "What will finally be at issue in the coming of Jesus Christ to the last judgment of the quick and the dead, in the resurrection of the flesh and the manifestation of the life everlasting, will be not merely the consummation but the universality of the renewal which has come to [humanity] here and now" (IV/3, 675). The future, of course, is constantly breaking upon us, even now. But once the penultimate becomes *schlechthinige Zukunft*, "utter future" (IV/4, 40 = *KD*, 44), reconciliation will be one with redemption. The dead will arise immortal, without contradiction and without shadow.

In fine, Barth teaches that humans have already acquired integrity through the reconciling work of the One who knit them to Himself, and being thus conjoined to His deity, they await only His coming, at which they will be manifested with Him. On that Day they will they gain a final, direct, universal, and undialectical awareness of Christ, and with it, comprehension of their own selfsame histories. For the human too the noetic proceeds from the ontic, and that noetic comes with the force of an ontic. Jesus Christ's presence becomes effective presence. Our proximity to Him is made manifest. With His appearance our hidden glory rises to the surface.

Having delineated Barth's understanding of the resurrection of the flesh as the manifestation of one's integrity with the divine in the manifest presence (parousia) of Christ, I now want to hone in on two troubling consequences. A lesser critique involves the point that Barth does not (or cannot) attribute the same range of meaning to our manifestation that he does to Jesus'. My more fundamental criticism is that Barth risks spiritualizing the Christian hope with his noetic thrust because, at its root, he compromises human creatureliness by trading in the currency of divine presence.

First to the lesser critique. Barth does not spell out our manifestation with the same, full character of Jesus'. Our manifestation is a vindication, he says. But before whom? It is a publicizing, he says. But to whom? Human manifestation is a showing forth of our true identity to God, certainly, and also to ourselves; we are freed from the ambiguity of carnal existence and come to a state of true comprehension of God and self so that, radiating the covenantal glory, we participate in the divine life and therefore no longer suffer from indignity and pain. But our coming manifestation lacks an important meaning of revelation, for at the center of Barth's description of Jesus Christ's own manifestation is the notion that He reveals Himself *to others*. He moves toward the saints, awakening and enlightening them. To be fully consistent, then, Barth would have to make more explicit provision for the way in which the general resurrection manifests our life to our fellow humans, the mutual display and fellowship of those who enter eternal life. Are we not raised together (Heb 11:40)? Do we not commune together in the promised land, in the New Jerusalem (Rev 21)? Will we not be—and are we not now, provisionally speaking—raised to one another?[44] Manifestation is at its heart a communication between self and other selves. In Barth's defense, much of this could have been slated for *CD* V.

My more serious objection, however, has to do the inherent compromise of creatureliness when one bases glorification strictly in terms of divine presence. To spell out my critique, let me first make a classification. Barth's concern for the manifestation of integrated being, the disclosure of our union with God in Christ, leads me to conclude something that at first seems impossible in *CD*: that Barth teaches something like a doctrine of deification, a saving *theōsis* at the heart of reconciliation and redemption. Like Origen, Athanasius, the Cappadocian fathers, Cyril and the later Alexandrian tradition, Barth orients his soteriology to the exchange of predicates effected by human closeness to God. Humans are glorified as they partake of the *divine* nature:

> What God is, He wills to be for man also. What belongs to Him He wills to communicate to man also. What He can do is meant to benefit man also. No one and nothing is to be so close to man as He. No one and nothing is to separate him from Him. And in fellowship with Him every need of man is to be met; he is to be refreshed, exalted and glorified far beyond all need. This, indeed, is what is allotted to him in the promise fulfilled in the resurrection of Jesus Christ. (II/2, 238)

44. Knight, "Time and Persons in the Economy of God," 134–36.

Only gradually have scholars begun to acknowledge deification as a real theme in Barth's works. In 1976 Eberhard Jüngel described Barth's doctrine of salvation as "the taking up of humanity into the event of the being of God," though he flinched at the word *theōsis*.[45] More recently, the kind of saving mystery inherent in the Word of God has led George Hunsinger to say that Barth's notion of divine encounter "comes within a hair of the traditional Eastern Orthodox understanding."[46] Most significantly, Adam Neder argues that Barth's participatory soteriology, for all its Reformational and Reformed distinctives, meets all the basic standards of a doctrine of deification.[47]

We should tread carefully here out of respect for Barth's own analysis. After all, he issued strident disavowals of the term "deification."[48] His cannons were perennially aimed at the apotheosis of nature endemic in romantic and idealistic Neo-Protestantism, Roman Catholic thought, and in the myriad theologies reliant upon natural theology. If we pair Barth and a doctrine of deification, then, we must also note three stern qualifications. First, deification is entirely God's gift. In this unilateral relationship no room remains for synergism.[49] If there is a communion, it is a *communio gratiarum*, a definite giver and a definite recipient. God establishes a union with the creature only by His own initiative and grace, and only in a way that sustains a marked priority (or asymmetry) within the fellowship. Two, in deification God imparts to humans the divine nature not by extending His substance but by bringing them into the covenantal relationship so they can reflect His image. At no point can humans be confused or mixed with God, moving up a divine hierarchy into the Godhead.[50] Instead, by

45. Jüngel, *God's Being Is in Becoming*, 75.

46. Hunsinger, *How to Read Karl Barth*, 175.

47. Neder, *Participation in Christ*, 91f.

48. E.g. I/1, 238ff.; II/1, 531; II/2, 577; III/4, 474; IV/2, 81–82, 106, 377. Barth's microscopically precise parsing regularly fails to impress, e.g., "As He adopts [the human essence], making it His own existence in His divine nature, He does not deify it, but He exalts it into the *consortium divinitatis*, into an inward and indestructible fellowship with His Godhead" (IV/2, 100).

49. E.g., I/2, 768; II/1, 670; IV/2, 88ff. This is a serious divergence from Orthodoxy, stemming from Barth's eschatological presentation of the doctrine, which makes salvation a coming glory given in hope rather than a progressive path (Neder, *Participation in Christ*, 89).

50. Barth protests an elevation of human nature to equality with God—but so do Eastern Orthodox theologians, in the form of the Palamite distinction of "essence" and "glory." Moreover, as Andrew Louth clarifies about Pseudo-Dionysius, "[O]ne 'ascends' *into* the hierarchy rather than up it" (Louth, *The Origins of the Christian Mystical Tradition*, 171).

faith, they show forth God: "In their existence they do not themselves become gods, but creaturely reflections of the divine glory and therefore of the divine being" (II/1, 673).[51] Barth struggles to explain how the human imaging of God's being never encroaches on either one's basic definition, but he is diligent in upholding the "correspondence" which never violates the "infinite qualitative distinction" (II/2, 577). Three, this reflection happens only because of the pre-established work of Christ. The illumination of the person transpires only because of the finished work and active mediation of the incarnate One, who alone among humans is God. In the Mediator humans are made divine, but Jesus Christ remains exclusively consubstantial with the Father and the Holy Spirit. Therefore, one's *theōsis* is indirect and secondary, a glory derived from Him who possesses these things directly and primarily. Only through Jesus' humanity (which is the humanity directly united to God) does one enter into the divine benefits.[52] We are not so much deified as "Christified." In sum, Barth's three qualifications channel deification through a Reformational lens: humans participate in God according to the principles of *sola gratia, sola fidei, soli Christo*. Only under these terms does Barth tread the Alexandrian route toward deification.

All well and good—but do these provisos guarantee a distinctly *human* fulfillment? Here lies my objection. It seems to me that Barth's filters, though helpful, do not vouchsafe the basic platform of human life that is corporeality, for deification seeks to fulfill human life not through the restoration of its natural identity but through the impartation of a supernatural quality. Supposedly the human person reaches his or her goal when suffused by God and translated into the divine mode. Supposedly the aim of human life is to obtain God's eternity (i.e., His "omnipresence") and His powers of comprehension (i.e., His "omniscience"). In both cases, *the creature as such is meant to exceed itself* through divine participation. By Barth's definition, the human is supposed to achieve its true identity by surpassing its native mode. This surpassing-ness is the very problem. I contend that Barth, like so many of the Alexandrians, brings down so much heaven as to wipe away earth. In breaking open the dam of God's heavenly perfections, the human identity is flooded as it were, uprooted, displaced, carried away.

---

51. Barth rejects the standard Eastern Orthodox distinction of essence and energies (e.g., II/1, 331–32), replacing it with a "historically oriented" solution (McCormack, *Orthodox and Modern*, 237).

52. E.g., IV/2, 100. Cf. Torrance, *Space, Time and Resurrection*, 136.

Christ-alchemy

Posing as the resurrection of the flesh, Barthian deification feels very much like a sleight of hand: The human fulfils creatureliness—by becoming divinized! The quotidian becomes perfectly normal—by operating according to the divine qualities! The flesh is raised—by being raised into the spiritual mode! Like other Alexandrian-leaning Christologies, Barth maneuvers through a doctrine of Christ that would define humanity through divinity, i.e., humanity submerged in divinity. Like most versions of deification, Barth's description of the human entry into a divine mode (however much mediated) fulfills the creaturely definition precisely by taking the creature *beyond* that definition. In gaining eternity the human loses time—but supposedly obtains it in a supreme sense. In gaining contemporaneity the human loses fleshly space and process—but supposedly obtains on a higher level. Through a kind of Christ-alchemy, Barth plunges humans into the humanity of God, in order that human existence might show its divine basis and be carried about in deity, glowing like gold.

Barth's reliance upon the idea of exaltation in God's presence comes through in his overly noetic language about the resurrection. As we have seen already, "manifestation" looks back to the already-established reality of participation rather than pressing forward to the as yet unfulfilled glorification. God's presence to us simply needs to become "present." But in this paradigm the resurrection, an event concerning knowledge and consciousness, conveys a spiritualization of the Christian hope. In a roundabout way Barth equates resurrection with the beatific contemplation of God and ourselves, concentrating too much on *visio Dei* (vision of God) and *fruitio Dei* (desire for God)[53]—but not nearly enough on *vita corporis* and *fruitio terrae*. Nothing new comes to the human in Barth's version of the resurrection. The human simply sees and is seen. In chapter 1 we noticed how Augustine and others noeticized the afterlife by making vision (vision of God, vision of self, vision of the world) the primary objective. The body may tag along with the perceptive soul, but flesh is an auxiliary component of the all-seeing self. In like manner, Barth's celestial future is a matter of *viewing* that which was and was done at the expense of a further *being* and *doing* on earth.

It comes as no surprise that various commentators have described Barth's anthropological shortcomings in Christological terms. An ally as strong as T. F. Torrance has a hard time shaking off "a suspicion of docetism" in response to *CD* IV,[54] and Oliver O'Donovan, for all his praise

---

53. *UCR* III, 485–86; II/1, 653ff.
54. Torrance, "My Interaction with Karl Barth," 62.

of Barth's epistemology, distances himself from an ontology which begets "disturbing results in a series of frankly Apollinarian Christological conceptions."[55] Most precise in his evaluation, I think, is Douglas Farrow, who finds Barth's actualizing of the two natures of Jesus Christ to have "a worrying Eutychian tendency."[56] That is, rather than being preserved or expunged, the human nature tends to be absorbed into the divine nature. A sad irony lingers in this, for Barth opens up communication between Christ's deity and humanity for the very reason of *avoiding* docetic tendencies, in order to avoid episodic interpretations of the incarnation or the worship of a *Deus absconditus* behind the *Deus revelatus*.[57] God's own being (His eternal being) is defined by His free act to become human. He was and is and ever will be the incarnate God, Barth demands. But by equating the deity of Jesus Christ fully with His finished human history (what Farrow calls "the Chalcedonian clamp"[58]), a distinction of natures becomes impossible. The human essence, construed as a history of the encounter with the divine rather than properties and powers, exists as a sub-essence within the Son's God-ness rather than a concrete otherness.[59] More specifically, now *the slippage of Christ's humanity into deity happens eternally*, at every point, not just at Christ's conception or baptism or resurrection or ascension, as older Eutychianizing accounts presented it. All that prevents the man Jesus from existing wholly "in the mode of God" is His willingness to be temporarily given to concealment in the incarnation. Once that "veil" is lifted at the resurrection, Jesus' domineering divinity takes over functionally. Barth claims that Christ's humanity-in-God-mode at the resurrection does not expunge human qualities, for the flesh remains established by virtue of the hypostatic union. But, in Barth's portrayal, has the flesh of Jesus really be established at His resurrection, or has it been dissolved and made an accident of His primary essence? Jesus' fleshy humanity accompanies His deity at all times, yes, but accompanies it as a solute stirred into a solvent.

Barth's Eutychean slippage affects all humans in the end time. A divine re-predication "manifested" at the general resurrection calls into question whether the subject continues to exist in a creaturely mode. Time and space no longer exist as the medium for the unfolding of earthly

---

55. O'Donovan, *Resurrection and Moral Order*, 87.

56. Farrow, *Ascension and Ecclesia*, 295.

57. Ibid., 243.

58. Ibid., 247.

59. van Driel, *Incarnation Anyway*, 104–5.

phenomena. Movement and history and relationship-building in the body cease. The flesh is only the basic "I" in a nominal, honorary sense, as something from the past held onto as a celestial keepsake. As with Christ's resurrection, Barth's general resurrection demotes the flesh to the level of a colorant, a lingering but faded quality. Or is it rather that the flesh is a pliable, neutral plastic, ready to be suffused and overtaken?

I do not accuse Barth of stripping away the flesh entirely in the human proximity to the divine. That would be hurling at Barth far too severe an accusation. It is not too much to say, however, that his eschatological revelation of human existence disperses the body as far and wide as God. The dead are raised, but raised not as flesh so much as something flesh-like. With the human broadcast something is lost in translation.

5

The Resurrection of the Flesh
as Incorporation

"I AM THE RESURRECTION and the life," announces Jesus (John 11:25). Such a claim means that He has authority to give resurrection and life, of course, though the force of such a statement invites speculation about how Jesus Christ's very being itself constitutes resurrection and life. In the two preceding chapters we watched Barth as he examined Christ's resurrection in the passive sense ("He was raised) and the more active sense ("He arose . . . and showed Himself"). A third aspect remains, one in which Barth attempts to plumb the heart of the mystery, namely, Jesus as resurrection. In this third, loftiest sense, Barth speaks of the resurrection of the flesh as the fullness of participation, as an *incorporation* into Jesus Christ through the Holy Spirit.

Adam Neder has proposed that the theme of divine communion "belongs to the fundamental core of Barth's theology."[1] I agree. In Barth's view, since humans have no life in themselves and because they are creatures, they need to drink from the heavenly wellspring in order to have genuine life. Without involvement in God's life they are doomed to perish, for ontological isolation is perdition and a plunge into nothingness, while participation in God is true life. Such participation in its full sense is what Barth means by the coming resurrection. It should be clear by now that Barth has little interest in a discrete doctrine of the general resurrection. Rather, his purpose is to demonstrate how Jesus Christ's incorporative being *is* resurrection, and how all those who are connected to Him are beneficiaries of His life, i.e., they are risen in Christ. Along these lines,

---

1. Neder, *Participation in Christ*, xii. Cf. Migliore, "*Participatio Christi*," 287–307.

Barth measures resurrection in terms of the sharing of predicates through relational transfer rather than the historic Christian description of resurrection as a transformation of substance through remediation.

We remind ourselves of where we have been. In chapter 3 we observed how the resurrection, conceived as duration, "raises" time into eternity, preserving delimited human time through divine contemporaneousness. Yet, problematically, such an omnitemporal span appeared to depreciate time as such, since the continuum of spatial-earthly history is terminated and transcended in the eschaton. In chapter 4 we heard from Barth how the manifestation of the resurrection "raises" to the surface the secret of sanctified human history, bringing one's grace-given, divine predicates out into the open. However, human identity hardly seems to retain its earthly shape in such a celestial perception and deific display. With eternalization and manifestation alike it was hard to conceive of the way in which Barth was affirming the flesh in the resurrection except as a footnote, as an accident, as some lingering texture. While not unappreciative of the advances of Barth's dogmatic efforts, this study has demanded of him something more concrete in the eschaton, a resurrection body no less dense than flesh.

In a third and final approach we focus on how Barth ranges the resurrection with incorporation, the way in which men and women are included in Jesus' body, are vivified in Him, and therefore correspond to His glorified life by being taken into that life. In this chapter I begin with the communion of the Holy Spirit. As God who has and is perfect communion, the Spirit (whose ministry is coincidental with Christ's resurrection) orchestrates fellowship with Himself and with others. Barth thereby speaks of Jesus Christ's own resurrection as an incorporative movement, implementing spiritual communion in His outgoing event of revelation. To wring more from Barth's doctrine of the end, I exploit some parallels between the doctrine of election and the resurrection of Christ, noting how each pneumatic opening of God's grace in time collapses in a great recapitulation. From there I touch on how for Barth eschato-pneumatic relations answer the problem of human isolation, for by the resurrection Christ in-corporates men and women into His own body. This chapter brings the study to a culmination, since eternalization and manifestation are expressions of a more central mystery: the human's mystical position within God. Incorporation extends outward as the conceptual umbrella for eternalization and manifestation.

With the heart of the matter lies the heart of my critique. The kind of onto-relational paradigm Barth shoots for with incorporation endangers particularity itself. Absorption threatens on multiple fronts: of the resurrection into the Spirit, of the Spirit into the Son, and ultimately of every human into Christ. First, so central is the concept of participatory incorporation for Barth that the very idea of the resurrection blends into the Holy Spirit, who is described as the power of this participation. Second, the logic of inclusion into Christ in God threatens the Holy Spirit Himself, who figures as little more than the emanated Christ in His connective presence. Finally, I will show how Barth's push for incorporation leads him to an eschatological panentheism: all things are moving into God through the Son. As the general resurrection suggests a final unity with God, in the end only the Christ-monad remains. Rather than resurrection securing a plurality of bodies, it has done the opposite, obscuring the distinction between God and humanity in the end. Without time, creaturely process, or hard corporeal distinction in the final state, human identity teeters on the brink of absorption into God. In all this the flesh factors in as a fanciful adjunct.

THE COMMUNION OF THE SPIRIT

God reveals Himself a third time, as the Holy Spirit, as the Redeemer who dwells in us, as the God who sets us free, who makes us into children of God just as antecedently He is in Himself "the Spirit of the love of God the Father and the Son" (I/1, 448). In the Holy Spirit, God the Father establishes communion between an earthly people and the Lord Jesus. The Father is free to give eternal life to His created people. The Son is free to give His integrity to His reconciled bride. But the Father's will and Son's work come to fruition only because the Holy Spirit effects communion between the separated parties. Fellowship is the Spirit's business. Truly, "Barth's theology of the Holy Spirit is a theology of *koinonia*, and *koinonia* is the essence of the Spirit's work."[2]

It is not my intention to elaborate on Barth's pneumatology, in part because it has been treated at length elsewhere,[3] in part because Barth himself makes little effort to isolate the doctrine. But I suggest something that clarifies his pneumatology even as it muddies it: the interchangeability

2. Hunsinger, *Disruptive Grace*, 185.

3. Ibid., 148–85; Rosato, *The Spirit as Lord*; Migliore, *"Vinculum Pacis,"* 131–51; Thompson, *The Holy Spirit in the Theology of Karl Barth.*

of the terms *Holy Spirit* and *resurrection*. In Barth's dogmatics they share the exact revelatory function and languish in a common nebulousness. In what follows I name four parallel functions in Barth's dogmatics, then go on to show how the ministrations of the Holy Spirit tend to eclipse the resurrection, and how Jesus' resurrection-presence in turn overtakes the Holy Spirit. In each case, particularity is at stake.

First, we address the equivalence of the resurrection and the Spirit. In chapter 2 I pointed out the extent to which resurrection and revelation were interchangeable terms. Moving to Barth's mature work, the same can be said of the resurrection of Jesus and the work of the Holy Spirit. I detect, roughly coincidental with the part-volumes of *CD* IV, four common functions: replication, nourishment, expansion, and communicative presence.

In IV/1 we find that the Holy Spirit and the resurrection both orchestrate a *replication*. In this part-volume Barth picks up the theme that Jesus Christ is the Son of God because He is the repetition of God.[4] The pneumatic/eschatological repetition, however, is one in which Jesus Christ surpasses Himself in order to reach others in a subjective appropriation of salvation. That the world might come to the knowledge of Jesus Christ in His finished work, He is given (or from another perspective, takes up) a glorious ministry after the cross of Calvary. A transcendent echo of Jesus' finished life commences at Easter, described either as a product of the resurrection or the product of the Holy Spirit. The raising of Jesus rehearses His life, which is the same as the subjective repetition of the once-for-all Christ-event in the Holy Spirit. More than a mere vocalization, the resurrection is the going-forth of Christ Himself, the glorious transcendence of His death. If I may borrow the repetition language of I/I, Christ repeats Himself and so sends the Spirit, or, alternatively, He repeats Himself and so goes forth in resurrection power. His protracted being beyond death "is the form of His action in which this action continues, in which it is made present to the man to whom He gives Himself," wherein the person is made a participant and contemporary of Jesus Christ (IV/1, 468). Jesus' awakening leads to a consequent bestowal of faith, gathering the community, for His *Jenseits* opens up an aperture through which others may find spiritual communion. And Christ's own excess results in an analogous echo on the part of His followers: the apostles can "reproduce" the gospel message (IV/1, 726) by preaching "in the power of His resurrection," which is "the force and authority of the verdict of the Holy Spirit" (IV/1,

---

4. E.g. IV/1, 205, 209; IV/2, 341. I am, of course, drawing a line back to Barth's earlier trinitarian language (see §9 in I/1).

320). Barth talks about the replication-movement either pneumatically or eschatologically. In each case Christians are caught up in the reverberations of Jesus' own overflowing history.

In IV/2, the resurrection and the Holy Spirit alike fulfill the ministry of *nourishment*. The Son upbuilds the community in His own exaltation, reorienting people in the royal way of love. Christians are swept up in their determination toward eternal life. Barth's shift between resurrection and Spirit is shockingly seamless in this part-volume, most dramatically in the middle of §64.4 "The Direction of the Son." There Barth is busy spelling out the many benefits of Christ's communicated power in the resurrection when, very abruptly, he changes subjects and announces, "The power whose operation is presupposed in the New Testament is the outgoing and receiving and presence and action of *the Holy Spirit*" (IV/2, 319, emphasis added)—and goes on to speak entirely in pneumatological discourse. The name changes but the functions remain the same. By the Spirit of God we are sanctified, edified, set on a course of holiness because He is the ligament by which we are bonded to Christ. The Spirit identifies us, warns us, and instructs us in the path of peace. Yet all of this could just as well be said to have been accomplished by Jesus' resurrection: Christians may move forward "by the direction which is given us by the existence of Jesus Christ, in and with His resurrection, in and with the witness and work of the Holy Spirit" (IV/2, 381). The two equivalent forces accomplish the same process of nourishment by attaching the branches to the vine.

Each also empowers Christians for *mission* in IV/3. The "promise" of the resurrection is God's gift of vocation to the reconciled ones, which is also the sending of the community in the Spirit.[5] As for the resurrection of Jesus Christ, He launches out from His place "to embrace ours too, to comprehend us men," performing "His prophetic work" (IV/3, 281). The resurrection power of the Victor is not just the power of His mission; it is ours too. By Jesus' resurrection Christians are plugged into the energy of His outgoing motion. But this prophetic movement Barth also attributes to the Holy Spirit, who reaches people with the Light of Life. Again, the life given by the Spirit and the life from the resurrection are different "forms" of the same energy. "As the Resurrected from the dead Jesus Christ is virtually engaged already in the outpouring of the Holy Spirit," says Barth, bracing his terminological merger, "and in the outpouring of the Holy

---

5. Though I appreciate Barth's use of Lukan language (Luke 24:49; Acts 2:33–39), I would suggest to him that he re-title §69.4 as "The Promise of the Resurrection" so as to repair the break in format. And why not, since there in content he keeps within the language of the resurrection, leaving the bulk of the pneumatic discourse to §72?

Spirit He is engaged in the resurrection of all the dead and the execution of the last judgment" (IV/3, 296). Irrespective of its eschatological or pneumatological phrasing, the movement of Christ to others concerns the mission of Jesus in the incorporative magnification of His glory. Incorporation is the world's future.

Replication, nourishment, and expansion can be said to culminate in a fourth and comprehensive parallel between the resurrection of Jesus and the work of the Holy Spirit, viz., *communicative presence*. We have already noted Barth's classification of Christ's manifestation in a three-fold parousia (Easter/pneumatic presence/consummation). In IV/4 Barth uses this syntax to identify the resurrection and the Holy Spirit: "These are the two factors, or, as one may and should finally say, the two forms of the one factor, in whose power and on a divine basis men become faithful to God instead of unfaithful to Him, and the foundation of the Christian life takes place" (IV/4, 30). As Jesus Christ is present to them in the power of the parousia, women and men respond and become available to Him as His genuine partners. Jesus' resurrection powers the Church—which is the Spirit's power. In Jesus' resurrection the community dies and is raised—by the baptism of the Spirit. By the resurrection humans are included into the divine *koinonia*—which is the community of the Spirit. The resurrection energizes human ethics—as does the Spirit. The Holy Spirit has more than just "an eschatological form."[6] He is the living eschaton of Jesus with others.

What consequences follow if resurrection and Spirit are one? To start, the resurrection, deployed as a participatory power, loses importance in light of the common operation of the Spirit. Resurrection carries the sense of incorporative connectedness in Barth's schema, but, in Scripture as well as tradition, the ministry of connectivity can be situated far more easily within the doctrine of the Holy Spirit. Indeed, Barth's eschatology as a discrete locus risks being eclipsed altogether. Barth retains resurrection as a kind of *Donnerwort* that moves theological conversations into awareness of the eschatological tension characteristic of revelation. By the end of *CD*, however, one wonders if resurrection, especially the general resurrection, deserves any systematic attention. If the future of humanity has to do with achieving divine duration, why not appeal directly to the essence of things—to life in the Spirit? If being present to God by the Spirit of God is what it means to be manifested in Christ, then why make a cumbersome appeal to the body of Easter and the bodies of the eschaton? If the pneumatic, subjective event is the real thing, why underscore the objective

6. Hunsinger, *Disruptive Grace*, 173–79.

event of Jesus' resurrection, whose quasi-historical claims make it sound so much like a mythical fixture?[7] And if the point is the *corpus in Christo*, lifted up in the Spirit, why bother homing in on the *corpus ex terrae* element at all?

Despite the ubiquity of the concept of resurrection throughout Barth's writings, only in recent years has anyone presented the case that resurrection is the linchpin of his work (R. Dale Dawson's treatment in *The Resurrection in Karl Barth*). A number of people, however, have filed resurrection under pneumatology and made the latter the key to his system. Consider how Philip Rosato glosses over eschatology to describe the Holy Spirit as Barth's *Vermittlungsprinzip*, his mediating principle,[8] or how Daniel Migliore passes over the resurrection of Jesus to concentrate on the Holy Spirit as Barth's "pneumatological counterpart [*pneumatologische Gegenbegriff*]" to his regulative Chalcedonian Christology,[9] or how Thomas Freyer perceives the entire organization of Barth's mature work within the logic of the Spirit.[10] If the resurrection-movement of Jesus is fundamentally equivalent to the movement of the Holy Spirit, then it is not out of bounds for Barth to relegate the resurrection of the flesh to the status of a pneumatological sub-effect in salvation, one in which human life simply retains a certain fleshiness in its pneumatic communion.

7. If indeed the resurrection becomes a subset of pneumatological presence, then it is little wonder that Barth struggled over so much of his career to affirm the empty tomb and the bodily vivification of Jesus. These "facts" are not earthly data at all; they belong to the life of the Spirit. They are moments projected and concentrated through the lens of the Spirit, henceforth to be discerned spiritually. That so many evangelical theologians in America were at loggerheads with Barth over the historical aspects of the resurrection had to do with Barth's unfamiliar attempt of packaging the resurrection in terms of the pneumatic moment of revelation. In a Spirit-ualized rubric the concrete elements of the Easter narrative dissipate into something subjective and ethereal. (For representative examples of the resistance to Barth's account of the resurrection, see Barth, *Karl Barth Letters, 1961–1968*, 7–8, 42–43; Van Til, *Christianity and Barthianism*, 90–113; Obitts, "Historical Explanation and Barth on Christ's Resurrection," 365–77). Furthermore, is not Barth's struggle against Bultmann to maintain objectivity and a semblance of bodiliness in Christ's resurrection a product of the fact that both of them shift eschatology to the bureau of pneumatology?

8. Rosato, *The Spirit as Lord*, 18. The resurrection and return of Christ play secondary roles to the middle term, "the legitimate theological center of his ecclesiology" (p. 120). It should be noted, however, that Rosato concludes that Barth's pneumatic pole does not hold up (outside of the doctrine of creation at least), making Barth guilty of interpreting everything "pan-christologically" (p. 183).

9. See Migliore, "*Vinculum Pacis*," 150ff.

10. Freyer, *Pneumatologie als Strukturprinzip der Dogmatik*.

Yet the disappearance of resurrection into the Spirit is not all. A double penumbra is in effect. If the resurrection vanishes into the Spirit, it can also be said that the Spirit sometimes vanishes into the enormity of the risen Christ. He in His prophetic ministry is the real arbiter of revelation to the subjective sphere, overflowing all boundaries in the power of His resurrected being, so much so that the Third Person feels redundant.

In increasing measure, the Holy Spirit appears in Barth's dogmatics as an appendage to the Son. The Spirit is pervasively the Spirit of Christ. Christ sends Him; Christ directs Him; Christ operates through Him; Christ redounds in Him. "He is the Holy Spirit in this supreme sense," says Barth, "because He is no other than the presence and action of Jesus Christ Himself: His stretched out arm; He Himself in the power of His resurrection, i.e., in the power of His revelation as it begins in and with the power of His resurrection and continues its work from this point" (IV/2, 322–23). The Holy Spirit is described as "the Spirit of the Word itself" (I/2, 239), "the self-expression of the man Jesus" (IV/2, 331), and "the living Lord Jesus Christ Himself in the work of the sanctification of His particular people" (IV/2, 552). For all His purported agency, the Holy Spirit begins to sound more like a function of Christ than one co-equal with Him.

Barth could and did tap into biblical arguments for a Christological pneumatology.[11] After all, the Spirit is the baptism administered by Christ (Mark 1:8), is sent and spirated by Christ (John 16:26, 20:22), seeks to glorify Christ (John 16:14), is called the Spirit of Christ (Rom 8:9; 1 Pet 1:11), and, in a passage cited often by Barth, may even be named equivocally with Christ (2 Cor 3:17–18). With good reason did Barth latch onto passages where Christ and the Holy Spirit are mentioned together, fearing heterodox theological programs that would invoke the Spirit as a creaturely spirit rather than the Son's. Had not pneumatology been the door to theological abstraction, to natural theology, and therein to the host of errors, both ancient and modern? For Barth, then, the traditional belief that the ascended Christ sends the promised Spirit was not enough. An invulnerable identity of the Spirit as the Spirit of Christ had to be forged so as to slam the door on unchristian metaphysics and mysticism.

In my mind, Barth fuses together Easter (an event obviously pertaining to Jesus) with Pentecost (an event obviously pertaining to the Spirit) to stem the theological hemorrhaging of the nineteenth century. The Spirit is always the Spirit of the risen Son, and therefore not an independent or

11. See especially *CD* §§12 and 64.4.

additional force of God that might justify anthropocentrism, nationalism, or any other perversion of Christianity. The merger of the Spirit's ministry and filial resurrection also—let us not forget Barth's roots!—solves the epistemological quandaries of religious knowledge by supplying an uncontestable closeness between the perceiving subject and Christ. Christ Himself comes to us in the moment of revelation, not mediately through the Spirit but immediately with the Spirit. For Barth, Jesus fulfills in a straightforward way the promise that he would be with the Church always (Matt 28:20), in that Jesus' life, His appearances in the paschal forty days, and His ongoing pneumatic presence all figure as part of His "extensive" story.[12]

The price for such Jesus-immediacy is high, however. Barth's talk of the Spirit tends to slip into talk about the living ministry of Jesus Christ in the power of His resurrection. At best the Spirit and the risen Christ work indistinguishably and in full communion. At worst the Spirit begins to look like a commodity or even subset of the Son, virtually indistinguishable from Him in the Easter mission. Robert Jenson raises this criticism when he says that Barth, instead of trusting that the Spirit can remain Himself as He breaks into others' spheres, employs a "tortuous dialectic . . . in order to locate the proclamation's objectivity in the Resurrection of the Son."[13] While I do not care to comment on Barth's Augustinianism, the validity of the *filioque* or the limitations of the Protestant tradition, I want to underscore Jenson's complaint that the resurrection (as Barth construes it) lubricates the slippage of the Spirit into the Son. In the reduplicative economy of the resurrection the Spirit gets cast as God's revealedness; in the transcendent space-time of the Son the Spirit becomes Christ's risenness; in the *ephapax* of Christ's opus the Spirit's music is but a rehearsal; in the eschatological twilight the Spirit looks very much like a limb of the moving Son. It is true that for Barth the Spirit performs an indispensable ministry in the earth so long as there is a "not yet" to the realized reality of Jesus Christ. The Spirit, the arm of Christ, reaches out and harvests the children of God. But once the arm works incorporation, what then its use? When the End comes, is He to be retracted, becoming an inner relation of Christ?

---

12. Cf. Freyer, *Pneumatologie als Strukturprinzip der Dogmatik*, 298.

13. Jenson, "You Wonder Where the Spirit Went," 298.

THE INCORPORATION OF THE RISEN CHRIST

What is clear in Barth's work is the sense of the *movement* of the Risen One to bring others with, alongside, and into Him. Already we have seen how the resurrection (or the outpouring of the Holy Spirit) is the event in which Jesus communicates His objective, *de jure* work to the subjective, *de facto* realm of other individuals. He is the Word, and through the resurrection He speaks Himself to us. Certainly this is true for *justification* and *sanctification* (the soteriological elements of IV/1 and IV/2), being dynamically enacted in us as Christ makes Himself present in our sphere. Yet there is a third, comprehensive sense in which Jesus communicates His gifts to us: He calls us to Himself and makes us part of His own, dynamic identity. In the resurrection He exercises His *vocation* (the soteriological element of IV/3), going out as the Light of Life, illuminating others so that they might be light-bearers with and in Him. For Barth Jesus Christ *is* the resurrection; "is" in the strong sense. To speak of His resurrection is to speak of Him in the act of sharing Himself through the incorporation of other humans into His life-giving being.

Here I do not want to duplicate Dawson's able exposition of Barth's answer to the "evangelical problem."[14] Rather, I want to map out the way Barth speaks of the resurrection in terms of an incorporative project, i.e., an expansion and contraction of Christ's body. To draw out the nature of this dynamic, I will look at election as a model of this kind of expanding and contracting circle. Because Jesus Christ stands as the encapsulating archetype and teleotype of all of God's ways, and because all things are ultimately incorporated into the representative Christ-monad from which they came, we are forced to enquire about what manner of recapitulation is at work in Barth, and what we are to make of the resultant panenchristism when all things are drawn into Christ at the completion of His resurrection-mission. This discussion prepares us for the bottom-line question: Is there room for individual identities in the absolute eschaton?

Let us start by remembering that Barth speaks of "resurrection" in many ways, and often fails to clarify the exact sense with which he employs it.[15] In general he uses it in three ways: 1) the *awakening* of Jesus Christ,

---

14. Dawson, *The Resurrection in Karl Barth*, 83ff.

15. I concur with Bertold Klappert and R. Dale Dawson that Barth, some inconsistency notwithstanding, made a theoretical distinction between the *Auferweckung* and the *Auferstehung*, the resurrection-awakening of the passive Jesus Christ and the resurrection-revelation of the active Jesus Christ, respectively. But even *Auferstehung* has its variegation.

which is an eternal decision apart from any manifestation, 2) the *appearances* of Jesus Christ in the forty days which establish the Church, and 3) the *pneumatic widening* of Jesus Christ from Pentecost forward in which He wins many by His prophetic power. This concentric pattern (typical in Barth's work) addresses the divine, the communal, and the individual levels. As the resurrection movement, these circles describe an *expansion* of Christ's outgoing glory. Yet one more expression of the resurrection is at work, a final *contraction*, 4) the *consummation* of Jesus Christ in His definitive enclosure of all space and time at His return. The circle expands, then closes.[16]

This concept deserves some unpacking. As for the epicenter of the circle, the resurrection narrative begins not on Sunday morning for Barth, but in the eternal counsel of God, before time as it were, in non-temporal eternity. Christ's resurrection happens in this suprahistorical realm, for "the event of Easter has to be understood primarily as the raising which happens to Jesus Christ" apart from the created world, an occurrence "first and foremost in God Himself" (IV/1, 303).[17] In this sovereign, irrevocable act within the Godhead, the Father acted (to use the naïve past tense) upon the Son, and the Son gladly submitted to this action. This divine moment in eternity involved a real choice. Would God decide to reveal the Reconciler to the world? The finished action of the Messiah could have been "shut up in Him" (IV/3, 282), but God, freely and joyfully, apart from any human agency, executed His verdict. He appointed His Son to go out to the world to have others share in His glory. In the beginning, God decided not only to reconcile humanity to Himself, but also to show that reconciliation in their realm. In the beginning, one might say, Jesus Christ awoke. Therefore, in a moment strangely coincidental with predestination, the Father raised the Son from the dead. He "elects the tomb in the garden as the scene of His being the living God" (II/2, 165). By doing so, the Son "emerged from the concealment of His particular existence as an inclusive being and action enfolding the world, the humanity distinct from Himself and us all" (IV/3, 283). God retains His aseity in the resurrection, but because of the eternal moment of awakening, Jesus Christ's being can be an

16. This is not to be confused with the three-fold parousia described in IV/3 and IV/4. Barth does not include the *Auferweckung* as a form of Christ's manifestation.

17. Barth's important *extra nos* is on one side a guard against subjectivizing readings of the resurrection (including Herrmann's and Bultmann's) in which Jesus Christ's history is dissolved in our own; on the other side is a protection against historicization (whether Schleiermacher's or Cornelius Van Til's) of those who would make Jesus' resurrection into a simple resuscitation and thus a mere instance of world-process.

inclusive being. His action is an including action. The decision *extra nos* is the radical designation of Jesus Christ as the some-body who moves out to em-body others in His own original body.

In the second ring Jesus Christ goes forth to establish the proto-community. Now awakened and commissioned with the sharing of His glory, Christ brings to Himself a body of believers. He appears to His disciples over the course of forty days, assembling the first community between Easter morning and the ascension. He illuminates them and delivers from their ignorance by showing Himself alive, the true Lord of Life. Barth is not concerned to grant these forty days too much of a historical character or to ground apostolic authority in the Son's appearances.[18] Rather, he understands the forty days as the prototypical time of revelation to the community, the founding of the Church, the forming of a nucleus among those who knew Him in the flesh before that fateful Sunday. There were some who doubted, of course (Matt 28:17), and Jesus did not appear to all (Acts 10:40–42), but such facts do not concern Barth, who understands the second moment of the resurrection as an effective launching of the Christian community, as a first instance of incorporation, as something officially made visible and audible and therefore made known to all.[19]

Expanding to the third ring, Jesus Christ incorporates individuals within His spacious body, a move enacted with Pentecost and the age of the Spirit. "It is not enough that the history of Jesus Christ should be objectively revealed to all men," says Barth. "What God wills in this history and with its manifestation is that all men should be saved, that they should be brought subjectively to the truth" (IV/4, 29). Fulfilling His prophetic office in the regenerative power of the resurrection, Jesus Christ brings His people historically into the community by bringing them alongside Himself, taking them up in His pneumatic "forward."[20] His members are spiritually animated, illuminated, and made witnesses of the risen Christ.

18. He grants to this stage a *terminus a quo* and a *terminus ad quem*, even a historical margin, though Barth interprets the resurrection accounts "typically," in the genre of "saga" (III/2, 452).

19. Revelation in the forty days has a certain representative nature (e.g., II/2, 256; IV/3, 371).

20. "The Holy Spirit is the *forward* which majestically awakens, enlightens, leads, pushes, and impels, which God has spoken in the resurrection of Jesus from the dead, which he has spoken and still speaks to the world of humanity: *forward* to the new coming of Jesus and the kingdom. . . . [The Spirit] is God himself in the same act in which in the Easter event he confessed his completed work in the history of Jesus Christ with the promise that he will confess it again universally and definitively" (Barth, *The Christian Life*, 256).

They undergo a process "in proximity and analogy to what befell Jesus Christ in His resurrection" (IV/3, 511). I emphasize that in describing the animation of humans Barth has not stepped outside the circle of Christology. Jesus Christ simply moves into the "remaining sphere" of individuals (IV/3, 276) and individuals "come into the sphere of this incomparable power of His" (IV/3, 185). Humans become participants in His life as He takes them under His care. They know Him because the Living One comprehends them. That is what the incorporating Son of God does: He *comprehends* others.

At this point, having taken into account the three rings, it appears that Jesus Christ's resurrection is extroversive, enabling, and multiplicative in nature. "For Barth, [Jesus'] reality is the condition for the possibility of real possibility," says Adam Neder, and this is certainly true of the resurrection inertia.[21] The resurrection winds blow to every corner of the cosmos, from the christological sphere *in atomo* to the anthropological sphere *in globo*, a pneumatic opening of the Christ event.

But one should make sure not to gloss over Barth's ascription of an introversive, assimilating, and monistic character to the resurrection. Jesus Christ does more than go out to liberate others and place them in orbit around Him. He also collects them. The divine, communal, and individual rings all lead to the fourth ring, the consummation, in which incorporation achieves its end. It is not really a ring at all, but a sealing and hardening of the rings, an end to their expansion. The final movement of resurrection ends all time and space, process and continuation. At the final revelation parousia a person's "future is present," when his or her "present has no more future" (IV/3, 916). Christ's incorporative resurrection concludes with an eschatological collapse in which everything is collected. In the remainder of this age the risen Christ moves out in the Holy Spirit to awaken and edify and send others out in joyful agency, but with the end comes an end to time, whether by bodily death or by the rapture at Christ's return.[22] The life that was lived by the human, knit to Christ, recedes into the eternal God. Like a terribly aged star, a spent red giant, the

---

21. Neder, *Participation in Christ*, 46. Barth's Platonistic language is intended to open up being and action; under the wing of Christ's resurrection humans exist "in this secondary, derived, indirect history, but a history which takes place *realissime* in its relation to that primal history" (III/2, 162).

22. Reluctantly, Barth finally confesses that there is no functional difference between personal death and the cosmic end (IV/3, 924–28). How would we expect anything but equivalence, if the eternalization of one's earthly life between the termini of conception and death has already been secured through identification with Christ?

to tal Christ

whole of creation collapses back to its core: "We wait for our inclusion in this . . . one indivisible, divine, sovereign act which comprehends [*umsassenden*] at once both the living and the dead."[23] The resurrection of the dead will reveal "His particular existence as an inclusive being and action enfolding the world" (IV/3, 283), which has its final collective expression at His return, when all creation manifests its "evident subjection by His judgment" (IV/3, 319). The collapse of the cosmos need not be seen with dread but with joy, for it means positively that our non-being can be "a return to the same God who called us out of non-being" (III/2, 595).

The consummation is a con-summation. In chapter 3 we saw how one's temporal history is to be summed up in eternity. But for Barth the coming summation addresses more than a reintegration of an individual's fragmented time; it is to be Christ's own self-summation through the full integration of His reconciled community. Toward this final reality, Barth prefers the language of the *totus Christus*, the total Christ.[24] Christ has an identity apart from others, no doubt, a *solus Christus* in His own flesh (a flesh willed in eternity by the electing God), and others have their own histories as they receive being from God. Yet Jesus Christ's resurrection-movement is all along a mission to bring together a community in His encompassing humanity, aimed to include the many in the one *totus Christus*. In post-temporal existence this totality exhibits unity of the highest degree, a simple expression of the Christ-act, the living fellowship of Christ and His people in a singular, eternal form. In the dregs of this age the resurrection power of the Holy Spirit knits together the rebellious parts of the ecclesia to its Head. But all of this simply presages the final consummation in which bodies are contained wholly and incontestably within Christ. The collective life of Christ's people is sealed (or revealed) with a perimeter:

> Does not His resurrection usher in the last day, when even the believer in Jesus can only live a life hidden with God in Christ? Do not His coming again in glory and the consequent revelation of this hidden life mark the end of this last day and time, the handing over of the kingdom of the Son to the Father? . . . Our past and limited life, which did not begin before time and does not continue beyond it, our real but only life, will then fully, definitively and manifestly participate in that *kainotēs zōēs* (Rom. 64). It will then be eternal life in God and in fellowship with Him. (III/2, 624)

23. Barth, *Epistle to the Philippians*, 117 (= Ger., 115).
24. E.g., IV/2, 60, 658, 675; IV/3, 216, 758.

The coming divine incorporation is not another production in time or something superadded to time. Rather, Jesus' final resurrection moment lassoes time, withdrawing all into "eternal life in God," "a life hidden with God in Christ." The summation of time, the final participation, will be a participation with an event horizon: God will be all in all.

Barth writes sparingly about the final, incorporating move of resurrection which brings about Christ-assimilation. Why? One might argue that Barth died before penning his doctrine of redemption (volume V of the *Church Dogmatics*), which he may have wanted to use as a careful explanation of the coming recapitulation. More likely, he felt that detailing the final, sagic moment of the parousia would involve too much speculation. But I suspect that behind Barth's reluctance lay a problem he created for himself, namely, the intractability of the eschatological *totus Christus*. Barth cannot describe the details of life in the end because, quite simply, there are no details to relay. Human particularity disappears in the ultimate moment. Jesus Christ in the final incorporation gathers His body with a gravity that can only lead to compression, immobilization, and assimilation of human identities. The flesh of the redeemed can be narrated in the past tense, but, as an exposition of the eternal present, such human lives resist differentiation or description. Flesh and bones converge and vanish into the eternal light.

One way of pressing the question is to bring in for comparison the similar closure inherent in Barth's doctrine of election. First, to summarize some important aspects of II/2,[25] Barth structures his doctrine of election in terms of three extroversive, concentric circles: divine, communal, individual. At the center is Jesus Christ, the subject and object of election. In the divine moment, God elects Himself to be the Representative and Savior of humanity without human agency, strictly within the Godhead (§33). From "before" any act of creation, God made Himself the archetype, the One in whom all were elected and included. Jesus Christ is there in the beginning as the electing God and the elected man, so no other will of God for humanity exists outside of Him. From all eternity He is the supralapsarianistic *decretum absolutum* of God; the Father wills Him to represent the whole of humanity. This single divine election includes within it a dual image in the communal election (*CD*, §34). Humanity has within it the non-elect and the elect, or Israel and the Church. Israel is

---

25. For more about the comprehensive impact of *CD* II/2, see the early standout study, Osaki, *Die Prädestinationslehre Karl Barths*. For a more recent and provocative interpretation, see McCormack, *Orthodox and Modern*, 183–233.

appointed for judgment, hearing and representing the passing man. The Church is appointed to mercy, belief, and the coming form of man. While there is a tangible Israel and tangible Church, Barth sees all of humankind encountered by the Word as a combination of both. The communal aspect expands to the third ring, individual election (*CD*, §35). Particular men and women are the true target of the election of grace. Their reconciliation with God and their activation as agents freed for righteousness is the aim of God's eternal election. Nevertheless, their own personal expression as elect or non-elect is overshadowed by the communal participation, which in turn is overshadowed by election in Jesus Christ. The full range of God's electing purposes converge upon this one Representative: "His election is the original and all-inclusive election; the election which is absolutely unique, but which in this very uniqueness is universally meaningful and efficacious, because it is the election of Him who Himself elects. Of none other of the elect can it be said that his election carries in it and with it the election of the rest" (II/2, 117).

This election plays out historically: Jesus Christ stands alone. He alone is the elect Representative—on behalf of reprobate humanity. He lives as the unique Head of humanity—by dying on the cross. He alone is anointed—for abandonment. He alone stands before God—to be judged. All stand against Him; none is with Him. But precisely at Golgotha all are *in* Him:

> "In Him" does not simply mean with Him, together with Him, in His company. Nor does it mean only through Him, by means of that which He as elected man can be and do for them. "In Him" means in His person, in His will, in His own divine choice, in the basic decision of God which He fulfils over against every man. (II/2, 116–17)

Christ takes the largest circle of individuals, all who make up the elect and the rejected communities, and withdraws them into Himself, sealing them in Himself by His atoning death. In Christ's substitutionary death "He is quite alone amongst us, the only One who is judged and condemned and rejected, just as He is the only One who has come and acts amongst us as the Judge" (IV/1, 237–38). The crucifixion of Jesus Christ is His drawing the perimeter of reconciliation around all, thus collapsing all into His pierced Body.

From here we may proceed with a comparison between election and resurrection. Indeed, I think there are good reasons to make the bold claim that the election of Jesus Christ and His resurrection are really just different aspects of the one decision wrought by the eternal God. Are not both from eternity and, in an important sense, happenings in eternity?[26] (Linking election and resurrection helps situate Barth's otherwise awkward discourse about the non-historical event of Jesus' awakening by the Father in IV/1.[27]) Moreover, cannot each be spoken of as the ground of the authority of Jesus Christ's incarnate life?[28] Though Barth does not highlight their concurrence, election and resurrection could be conceived of as an eternally coincidental event, and therefore a double-axiom of the gospel, situated on either side of eternity with Christ's incarnate history as the decision's content.

More to the point in this study, the parallel between election and resurrection holds true in terms of the *pattern* in which each plays out: both election and resurrection are *incorporative* decision-events in which humans are included in Christ. In the outer movement, each expands from (or develops within) the divine choosing of Jesus Christ, which has its resultant communal and individual inclusions. Election's set of concentric circles plays out the drama of reconciliation: the eternal decree in Jesus fructified from the One to the many through the creation of Adam, the population of the earth through Noah, then on to the manifold blessing

26. Cf. Eitel, "The Resurrection of Jesus Christ," 38–40, 43ff. Eitel goes on to do with resurrection what McCormack does with election: God's redemptive movement *is* His actualistic, triune being. The expansion of the divine decision into time corresponds to (and is the "historicization" of) the eternal awakening.

27. I am thinking specifically about how this equation clarifies the difficulty with Dawson's interesting reconstructive work. He would have Barth forge a stronger link between the resurrection and the reconciling work of Jesus Christ in order to secure the ontic nature of the resurrection (and with it, a better sense of the trinitarian action on the cross). To accomplish this, Dawson suggests that the *Auferweckung* (the intra-divine awakening, as distinguished from the ensuing revelatory movement, *Auferstehung*) be classified as a moment of ontic reconciliation rather than as part and parcel of the noetic, prophetic ministry (*The Resurrection in Karl Barth*, 211–15). Dawson's reclassification would be successful were it not for the fundamental identity of awakening with the eternal *election*, not the history of *reconciliation* worked by Christ on earth. If he desires to append Jesus' awakening to the reconciling work of the cross, it can only be done indirectly, secondarily, mediated through the eternal fiat, not as part of the historical reconciling work of God as such.

28. "That which God as [the world's] Creator wills and willed from all eternity . . . is what is event and revelation in the history of Jesus Christ. *Its direct origin in God's eternal election, decision and act* is what gives its voice authority. This is its distinctive feature. This is what gives it the contours which mark it off from other facts. *This is the mystery of the awakening of Jesus Christ from the dead*, and therefore of His unconquerable and indestructible life, and therefore of the newness and originality with which He confronts the world and primarily and supremely Christians, and therefore of the beginning of the history of light shining in the darkness" (IV/3, 227, emphasis added).

given to Abraham.[29] However, a thinning of the visibly elect community occurs through Moses and David, the kings and prophets, ultimately leading back to the single history of the New Adam. Israel's actors in the history of salvation narrow until, with the scattering of the disciples from the Garden of Gethsemane, only Jesus remained. Upon this one cruci-fied Representative rested the whole task of reconciliation. The circles of election contracted back to the single point on Golgotha, the telos of the divine election, thereby enacting God's gracious election.

As for the resurrection of Jesus, the same elective expansion occurs, this time from the divine, single point in the awakening to the second, communal ring during the forty days of appearance to the inclusion of all sorts of individuals at the outpouring of the Spirit. The now-established Church expands into all the world with Christ in His prophetic mission. But for how long? When will the resurrection of Jesus cease to be an inclu-sive opening, and become an inclusive convergence back to the singular? When will, as with election, the many converge to the One?

As long as time continues it makes sense to speak of a dynamic go-ing-out. But once time ends, will not all of Christ's people be drawn back into their Representative? Will it not be Him and Him alone? The return of Christ will be the re-turning of humanity into Christ. Every individual will be compressed into the One, the single point. In conclusion, if Barth's pattern of resurrection follows his pattern of election, then every human person will someday be withdrawn into the unitary Christ-body.

The punctiliar nature of the concluding resurrection I find to be a haunting prospect. If Barth's doctrine of redemption follows the pattern of reconciliation, then there is no human remainder in the Beyond, no being outside of Jesus' representative being, no bodies outside of Jesus' represen-tative body. Humans' brains and bones, personalities and processes fuse into Jesus Christ's singular, teleological representation. And in this respect is not Barth skirting the same predicament as Origen, whose matching of post-existence with pre-existence tended to reduce individual humans into divine accessories?

Let us be clear about the bone of contention. Barth has not come out and taught a total absorption to a simple Christ-monad. He prefers the (ecclesiastical) concept of the *totus Christus*, which has a correspond-ing incarnational logic of unity, distinction, and priority.[30] But when his logic is pressed, all of his fleshly and creaturely histories, when drawn to

29. See II/2, 54ff.

30. Cf. Bender, *Karl Barth's Christological Ecclesiology*, 202–5.

the omega point, fuse into a singularity. In this eschatological singularity Barth seems satisfied to speak of a lingering *differentiation within Christ's body*. In contrast, I am insisting upon a *plurality of bodies*. I question whether a spectrum of persons within the person of Christ can actually be said to exist if time, process and flesh have ended. It is not enough to describe a macro-body in differentiation. Resurrection bodies are to be *our* subjective appropriation of salvation. We are to have our mortal flesh raised immortal. *Our own flesh* is reanimated. There are to be *living bodies* upon the New Earth. Our affiliation with Christ in the End will be a standing side by side and a gazing face to face, just as a stricken Job prophesied: "Even after my skin is destroyed, yet from my flesh I shall see God; whom I myself shall behold, and whom my eyes will see and not another" (Job 19:26–27, NASB). If Barth's monism is the case, then I have a hard time seeing how the compressed differentiation of the One permits the statement "I myself" in a comparable or fuller way than is presently possible.

Barth was not a pantheist. Though he spent time in the schools of Schleiermacher, Eichendorff, and Novalis, and though he could call himself a romantic of sorts,[31] he never considered the "Immediate" to be a reality accessible from this side. If the creature is to be, as Schleiermacher contended, one with the infinite in the midst of the finite, eternal in a moment, such unity with the eternal is given only *in hope*. It is not yet apparent how all things are in God and are being folded into Him; they are not presently interchangeable with the One. Unity between God and humanity is a *coming* reality. The eschatological character of revelation destroys any alliance between it and the *deus sive natura* of Spinoza and the young Schelling. More decisively, Barth speaks of a radical *diastasis* all along between the Creator and the creature, between the unconditioned and the conditioned. The movement from the former to the latter is always a matter of grace: "We have always to remember that God's glory really consists in His self-giving, and that this has its centre and meaning in God's Son, Jesus Christ, and that the name of Jesus Christ stands for the event in which man, and in man the whole of creation, is awakened and called and enabled to participate in the being of God" (II/1, 670). If participation, then not pantheism.

But is Barth a panentheist? Does he hold the belief that God "includes and penetrates the whole universe, so that every part exists in Him, but His Being is more than, and not exhausted by, the universe"?[32] Here

31. See Busch, *Karl Barth*, 40.
32. Cooper, *Panentheism*, 27.

a monism of the second person

we must walk the theoretical tightrope with Barth. All things come from God and are sustained in God. All things are related to their Primal Origin and apart from Him have no subsistence. But God's *Wesen* is at no point identical with the creature's, and any communication between the Creator and creature happens through the strictly calibrated exchange of properties in Jesus Christ. Thus Barth claims to reject panentheism from the outset: "God does not form a whole with any other being either in identity with it or as compounding or merging with it to constitute a synthesis— the object of that master-concept, so often sought and found, which comprehends both God and what is not God" (II/1, 312). Void and bankrupt are all theological attempts to equate world-process with the eternal, even if that be panentheism's finest exponent, Hegel, who in identifying history and Spirit loses the identity of each.[33] All along the way Barth claims to follow a path that posits the hard demarcation of Creator and creature, couching it in the mediating union of Jesus Christ.

Not everyone agrees with Barth's self-assessment, however. According to Richard Roberts, Barth's attempts to escape Idealism in the 1920s failed. The author of *Der Römerbrief* pries himself from the clutches of Schleiermacher only to fall into the synthetic ontology of the Idealists. "Just as with Hegel the danger of reduction constantly threatened such a synthesis on the level of pure thought, so with Barth there is the threat of reduction of the diverse totality of being into the realm of the divine being in us," claims Roberts, who sees in Barth "the inevitable suppression of the real distinction of immanence and transcendence in the name of a higher reality."[34] To give a measure of honor to the created world, Barth posits an ontology in which historical action gives definition to eternity. But even here actualism has a Platonic recoil back into the Idea, for time itself has its *plenum* only in eternity. Plurality contracts into the monad. Sensing this threat, Barth attempts to prop open the closing aperture with Christ's own indestructible historical narrative (including the resurrection appearances), so that the concretions of life in ongoing time are "not merely the supra-philosophical expression of the divine being and the resolution of antitheses."[35] But the transfer of monism to the Second Person fails to mitigate the collapse, says Roberts. Time and particularity eventually succumb to eternity. While I do not share Robert's cynicism about Barth's overall project, I think he accurately gauges the monistic pull of Barth's

33. Haga, *Theodizee und Geschichtstheologie*, 234.

34. Roberts, *A Theology on Its Way?*, 7.

35. Ibid., 30.

ontology when speaking of the End. If all things are determined by God's own being and finally incorporated within His own being, i.e., if all things exist in God as their *archē* and come to rest in God as their *telos*, then an indecipherable unity melds the creature and the Creator at the omega-point, regardless of how much partitioning and expansion transpired in the penultimate epoch.

Bruce McCormack's prediction, that Barth's doctrine of election will be his most enduring contribution to theology, is likely true.[36] Through such a pivotal move, creation (and therefore anthropology) can be spoken of as radically defined by God's own decision in the Son. But it seems to me that there are different ways to speak of Jesus Christ as the archetype and teleotype of creation. Just how does this Elected One represent others? By what qualification is He the stand-in for every human? To what kind of being is He elected? And here is the difficulty: Barth's doctrine of election has a panentheistic thrust because he makes Jesus Christ the One *elected to assume human essence.* For instance, he says, "[W]hat the eternal Word made His own . . . was not a man, but man's nature, man's being, and so not a second existence but a second possibility of existence, to wit, that of a man" (I/2, 163). Again, human essence is the "sum of . . . relationships" as defined in Christ (III/2, 40). Of course, Barth steers away from classical approaches to metaphysics and drives toward history and ethics. Nevertheless, he is consistent in making Jesus Christ the archetype of humanity: "What God the Son assumed into unity with Himself and His divine being was and is—in a specific individual form elected and prepared for this purpose—not merely 'a man' but the *humanum* [*das Menschliche*], the being and essence [*Sein und Wesen*], the nature and kind, which is that of all men, which characterizes them all as men, and distinguishes them from other creatures" (IV/2, 48 = *KD*, 51). That is how Barth solves the universal-particular problem, by making Jesus Christ the universal which defines all the particulars by making them participate in the being of the universal form. Therefore his ontology is at its roots a kind of panenchristism. All things move from Him and through Him and to Him, since He is elected as the ontological archetype, the realest level of being from which all other things derive their reality. Other humans are humans not because they are *like* Him, but because they are *in* Him, because they participate in His human essence. Once time and the veil of death are taken away, Christ the Head will exert His manifest reign over His body, and God will be all in all. That is the result of the combination of a

36. McCormack, *Orthodox and Modern*, 183.

Christological doctrine of election and a strong sense of the assumption of the human nature.

My concern is not Barth's conception of election as such, then, but the consequences of interpreting Christ's representative being in so totalizing a way. I will not deny for a second that Barth's panenchristism generates human existence and freedom and correspondence in creaturely time, since all things are enabled to happen within the historical opening. Many things are permitted to unfold in the extent of the Christ-event. The resurrection of Jesus Christ opens up His lively and empowering story, facilitating enumeration within His own spacious mission. As one Barth commentator puts it, humans have their being along the lines of a kind of enhypostatic ethical dynamic.[37] This I concede and celebrate. But I am not at all clear as to how Barth sees human flourishing to continue in any real way at the return of Christ. At the final closure of time, Jesus culminates and seals and ends all activity. His history is no longer history-begetting but history-collecting. The circles retreat into a point. Edwin Chr. van Driel voices a similar worry, that ontological encapsulation in Jesus Christ poses a threat to human agency as soon as the parousia takes place in its final form.[38] In the End, all flesh is concluded and made subsidiary to the one ascended being of Jesus. In this Barth's reliance on participation has gone too far.

Barth's quasi-panentheistic features are not at all unheard of within the Christian tradition, which in its Alexandrian trajectory has been heavily reliant upon Neo-Platonic categories. Like many of the eastern Church fathers, Barth distances himself from Neo-Platonism even as he moves toward it. Barth steps away from Plotinus's theory of emanations—yet he categorizes all being in terms of participation in the divine through Christ. Barth rejects a metaphysical hierarchy of being with his rejection of the *analogia entis*—even as he draws up an *analogia eventus*.[39]

37. Webster, *Barth's Moral Theology*, 89ff.

38. "Included in [Christ], every human nature is assumed, elevated, and exalted. But what about the human agents who are the subjects of these human natures? They did not exist yet when their histories started. Presumably, they were not objects of assumption. And indeed, they are not preserved in the eschaton. Their histories are; they are not. In this proposal, human agents seem to fall outside the reach of salvation" (van Driel, *Incarnation Anyway*, 141).

39. "Indeed, I remember that Barth enthusiastically welcomed a remark of the late Dorothy Sayers, in her broadcast plays, that we are dealing here [in the act of God in Jesus] with 'the only thing that ever really happened.' Although Barth rejected the *analogia entis*, he has had his own doctrine of event-hood!" (MacKinnon, "Further Reflections," 110).

To Barth's credit, he affirms the material body more than most Neo-Platonic philosophers, who accorded the material world an ambiguous moral standing by speaking of it as the boundary of perception and the edge of evil. Also importantly, Barth is on guard against a panentheistic absorption of the human nature. Yet when it comes to the all-in-all of God, Barth's eschatology shows forth the typical haziness of panentheism's eschaton:

> From those to whom He wills to be all in all, [God] strips everything else. This is what we must experience in death, under the sign of His judgment. We do not know what and how we shall be when we are no more and have no more time for being in virtue of our death. . . . We can make no dispositions concerning our future when we shall have no more future. We can only cling to the fact, but we can really do so, that even in our death and as its Lord He will be our gracious God, the God who is for us, and that this is the ineffable sum of all goodness." (III/2, 609–10)

What little Barth is willing to say about the final state sounds very much like the panentheist's limp retort to death, viz., that death (just like life) is overcome by the "ineffable" truth of our solidarity with the divine being. I do not mean to accuse too boldly. I merely suggest this: Barth's eschatologic makes him cousin to the family of panentheists.[40]

Since critique is clearly moving beyond Barth's Christology to his anthropology, let me simply reiterate that for him Jesus Christ's resurrection is incorporation. On one level (corresponding to my chapter 3), Christ is incorporated. He is claimed by the Holy Spirit and made eternal in body and soul. But the greater meaning for Barth (closer to the content of chapter 4) is that Jesus Christ goes forth in His resurrection power to incorporate others into His saving work. Through His Holy Spirit He labors to expand the scope of His own earthly-historical body, which is a collection into His own body, a collection that will someday conclude with a final recapitulation. Jesus Christ's resurrection is His inclusive power which binds others, carries them along, and holds them in Himself.

THE ISOLATION OF THE HUMAN

More remains to be said about disappearing differentiation in the general resurrection, but let us first consider Barth's portrayal of the predicament

---

40. Should it surprise us if a good number of Barth's own theological descendents—I think of Moltmann, Pannenberg, and Jenson—have developed more openly panentheistic models of salvation, *and done so through the doctrine of the resurrection*?

of human beings as such. Hitherto we have noted how humans are impaired in their pure creaturely state by temporal limitation and ambiguity. A third aspect of impairment is the threat of isolation, a threat inherent within creaturely selfhood. When humans attempt to assert their flimsy independence from God, making their created state autonomous and therefore sinful, they are plunged into a terrifying spiral of destructive loneliness.

Humans need divine communion. What the being of Jesus Christ teaches us is that humanity exists and has its righteousness through dependence upon God. In fact, His existence as a human is wholly contingent on Him being the God who takes this human existence to Himself. According to Barth, what Christ reveals is that we are appointed for the same kind of dependence to sustain our human calling, and that He Himself provides the avenue to fulfill our humanity. Through Him we find the possibility of covenantal fellowship with God, and, through God, with others.

One of the more difficult aspects of Barth's thought involves the affirmation of creation's being made good without the affirmation of its inherent goodness. Creation's moral status depends not on its thing-ness but on its connection with God, who is its Primal Origin and continual source of life.

> Creation is a benefit inasmuch as it is based upon and attains its end in the divine covenant with man. Thus even the creature does not merely exist, but does so as the sphere and object of the covenant, as the being to whom God has devoted His goodwill and whom He has destined to share in the overflowing of His own fulness of life and love. To be a creature means to be determined to this end, to be affirmed, elected and accepted by God." (III/1, 363–64)

Humanity epitomizes dependence on God, for the dignity of humanity is its intimate fellowship with God. Only by being with God can the human be truly human.

> If it is forgotten, if we think of man in isolation from and independent of God, we are no longer thinking about real man. Man exists only in his relation with God. And this relation is not peripheral but central, not incidental but essential to that which makes him a real man, himself. He is to the extent that not he himself but God is His sovereign Lord, and his own sovereignty flows from God. (III/2, 123)

The human is the creature ordained specially to be from God, with God, and to God. He or she is appointed as the target of the Word of God, chosen to hear the Word and respond in gratitude. In the mystical communion of the event of the Word of God, a human is fully humanized, empowered, and radiant. The human receives *doxa* in this relationship and reciprocates to God a creaturely *doxa*.

In the modern world independence is often held out as the highest virtue in life, a trend of which Barth was well aware.[41] Barth's theological anthropology is a furious retort: independence (by which he means a disregard for spiritual communion with God) is fatal. If the creature ignores its neediness and tries to strike out on its own, it brings death upon itself. It wanders into the wilderness of nothingness. It leaves the bond of participation and chooses suicide. One might object that we, unlike Christ, do not by nature have His inherent divine communion. But Eberhard Jüngel gives a good Barthian response:

> All other human beings certainly exist independently without needing to be divine. Yes, but look at how they exist! An "independent" human existence is an existence as a prisoner of sin. When we exist independently, we lose our humanity and ensure our own death.[42]

Humans attain their dignity through fellowship, not isolation.

We may speak of the human predicament only because we know of human fulfilment as revealed in Jesus Christ. The Word of God informs us of our wholly interrelational destiny. Again Barth adopts the form of triple concentric rings: divine, communal, individual. Pivotally, the divine calling of persons (§44 "Man as the Creature of God") starts with the connection and differentiation of God and humans. The truth of humanity, fully true only in the elect Jesus Christ, is that

> Deriving from God, man is in God, and therefore for God. We are not speaking of a predicate which he might have but perhaps might not have. Man is essentially for God because he is essentially from God and in God. (III/2, 71)

---

41. Barth makes the charge that eighteenth and nineteenth century moralistic individualism was entirely consistent with the absolutistic society (*PTNC*, 112–17). Later he names Friedrich Nietzsche the prophet of humanity-less individualism (III/2, 231–42).

42. Jüngel, *Karl Barth*, 134.

The divine calling in Jesus Christ sets the "ontological undertone" (III/2, 134) for the next ring of relatedness (§45 "Man and His Determination as the Covenant-Partner of God"). The second basic form of humanity is to have fellowship with one another, just as Jesus Christ was and is the man for others. People share in His likeness by echoing His for-ness toward the community. Through God our encounter is also with those who belong to God. Moreover, creation itself bears out this pattern in the dyadic relationship of male and female, man and woman.[43] Barth's treatment of the third ring, the individual (§46 "Man as Soul and Body), though arguably the weakest section of the *Church Dogmatics*, is impressed with a similar pattern of interrelation. By God's life-giving Spirit a person is the soul of one's body. Animated by God, inner and outer facets are unified, even as the differentiation and priority of soul over body is retained. Each of these circles—divine, communal, and individual—depends on the relationality granted in the being of Jesus Christ. So if humanity's definition as humanity has at its base a communion with the Almighty through election in Jesus Christ, if human society is the *analogia relationis* which is also the *imago Dei*, if human constitution relies upon the gift of spirit in order to be the soul of one's body, then human beings cannot stand alone.

They cannot. To choose autonomy is to choose the way of death which leads to eternal death. Along Augustinian lines, Barth teaches that self-definition is sin, and sin is *das Nichtige*, nothingness, the void. Nothingness is precisely the predicament of human beings. They jeopardize themselves at every turn through wanton self-seeking. They would be gods, feeding their own appetites for immortal idiocy. They would make their fellow humans into slaves of their own solipsistic imaginations. They would stray in order to pursue their illusions, and by doing so make themselves utterly contradictory.[44] Wrenched from proper Christo-relations, persons plunge into an egotistical nightmare.

---

43. If Barth has any constitutional aspect of the *imago Dei*, it can be found in dimorphic sexuality: "Man would not be man if he were no longer male and female, if his humanity did not consist in this concrete fellow-humanity, in this distinction and connexion. He has lived in no other way in time, and he can live in no other way in eternity. This is something which he cannot lose. For by it there stands or falls his creatureliness" (III/2, 296). Barth's departure from contemporary gender complementarianism involves his unwillingness to elaborate this thought into the positing of two different, sex-specific images of God. But his departure from contemporary gender egalitarianism stems from his unwillingness to conceive of relations without a sense of priority.

44. In fact, isolation makes people anomalous rather than inhuman (for taking on the status of an animal is not even a hypothetical option for the covenanted human).

However, the good news announces that the crucified Jesus Christ was the *only* isolated one.[45] He bore the ignominy of the world at Golgotha. He alone suffered Godforsakenness, and in this Godforsakenness He died alone. But for such service to God and humanity, God declared Him to be the Son of God through the resurrection of the dead. Jesus Christ rose with the full glory of a man in the communion of the Holy Spirit. In Barth's mind the resurrection is much more than a statement about the fate of the fallen Jesus. It is a public appointment of Jesus Christ to be the mediator of all things in their restoration to God through the power of His Holy Spirit. The resurrection is the transmission of life through Him who is resurrected, indeed, who *is* the resurrection. Any other person would overcome their isolation (that is, be raised from the dead) must achieve it by abiding in His life.

One of the more counterintuitive aspects of Barth's work has to do with his sense that covenantal relations are the full basis for human constitution. That is, if Barth has a philosophy of reality, it is a relational metaphysics, not a substance metaphysics. Relations not only precede substance, they *constitute* substance. At face value Barth would appear to read creation and covenant together as reciprocal sides. In *CD* III/1 he describes creation as the *äusserer Grund* ("the external basis") of the covenant and the covenant the *innerer Grund* ("the internal basis") of creation. But appearances can be misleading. In his explanation, Barth says that creation is merely the geographic presupposition of covenant, the non-descript stuff with which to work, but covenant (that is, relation) is "the material presupposition" of creation. Therefore, "If creation takes precedence historically, the covenant does so in substance" (III/1, 232). It is not that Barth rejects all talk of human substance; after all, he discusses human spirituality, male and female, soul and body. But all of these concretions are fixed according to a Christological blueprint. Their subsidiary relationship to and in Christ is what allows them to be real. The great scope of being derives from its primal relations. This is particularly and especially true for humans. Election leads to the *imago*. Christ's incarnation defines our fleshly lives. Participation in the Logos produces rationality. Union with His Spirit produces spirituality. In short, relations precede substance.

To sin is to make oneself impossible, to enter a category that does not exist. As such, sin is death.

45. Barth follows Calvin and the Reformed tradition in understanding Christ's descent into hell as part of His cry of dereliction on the cross (Lauber, *Barth on the Descent into Hell*, 10–12).

Karl Barth and the Resurrection of the Flesh

The seminal power of onto-relations (whether described as "covenant," "participation," or "fellowship") allows Barth to design his doctrine of humanity in a rather different way than earlier generations. This has genuine advantages over other models. Onto-relations prevent the growth of natural theology, for no generic anthropology can be posited if humanity acquires its definition through a bond to Christ. More specifically, substance metaphysics (in the form of personal immortality, rationality, creativity, or spirituality as bases of human identity), with its inevitable slant toward secularism, falls by the wayside.[46] My judgment is that Barth's approach is significantly healthier than other anthropologies.

But it is not without problems. Relational metaphysics attempts to relate things, but Barth does not make clear what kind of things are being related. The relational bond is supposed to supply the predication for things, but this begs the question: What is a thing is if it has no predicates before entering into relation with something else? This is a difficulty for Barth, who, in an attempt to set up a blockade against substantialist readings, seems to assume that the covenant is a *sufficient* condition for creation. The bond somehow posits that to which it is bound. Creation becomes a subsidiary function of covenant. What should not be lost on us here is Barth's Platonic structure, where the archetype (in this case, the covenant, the "material presupposition" and true "substance") overflows into the shadowy sub-realities of creation and sustains these inferior expressions by sharing an archetypal similitude. Like all Platonic systems, the physical world suffers—not because it is excluded *per se*, but because it becomes an appendage, an accessory, a derivation which in the end may or may not be needed by the higher stratum governing it in the first place.[47] It seems to me that, lest metaphysics become excessively referent-less, and lest the created order be understood as a lesser component of a divine tautology, Christians must reserve *some* room for asking about the contours of creational substance alongside divine relation.

Here Edwin Chr. van Driel's critique is helpful. He deduces from Barth's doctrinal moves an auxiliary doctrine, that the creature as such is always characterized by dis-integration. For

46. Substantialist accounts "fail either to perceive or to take seriously the fact that humanity derives exclusively from election, has no independent existence apart from Jesus Christ, and is actualized in faith and obedience" (Neder, *Participation in Christ*, 39).

47. More precisely, Barth's approach has many of the structural features of Neo-Platonism, which, lest we become too harsh, has been among the most generous philosophical systems to corporeality (cf. Bowery, "Body," 105).

all of what is not God necessarily lapses into evil unless God incorporates it into God's own being. Only one form of existence, divine existence, is equivalent to the good. No other form of being is good or will obtain the good, unless it comes to participate in divine being. Not even God can create such a being—all God can do is safeguard the being God created by giving it a share in the divine life. Creational life is governed by entropy.[48]

By ontological necessity creation is subject to death and decay, according to this perspective. Created things, by their essential lack of divine status, move toward nothingness. Therefore, says van Driel, for Barth there is no way to eradicate death without eradicating the creaturely order. The only way to stop "creational entropy" is to halt nature and have it "safely embedded in the divine life."[49]

If Barth tends to overstate relations, it is to pound in a key point: "The created world dissociated from its transcendent Creator loses its natural axis" (III/2, 11). I concur—but association does not have to be incorporation. Life "in Christ" can mean something other than sublation of the creature by non-creaturely transcendence. Our adoption, whether penultimate or ultimate, preserves the difference of creatures and the Creator. Just as the difference between the divine and human natures is not resolved into the divine in the hypostatic union (not even in Jesus' glorified state!), so the difference between our special human identity and Jesus' is not resolved in the participatory union (not even in Jesus' final recapitulation of His ecclesial body). Even as Christ's body, we are always related to Christ as some other-body. Is Barth able to preserve a real differentiation when speaking of humanity's future?

THE INCORPORATION OF THE RISEN HUMAN

We have heard several times now Barth's answer to human sinfulness: communion. Jesus Christ objectively reconciles humans to God, to each other, to themselves. The Holy Spirit (i.e., Jesus in the power of His resurrection) makes objective reality altogether great by expressing it subjectively. For Barth the entire way of life for humans may be summed up as participation in Christ,[50] as *relation* to Christ as it plays itself out in the

48. van Driel, *Incarnation Anyway*, 122.

49. Ibid., 123.

50. Cf. Hunsinger, *How to Read Karl Barth*, 114; though see the complaint about the participatory limitations of Barth's "revelation model" in Torrance, *Persons in Communion*, 307ff.

re-corporealization (handwritten)

event of life "in Him." Through the event of the Word of God the bodies of many are made part of Christ's one body. This is certainly true on a figurative, ecclesiastical level (1 Cor 12; Eph 4). But, I wonder, what does Barth's emphasis on incorporation into Christ's body do to resurrection at the final eschatological level? Does resurrection have the same meaning as the Scriptures' sense of re-corporealization in the resurrection of the dead? In this final section I prod Barth's doctrine of the end times to clarify its about bodies and Christ's one body.

Body is a complicated category for Barth. Bodies exist as particulars, of course, but, speaking cosmically, only because they are linked to the Head of the Body. Most fundamentally, *sōma* belongs to Jesus Christ, who, as the Head, is the bodily archetype. More than just a body, Jesus Christ is body. He defines what body is. By virtue of His eternal identity elected for humanity, His body is all-inclusive, "the archetypal man whom all threatened and enslaved men and creatures must follow. He alone is the promise for these many, the Head of a whole body" (III/2, 144). Moreover, *in* His archetypal body He supplies bodiliness. While Barth affirms the plain meaning of *sōma* too, he treats it as a subordinate expression enabled by the archetypal body of Jesus Christ. An individual's physical body is real, yes, but not as real as Jesus' body, which has a sense of being "the body which throws a shadow," "the one in many" (IV/1, 663).

Even late in his career Barth speaks with a kind of ambiguity about the resurrection body of Christ. He has and is a body like ours, yet, unlike any other, His body is also the prototypical macro-body. Easter in its extended meaning, then, is the em-bodying of other bodies into Christ's body:

> The content of Easter Day and the Easter season consisted in this, not in an "attesting miracle," not merely in a parthenogenesis of the Christian faith, but in the appearance of the body of Jesus Christ, which embraced their death in its death, their life in its life, their past and their future in itself, thus including them all in itself. As He encountered them in this corporeity, the disciples heard addressed to themselves as such, to the *ekklesia* which arose in virtue of it, the call which is the disclosure of the secret of His earthly-historical existence: "Ye are the body of Christ." (IV/1, 664)

Christ's body is magnified, extending from His own to the Church. The mission of the Holy Spirit is to facilitate this resurrective wave of Christ, calling a community "as His body, i.e., as His own earthly-historical form

The archetypal man (handwritten)

time + space closed

of existence" (IV/3, 681). Christ's resurrection, we might say, is the outgoing power of His body to include other bodies in His.

I think the more forthcoming way of expressing this is to say that there is but one resurrection. Technically speaking, Barth has no discrete eschatological doctrine of the resurrection of the dead. We will never be raised as Jesus Christ was raised. His was and will be the only resurrection. However, we may *participate* in that one resurrection by union with Him. We may and must be related to Him, enlivened by His animating energy. In a rather flagrant distortion of Heidelberg Catechism question 49, Barth says, "In Jesus Christ I am no longer at the point at which I can die; in Him our body is already in heaven" (DO, 155). That is, we have no resurrection awaiting us vis-à-vis Christ, only a future in the One who is resurrection.[51] Our resurrection is the showing forth of the one resurrection, which is Christ's manifest God-relation.

As I explained earlier, Barth wants to speak of resurrection as an extroversive event, by which I mean a movement of Christ moving outward and oriented toward others. From Easter through the forty days and then through the age of the outpouring of the Spirit, Jesus Christ calls others to be His body. In *CD* IV/3 especially, Barth's portrait of the Church is of a community called on mission, shining outward with the Light of Life. But Barth generally skirts the topic of the ultimate, when there is no more going-out, only a coming-in. §73 "The Holy Spirit and Christian Hope" is a discussion of how the Christian, as a member of Christ's community, may "*move* towards his final and yet also his immediate future in hope in Him," though Barth has little to say about how Christ will "*consummate* the revelation of the will of God fulfilled in Him" (IV/3, 902, emphasis added). His only word is that, at the return of Christ, time and space are *closed* (IV/3, 916), and Christ is revealed "universally" and "immediately" (IV/3, 903).

Barth cannot speak consistently about the resurrection of the dead, for in the final form of the resurrection the event is not outgoing, but subsuming. Then and there Christ's mission will be complete. Then and there His body, instead of going forward in action, will revert to Him in rest. The only truth at that time will be that all things exist in Christ, that God is all in all. What then can the return of Christ be but a recapitulation, a gathering into the One? What more can the resurrection be but the final manifestation of the fact that the ecclesiastical body is indeed the *plērōma* of Christ's *sōma* (IV/2, 659)?

51. Cf. Thompson, *Christ in Perspective*, 132.

Karl Barth and the Resurrection of the Flesh

And here the question of the flesh is of acute importance. So long as humans are alive in the flesh, in time and space, no question exists of their personal, physical identity even as they are incorporated into the risen Body of Jesus Christ. But when the end comes, when all things "return" to Christ at His "return," what is the place of individual identity? How do the many stay fixed as the many when resolved into the One? How is the consummate constitution of the single Christ-body also a resurrection of the flesh, of *our* particular instances of flesh? Barth somehow holds out hope that life in Christ's eschatological Body will not compress but express the fullness of the earthly human life. I sustain the judgment that Barth has demonstrated neither how nor to whom this expression would exist in the final state. CD V would have been burdened to spell out the eschatological unity-in-difference of Christ's ecclesial-cosmic body.

Barth professes belief in *resurrectionem carnis* so vociferously, I suspect, in part because he requires the flesh to supply a real texture to human lives in the the recapitulation of all things into Christ. Like any panentheistic account worth its salt, Barth's final sublation of history into eternity does not eliminate the fact that eternity has been serialized by time. Flesh breaks up the brightness of day in which all cats are white, so to speak. But—and this is the crux of the matter—from the standpoint of the Barthian Omega such differentiation is no more than *the preserved distinction of former histories in God*. Flesh "historicizes" humans' eternity, but only enough to preserve life as a monochromatic reproduction. Why? Because the Omega-point archives the time in which flesh existed. In the ultimate, the human dimensions in which flesh lived are compressed by the gravity of divine proximity. We have life in the flesh because the temporal provides *space* for us to live as particular creatures. But according to Barth, on the last Day human differentiation relies solely on the *spacing that once was*.[52]

For Barth, such differentiation is enough, but I am unconvinced. The highly relational terms of Barth's doctrine of the resurrection cast shadows

52. Gerhard Sauter explains that "one of the most serious interpretive problems" in the *Church Dogmatics* has to do with the foreclosure of human lives in the Christological perfect, not because of a problem of overrealized eschatology in the reconciling work of Jesus, but because Barth permits himself to speak of the future from God's perspective ("Why Is Karl Barth's *Church Dogmatics* Not a 'Theology of Hope'?," 425). Claiming such knowledge, and thus moving by imperceptible but triumphant degrees from the finite to the infinite, is "the characteristic move of ontotheology," says Walter Lowe, a move that reveals that one is not so interested in concreteness and contingency after all (Lowe, *Theology and Difference*, 121–22). Perhaps Barth has not taken into account just how paradoxical is the relation between God's will and God's rule in the rest of history (Jenson, *Alpha and Omega*, 151–57).

of doubt upon its standing as a resurrection of the flesh. Though not nearly so overt about Christ-monism as in his early work,[53] Barth's mature output also points to a final, monistic convergence. Once time and process and bodies pass, we are held solely in the human nature of the Logos; any distinctions are internal, intra-christic, and therefore nominal; the histories of the flesh, mummified in eternity, are—and are not—flesh. In John's vision, the resurrected saints receive their *own* names written on white stones (Rev 2:17). However, in Barth's presentation the name of Jesus Christ can be trumpeted so loudly that all other names and voices, however much denominated in this life, are inaudible in the resurrection.[54]

My concern about *CD* at this locus joins the concerns of those who have flagged Barth's eschatology as universalist. If Jesus Christ absolutizes salvation in His own election, work, and resurrection, will not all be saved? The inclusive force of the victorious Elect One hardly permits a distinction of soteriological futures for individuals. All are defined by Christ, and therefore must and will be brought to Him in eternity. Yet Barth rejects the doctrine of *apokatastasis* in its universalist sense. Any theology that speaks of an assured pan-salvation, he says, risks impinging upon God's freedom, speculates about the future, and confuses Christ and world-process.[55] A range of commentators thus label Barth's position as patently contradictory.[56]

As for a noteworthy defense of Barth on this point, Tom Greggs understands Barth's universalistic trajectory to preserve human particularity on the ground that Jesus Christ Himself is a particular. This point is discerned in Barth's rejoinder to Berkouwer in which he says that *CD* is

---

53. I am thinking of such passages as when Barth confesses that "Jesus Christ is the Redeemer, the individual standing existentially before God. In Him duality has become unity [*aus zweien eins gewordene Individuum*], for in Him rejection has been overcome and swallowed up in election" (*ER*, 417 = 2*Rö*, 402), or his comment, "That God is all in all, *is* not true, but must *become* true. Christian monism is not a knowledge that is presently possible, but a *coming* knowledge. If it is to be genuine, it must only be comprehended now as Christian dualism, as the tension between promise and fulfilment, between 'not yet' and 'one day'" (*RD*, 170).

54. Cf. Farrow, *Ascension and Ecclesia*, 243; McDowell, *Hope in Barth's Eschatology*, 224.

55. E.g. II/2, 417–18; IV/3, 477–78, 489, 713. Acts 3:21 speaks ambiguously about the time "of the restoration of all things [*apokatastaseōs pantōn*]," commencing after heaven has received Jesus for a time, though the Christian tradition since Origen has generally understood the term *apokatastasis* as a claim about the scope of salvation. For a genesis of the doctrine see Moore, "Origen of Alexandria and Apokatastasis."

56. E.g., Berkouwer, *The Triumph of Grace in the Theology of Karl Barth*, 116; Hick, *Death and Eternal Life*, 260f.; Crisp, "On Barth's Denial of Universalism," 18–29.

grace not a principle but a person

not centered around the triumph of grace (that is, a Christ-principle) but around the victorious, living person, Jesus Christ (IV/3, 174ff.). Greggs extrapolates from Barth's point by saying, "Since election is the election of a *person*, it is the determination of a person, and therefore the question arises of human self-determination which corresponds to this determination. Election in the person of Jesus allows the space for human freedom which a principle never can."[57] The sheer force of the objective content of this one individual Representative assures universal salvation even as it assures agency.[58] The weakness of Greggs' rejoinder, I think, stems from a certain underdevelopment of his own argument in two respects. First, for Barth at least, Jesus' own particularity has as much dissimilitude as similitude with our own. We are mere particulars, where He is archetypal, trans-particular in His particularity. Second, but more importantly, neither Barth nor Greggs has explained how other individual agencies retain their fullness *after* the terminal sublation into Jesus' eschatological simplicity. If the final parousia (post-temporal eternity) is ultimately equivalent to the predestinating decree (pre-temporal eternity), as Barth insinuates throughout his writing, then people at that point exist "in Christ" in a more minimal, representative sense.[59] What is lacking is an account of how the particularity of Jesus Christ props open enough space in His final, totalizing body to accommodate whole, living persons. Again, I have granted the success of Barth's ability to speak of a movement from simplicity to plurality in the Son, but a certain inability to sustain plurality in the movement back to simplicity.

Barth's confidence about the preservation of individual identity hinges so much on the allowances of participation in Christ. Particulars abide in the archetype of Christ's humanity. Personhood remains as it is embedded in the life of the incarnate Person. The event of an individual's salvation takes place in the revelatory Event. Barth uses this concept of participation effectively with his ethics, showing how human freedom is lodged in God's freedom, but I am unconvinced that his use of Neoplatonic/Augustinian

57. Greggs, "'Jesus Is Victor,'" 206. What Myk Habets says about T. F. Torrance could just as easily be applied to Barth, that participation in Christ is "the 'personalising' of the human being in *the* Person of the incarnate Son" (*Theosis in the Theology of Thomas Torrance*, 39).

58. Greggs, *Barth, Origin, and Universal Salvation*, 49–53.

59. In the end God will not be alone again as He was before creation, if only because "God will not cease to be the One who *has done* this first thing," viz., create (III/1, 43, emphasis added). But given the perichoresis of pre-temporal and post-temporal eternity (II/1, 640), how does the perfect tense really make the end less lonely than the beginning?

syntax translates into eschatological ontology. At the Omega moment at least, it is difficult to see how God's final being-in-action regenerates our own living, distinctive beings-in-action. Rather, God circumscribes them, sums them up, and puts them to an end.

I have insisted all along that we embrace the apparent meaning of the Church's creed: that Christ's redemptive work in the resurrection of the dead involves a raising of *specific* bodies and placing them in *specific* relations to God and to one another in a *specific*, earthly setting. However much the scriptural witness may speak of a newness in the coming way of life, it never speaks of redemption at a loss of the concrete dimensions which make up human individuality. Barth's human identifiers feel dangerously flimsy when he exchanges bodies for "differentiation" within Christ's Body, or when he trades fleshly plurality for a "distinction" of persons in Christ's person, or when he thinks that onto-relational "priority" suffices to establish the existence of identifiable human persons in eternity. Historical human bodies, absorbed into Christ representative history, become asymptotic.

In this chapter I have recognized the importance of the communion of the Spirit, and how Barth applies divine communion to the resurrection-movement of the Son to reach those in isolation and perdition. Barth again reaps a theological harvest by overlapping key concepts with the doctrine of resurrection. But this overlap comes with a multi-leveled problem of absorption. The resurrection disappears into the Spirit, the Spirit disappears into the risen Son, and, ultimately, all of humanity is subsumed into Christ's eschatological corpus. I have not registered concern with Barth's incorporative paradigm in the present age. In the throes of the dialectic of this world God and human agents are distinguished *temporarily* (in the double sense of that word). Though belonging to the kingdom of God in the moment of revelation, humans trudge along brokenly in space and time, i.e., in the flesh. They live in their fleshly limitations while God lives in the freedom of Spirit. But once they reach the final goal and have no other future except a future in the reticulated body of Christ, difference is severely relativized. Individual identities become nominal in Barth's panenchristism, for little can be said of delineation when human lives are subaltern to the one Christ-subject.

Our histories in our respective bodies will be preserved in Christ's body, Barth promises us. But is preservation the same as resurrection of the flesh? How does recapitulation into the body of Christ reanimate us as differentiated covenant-creatures? We will be fully alive, Barth assures us.

But *how* will we be alive? How will *we* be alive? Something indiscernible lurks at the Barthian future: not the enigma of the resurrection, but the puzzle of billions of bodies pressed together to infinite density.

6

A Future in the Flesh

WITH SPECIAL ARDOR KARL Barth sought to uphold human corporeality. In an age when it would have been easy to defer to a more generic Christian hope (the resurrection of the person, the resurrection of a body, the survival of the self, etc.), he professed the resurrection *of the flesh*. With increasing frequency and adamancy over the course of his career he affirmed the special, physical, historical nature of Jesus' identity in His resurrection, and with it, the special, physical, historical nature of our own identities in the coming resurrection. Against traditional reliance upon a concept of the immortality of an immaterial soul, Barth upheld the bodily constitution of the human in his or her future with God. Against the widespread demythologizing programs of twentieth century theologians, Barth found creative ways to defend the corporeal dimensions of the Church's historic beliefs.[1]

My sympathy for his program notwithstanding, I have picked at the Gordian knot that is Barth's doctrine of the resurrection of the flesh. As the layers of his theology are peeled back, I have registered various concerns, all centered around the looming feeling that the participatory eschatology he speaks of abrogates rather than fulfills human identity. Barth's intense conviction about the penetrating presence of the living Jesus Christ in revelation leads him to speak of a translation of Jesus' flesh into eternity. By extension, other humans through participation in the Risen One have their flesh translated into the eternal idiom. And there lies my concern:

1. As for the demythologizing programs of the twentieth century, I am thinking of Rudolf Bultmann, Paul Tillich, and Reinhold Niebuhr, not to mention the more moderate "bad business" of Emil Brunner. For a review of the "word and faith" position of Bultmann and John Knox, see Lorenzen, *Resurrection and Discipleship*, 36–63.

something is lost in translation. Barth's delineation of the resurrection of the dead yields a redeemed human being with a flesh-like quality—but only flesh-*like*.

SUMMARY OF CRITIQUES

The questions I have posed to Barth in this study boil down to three specific related concerns about the disappearance of the human. Against the concept of eternalization I posed *the problem of continuity*, since Barth's version of the resurrection abolishes the temporal mode of life native to human beings, and instead raises delimited human histories to pantemporal stasis. Second, against the concept of manifestation I pressed *the problem of creatureliness*, since Barth construes glorification so much in terms of a publication and knowledge of our deific qualities through fellowship with God rather than a restoration of human attributes. Third, against Barth's concept of incorporation I posed *the problem of particularity*, in which distinct human bodies, once their outgoing participative histories terminate, converge into the one body of Christ. That is, Barth's doctrine of the resurrection of the flesh triply threatens humanity's basic constitution by memorialization, by deification, and by recapitulation.

As for the problem of continuity, I observed in chapter 3 how Barth believes that the consummation will curtail all time, all process, all flesh as such. The process of creaturely life ceases with the final state; no further creational development is granted by God. Barth's actualistic account speaks of eternal life produced through the eternalization of a human's concrete temporal history. A person's history between birth and death is summed up and made to participate in God's Beyond. The resurrection, instead of a new supply of time to the person, is a gathering up of an earthly life into eternity, in which this earthly self somehow acquires the omnitemporal accessibility of the Risen One. Caught up in the simultaneity of Christ's own presence, persons transcend the flux of the world. For Barth, the resurrection of the flesh does not denote a resumption of human development, but a leap into the divine experience of all reality happening at once.

In contrast, I have contended that Barth's quest for historical resolution does not match the biblical imagination, which pines for a future both kinetic and sempiternal. Barth's concept of eternalization gropes after the elusive Platonic ideal of resolution but does not attain it, for the risen, collected history of a person would seem to repeat the horrors of suffering rather than overcome them. And even if these past horrors are edited from one's actual existence, Barth has not made a convincing case for the possibility of fresh historical action; not on Jesus' part in the forty days of His appearances, and certainly not for those of us who are raised when there is no more chronological time in which to act. More seriously, I demonstrated how Barth's speculation on limitation and eternalization requires one to see death as a natural phenomenon. *Thanatos* becomes an ally who resolves one's life and escorts one to the eternal mode of life. Even if God alone grants immortality, death has become His chief servant. In Barth's schema, the Christian hope for eternal life is barely distinguishable from a longing for death.

Barth does not hypothesize about an immortal, immutable human soul. He speaks of human identity as a transient journey in both body and soul, a being-in-act. Nonetheless, Barth understands this life as the template which becomes immutable at the resurrection. One's earlier kinetic identity is supposedly preserved by raising it beyond diachronic process. But let us not be blind to the fact that immutability, even if it characterizes a once-living history, is still immutability. Therefore, despite all of their reclaimed past actions, Barth's resurrected ones have a certain plastic quality to them; they are high fidelity recordings, fantastic holographic trophies; they are lives memorialized. In the end, human identities in the flesh are transcended—and thus bowdlerized. Translation into an eternal mode adds an impressive dimension, no doubt, something almost angelic, but the change also subtracts the basic temporal mode of human existence.[2] It seems more accurate to say that Barth has cast the resurrection as a kind of cryogenic pantomime. The flesh is in stasis, and heaven is its reliquary. The dead do not come back to life for Barth. No, their histories rise.

As for the problem of creatureliness, I observed in chapter 4 that Barth conceived of the coming resurrection as a manifestation of our true identities in Christ. Our isolation from God has been remedied in the integrated being of Jesus, who brings the divine nature to the human

2. Barth's "angelic time" would have a ring of liberation to it through its ability to straddle heaven and earth (Ford, *Barth and God's Story*, 145), were it not for the sense that the blessed dead, made denizens of heaven, do not seem to have real access to time. What is more, any entry into chronological time will become an obsolete possibility after Christ's return stops all process. At this very point Adrian Langdon wonders "how humans could exist, even in the state of glorification in the eschaton, without some form of temporality. In CD III/2, Barth defines human nature as *imago dei*, ensouled bodies, and existence in time. How can humanity exist if this universal *Existenzform* is taken away?" (Langdon, ""Our Contemporary from Now until Eternity," 17).

nature, healing the latter through the former. Christ's covenantal integrity was sealed with His death, but is now revealed by His resurrection power, penultimately in this age, fully at His consummate return. At the close of time we will be manifested with Him in glory, a glorification which Barth interprets as a disclosure of our already-exalted identity in Christ. On the final Day the whole truth will be made public. That is, we will perceive God as He is, and thus perceive ourselves caught up in His own dignity.

In contrast, I have argued that Barth's depiction of manifestation, for all his provisos, is a noetic unveiling at the expense of ontic trans-formation. Human flesh is not restored so much as its secret is revealed. Glorification becomes a matter of perception of God and self rather than a restoration of the life of the body. In fact, bodily glorification has become a rather obsolete dimension of salvation since the real matter for Barth is the exalted human nature already "raised" by Christ's incarnation, by the proximity of the human nature to the divine nature. All that needs to tran-spire is the final expression of Christ's parousia, His ultimate "manifest presence," His definitive and universal coming, at which point the saints will show forth their hidden, deimorphic glory. I have explored beneath the surface of Barth's presentation to get at its inner logic of proximity, i.e., his sense that salvation is, by definition, closeness to God and the sharing of His perfections. So far as his Christology and soteriology turn on the communication of predicates in the divine-human union, Barth writes in the Alexandrian or Lutheran mindset. Accordingly, I have raised the red flags of the Antiochene and Reformed schools. That is, Barth has a hard time explaining the divine and human natures in their differentia-tion, especially the human nature in its consummate state. When we are manifested with Christ and obtain His divine omniscience (among other things), how will we be fully human? What of our earthly dimensions once they have been subsumed in the divine life?

Barth's grammar of proximity tampers with creaturely boundaries. It makes human fullness dependent upon an elevation out of the earthly mode and a raising up of the consciousness to a divine plane of cognition. Barth's sense of the resurrection, then, is not unlike Plato's vision in the *Republic*: When the "real" world calls us from the darkened phenomenal world, we will see the truth behind the appearances, and understand our-selves as sharers of the great Reality. To accept Barth's proposal about the coming resurrection is to expect that God will call us from a cave (so to speak), not a tomb. Barth's insistence that we will stumble forth in soul *and* body is inconsequential: what really matters for him is that we will *see*, and that we will see *divinely*.

To the problem of particularity, in chapter 5 I investigated Barth's understanding of resurrection as incorporation. His mature work conceives of the resurrection as a movement of Christ outward, awakening others, edifying and enabling them to join Christ in His mission to the world. Jesus' resurrection seizes others in divine communion, uniting humans to Himself (and therefore to each other) in His earthly-historical body. I noted how Barth, when it comes to the resurrection-movement, has a difficult time demarcating the action of the risen Christ from the ministry of the Holy Spirit. The Christo-pneumatic power of the resurrection of the dead delivers the human being from isolation into fellowship with God. Bearing a panentheistic (better, panenchristic) pattern, Barth's anthropological ontology looks to relational categories (that is, participation in God's own being) to establish identity and reality.

Since he seemed tentative to spell out the incorporative line of thought all the way, I pressed Barth's eschatological patterns in *CD* to see what might come of human beings in the absolute future. I reasoned that if the expansion-contraction model of the event of election repeats itself in the event of resurrection (and I gave formal reasons to think it does), then the outgoing movement of the risen Christ convenes with a great closure at His return. The multiplication of bodies within His ecclesial body holds up in this age, since our spatio-temporal flesh marches along vis-à-vis dialectically with Christ's inclusive being. But once space and time end, once the dialectic is resolved, nothing can remain except the single, inclusive, representative body of Christ.

If there is any sense in which Barth can speak of individuated bodies in the eschaton, it is that once upon a time there were fleshly histories identifiable apart from Christ. In the end, only the integrated, recapitulated monad remains. That is, Barth has substituted differentiation within Christ's body for the raising of many bodies. Where the biblical imagination casts a specific future for specific individuals, Barth's writings allow for little more than nominal, intra-Christic identities. In this troubling paradigm, the quandary is not just whether all will be saved in the end, but to what extent there will be identities left to save.

If Barth's eschatology has careened off the tracks somewhere along the way, the derailment started with his equation of resurrection and revelation (the content of chapter 2). The merger can be detected quite directly, of course, when he speaks of the Christian hope in terms of manifestation.

But I find his resurrection-revelation equation to be decisive in a much greater sense. Very early in his theological career Barth latched onto the resurrection of the dead as a way of talking about the dialectical event of God and humanity in the moment of encounter. God sublates humanity— that is, He "dissolves and establishes" every human condition in the act of communicating Himself. Every dimension of the earthly mode must be completely abolished and reconfigured in divine categories. That pattern, amazingly enough, appears throughout Barth's mature doctrine of the resurrection of the flesh: in the end, human life is wholly stripped down and re-fabricated in God. Every articulation of life in the flesh is deconstructed and reconstituted with eternal syntax.

Is not the same sublation at work in Barth's concepts of eternalization, manifestation and incorporation? Human time is dissolved—but somehow transfiguration into eternity accounts for real time. Creaturehood as such is dissolved—but somehow the deified and manifested identity accounts for earthly parameters. Even specific humans bodies are dissolved in the end—but somehow the single incorporative Christ reconstitutes the outline of their own bodies. The dialectic, dramatically at work in the present age, comes full bore in the coming age. As a way of underscoring the sense of peace and resolution, Barth calls the final resurrection "an end to the dialectic" or "a completion of the dialectic"—but this is the most dangerous theological move possible. Since Barth has conceived of revelation-resurrection as a sublation into God, will not the resolution of the resurrection of the flesh mean a full conclusion of humanity into God? To complete the dialectical movement is to resolve human being too much in God's own being. In other words, Barth's fusion of the revelatory dialectic with the resurrection of the dead cannot produce an end that is not monistic. At best, the body in its space-time belongs to the coming age only as paraphernalia, as a colorant, as the texture of the eternal state. Human nature is translated with the Word of God into an inscrutable heavenly language, against Barth's desire to pronounce it with an earthly inflection. The flesh is hardly flesh anymore.

BARTH AND THE TWO TRAJECTORIES

For all his fantastic creativity, Barth's doctrine of the general resurrection can be situated among the two ancient views I outlined in chapter 1, the collection-of-the-flesh trajectory and the participation-of-the-flesh trajectory. It should be evident by now that he fits much better programmatically into the family of participationist theologians. While Barth manages to pull in some of the features of the collection view, the concepts of eternalization, manifestation, and incorporation operate in the core syntax of the more eastern, Alexandrian type.

First of all, eternalization turns on the dynamic of participation. As I explained in chapter 3, Barth postulates the transformation of time through its translation into the divine mode. The sublation of time into eternity is resurrection. Like Origen, Athanasius, and Maximus, Barth seeks the existence of the creature in God in the Beyond. Like them he sees the resurrection constituting a radical change, a full-scale *novum*. Interestingly, however, Barth leverages the participatory ontology to secure the ends of the collection view. Eternalization gathers the total human: every atom, every instant. This pulling together of all the bits of human existence in the body is even more total than what Jerome or Augustine or any representative of the collecting-the-flesh view ever imagined. In this way, Barth uses the Eastern resources to out-west the West! But my point here is that, like every mechanism of participationist eschatology, eternalization begins with the radical transformation of the creaturely being.

The resurrection as manifestation likewise fits better with the participation view. As I talked about at length in chapter 4, Barth understands glorification to be a product of the intimacy of the human nature with the divine. The exaltation of Jesus Christ occurs not with the resurrection, but aspectually throughout His incarnate life, from conception to crucifixion. The resurrection only manifests His exalted life. Likewise, human beings are already glorified through their participation in the divine nature through union with Christ, needing only to be revealed as such. Barth's reliance on the communication of properties to describe glorification, I argued, is wholly in line with the Alexandrian view, which is to say the participation view. Barth differs from other deificationists, of course, most notably in his rejection of glorification as a progressive, synergistic process. Yet his eschatology compares favorably with the likes of Origen, Athanasius, and Maximus, since for all of them resurrection is ultimately a matter of human ascension into the life of God. And again, Barth's talk of manifestation manages to address some of the Western concerns in a roundabout way, since the resurrection has so much to do with godly perception, something akin to Augustine's or Thomas' *visio Dei*.

Finally, the resurrection of the flesh as incorporation, which I detailed as much as possible in chapter 5, has entirely to do with the rubric of participation. Glorification comes through onto-relations with God through Jesus Christ in the power of the Spirit. Like the ancient Alexandrian theologians, Barth exposits resurrection as the glory inherent in the recapitulation of all things into Christ. Human life, even human life in the flesh, is conjoined pneumatically within the *totus Christus*. In the final state, human lives will resolve in God. In all this the power of participation is at work. Yet once again, Barth achieves a certain ecumenical scope by underscoring the body, just as the collection-view exponents did, making sure the whole person is brought into divine orbit.

To his credit, Barth articulates his doctrine of the resurrection of the flesh without philosophical speculation about a dualism of body and soul. An immaterial, immortal soul does not precede the body nor find beatific existence apart from it. Barth's fixation on a flesh-based anthropology resists any possible flight into a purely "spiritual" realm. He is nobler than the ancients in this regard.[3] Still, a lingering difficulty presents itself. Why does it feel, at the end of the day, as if Barth has succumbed to the spiritualizing trend and given us a word about going to heaven?

ASCENDING TO HEAVEN OR RAISED ON EARTH?

If Barth's doctrine of the general resurrection fails in the likeness of Christian theology's past failures, it certainly has to do with the sad fact that a hope centered around the vision of God makes the redemption of the body inconsequential. Of course, both of the types are eager to cover their bases, superadding corporeality to the human once having secured the spiritual dimension of human beatification. But that is the very flaw with each approach: superadded corporeality is ornamental. Once the soul (or Christified human) has been said to perceive God, the restoration of the body can be no more than an afterthought, a footnote about anthropic completion. In the traditional paradigms are we not coaxed to gaze past the redeemed bodily crust to the real salvation, that is, to the beatification of the human consciousness? If "eternal life in the presence of God" is what matters, will not resurrected flesh be an auxiliary appendage to the glorified person, an adjunct at best? Should it be any surprise that to this day such a widespread belief in "going to heaven" has supplanted the doctrine of the resurrection of the dead?

---

3. Though even here, I think, Barth's holism is more closely related to the participation view, in which all human components are relativized by the fact that they are together pulled into the ambit of the divine nature.

I have observed how Barth successfully distances himself from the crasser conceptions of going-to-heaven-when-I-die. He counters escapist tendencies with his actualistic ontology and an abiding sense of responsibility for the world. Nevertheless, I reiterate that Barth has pursued a glorification that comes about through proximity to God. Perfection occurs as humans are elevated and manifested as participants in the perfections of God. Glorification occurs as humans are caught up in the heavenly mode of life, living as God lives and seeing as He sees. What matters is that they are "with" God. Accordingly, if I may state it assertively, *Barth has given us a doctrine of personal ascension, not bodily resurrection*. He has taught that at the final trumpet a human will be eternalized, viz., "raised" to full participation in God's heavenly time. He has taught that a human will be manifested, viz., "raised" to full participation in God's heavenly, perceptive powers. And Barth has taught that in all this a human will be incorporated, viz., "raised" into participation with God through Christ's one exalted body. To my mind, that kind of translation is oriented very little toward the idea of "the resurrection from the dead" and very much toward the idea of being "in Christ." The latter, a Pauline watchword, could be said to encapsulate Barth's dogmatic sensibility. Now, the bodily dimension has its share in a human's in-Christness. Barth states that regularly enough. But the redemption of the physical body as such means little, for glorification concerns the more general, upward movement of a human's sublated history.[4] In Barth's dogmatics, the resurrection exists as a subset of the ascension, and therefore languishes.

One might suppose that my criticisms about Barth's less-than-fleshly picture of the future leads to a dismissal of the output of his eschatological project. Not necessarily. Barth's talk about the eschaton could be quite useful, I wonder, if one applies it to a doctrine of the *intermediate* state. Participatory categories like eternalization, manifestation, and incorporation might work well when it comes to explaining what happens to the dead saints between death and resurrection. Could not eternalization account for the fact that the dead are still alive to God (Luke 20:38)? Might not the divine-human proximity underneath the concept of manifestation

---

4. The theme of glorification-by-relationship, the ascended and ascending life, has been picked up by various modern theologians. Among Lutheran scholars, Robert W. Jenson affirms that "being in the kingdom and being perfectly in Christ will be the same thing" (Jenson, "The Great Transformation," 34). Aiming more generally at trinitarian participation, Ted Peters says, "The total relationality within the divine perichoresis . . . is life untrammeled by passage and death. When historicized, it results in victory over death through resurrection" (Peters, *God as Trinity*, 182).

help explain why Paul, wasting away, pined to "be away from the body and at home with the Lord" (2 Cor 5:8)? And is there not a sense in which incorporation into Christ contravenes death, insofar as Jesus says "everyone who lives and believes in me will never die" (John 11:26)? God sustains His own in death. The state of death cannot eclipse the victory of Jesus and His definition of others imparted in baptism. Even in death, Christians can also be alive by virtue of the fact that they are already dissolved and established, collected and remembered by the covenanting God. In such a way, Barth's resurrection categories might be co-opted and put into the service of explaining the intermediate state.

As it is, unfortunately, Barth's comments about immediate glorification at death betray the fact that he has conflated the intermediate and final states. Consider how towards the end of his life Barth makes some rather transparent comments about the dead having entered into their ultimate glory. Goethe may have erred significantly in his Enlightenment theology, but, "We can only say that as far as he himself is concerned he now knows better" (IV/2, 419). Or, mentioning dead friends, Barth opines, "There now shines on them the eternal light in which we, *adhuc peregrinantes*, shall some day need no more dogmatics" (IV/3, xiii). That is, even though Christ has not returned to earth, they have already been raised from the dead. Therefore, when Barth goes to talk about the final parousia, it is no more than a "direct" translation for all humankind to the divine glory, a translation which will have been hitherto accomplished by death.

> Whether we describe it as rapture or change, a direct transition to participation in the glory which comes to the creaturely world in and with the coming of Jesus Christ can be the end of the Christian instead of dying—*the same transition to the same participation in the same glory* which is awaited indirectly, in the passage from life through death to the resurrection, by those already dead, but in this other form by the Christians who will then be alive. . . . [A]longside the many dead who will then be raised, there will also be those who are still alive and who thus reach their end in this way. . . . Those who are already dead, but raised from the dead, will share this [change] with some who are still alive. (IV/3, 925, emphasis added)

For Barth, one is raised instantly at death.[5] The dead do not look forward to any further glorification. By implication, Barth must mean that when

---

5. Thus Barth can be spoken of as a major exponent of the "immediate resurrection" view (Cooper, *Body, Soul, and Life Everlasting*, 106).

Christ returns He will terminate the remainder of humanity and elevate them to the same heavenly status as the dead. Eternal life in death is the final state.

The serious and abiding flaw of his presentation, therefore, is not unlike the flaw of too many Christian eschatologies: Barth secures a heavenly future, and then, once past the celestial gates, smuggles in corporeal dimensions. Did we not even find the same tendency in some of the Church's great theologians, whether Origen or Augustine, Maximus or Thomas? Did they not send the saints to heaven and then, almost as an afterthought, ascribe something quasi-fleshly and quasi-earthly to their heavenly identity? But—and here every spiritualizing tendency must be repudiated—the intermediate state is not the final state. Eternal perdurance is not the same as everlasting life. The heavenly vision of God is not the same as the recreation of the world. Having a share in Christ's body is not the same as receiving from Him one's own resurrected body. In short, the Christian consolation is not the Christian hope.

The theological fallout from giving primacy to heaven-going over earthly resurrection is great. Several loci are damaged by it, especially the doctrine of humanity. If we humans are to hope for an eternal, blessed "presence" with God at death, then one inevitably questions to what extent we are at heart temporal, creaturely, particular entities. Doubt about our terrestrial parameters seeps into our doctrines of God, ecclesiology, and ethics. In exerting so much energy to escort humanity into God's heavenly sphere, we degrade our earthly identity. That is why I have militated against Barth's position, and why I have stressed so relentlessly the patristic *credo in carnis resurrectionem*. Where Barth hopes for resolution of the human through eternalized time, I believe the Scriptures affirm time's *resumption*. Where Barth would have a noetic revelation of our hidden, inner union with Christ, the gospel puts forward the hope of *reidentification*. Where Barth has toyed with the possibilities of pneumatic recapitulation, of embodiment into Christ's risen body, the gospel unapologetically holds out the hope of pneumatic *recorporealization*.

It is not the objective of my project to construct a better doctrine of the general resurrection. That would require another volume. However, it is appropriate to name several things that must be *undone* if such a project is to go forward. First, Barth's fusion of resurrection and revelation must be unbound. There are links between Easter and Pentecost, no doubt, but treating them as two expressions of the same parousia cannot bring about the proper doctrinal affirmations, especially about the final state. We must let resurrection be resurrection. Second, the idea of the exchange of properties between the Son's dual natures must be undone, at least so far as that exchange would make humanity operate according to a divine mode. The Word blesses humanity by becoming flesh, but the flesh never attains supra-creational transcendence. That is, we would do well to step back to a more Antiochene or Reformed understanding of the integrity of the human nature and divine nature in the one person of Christ, and the impossibility of their admixture or confusion in Him.[6] Third, the equation of the Son in His resurrection and the Spirit in His ministry must be undone. Jesus Christ must be understood in the distance of His heavenly session and pending return, where the Holy Spirit must be the one identified as the One who, interposing Himself during Jesus' corporeal absence from us, is God in direct interaction with humanity. That kind of distinction would permit the Spirit a better defined role and identity in the economy of salvation. Moreover, spacing between the Son and the Spirit would permit eschatology to be done more directly under the banner of pneumatology. In my mind, this matters because of the way Scripture speaks of the Holy Spirit's special relationship with earthly matter, even the way He addresses humans in their fleshly character. The *sōma pneumatikos* (1 Cor 15:44) is the transformed—but thoroughly human—body of flesh re-engineered and fueled by the Spirit. If we are to have real purchase on human renewal in the eschaton, it must be done with pneumatological currency.[7] As each Barthian conflation is pried apart, the possibility of speaking of everlasting life in the flesh reappears.

Karl Barth died on the tenth of December, 1968. The night before, while writing, he had been interrupted mid-sentence by a telephone call from his lifelong friend, Eduard Thurneysen. That sentence would never be finished. In the morning, Nelly Barth slipped into the bedroom to play a record of Mozart, with which she, in vain, attempted to wake her husband. During the night the great theologian had slipped from the flesh into the celestial Beyond. He went to be with the Victor. But little more remains to be said about Barth on that score. What can and may and must be said concerns this earthly side alone: that one day he too will rise and see the Lord's goodness in the land of the living.

---

6. Alternatively (but more perilously), along Alexandrian or Lutheran lines, one might deepen Barth's thoughts on the divine kenosis in order to understand the Son of God as sempiternally given to life in the human mode, so that Jesus Christ's future, as well as our own, secures a final, everlasting aeon on earth rather than in heaven.

7. Cf. van Driel, *Incarnation Anyway*, 161.

Bibliography

Anatolios, Khaled. *Athanasius: The Coherence of His Thought*. New York: Routledge, 1998.

Barth, Karl. "Afterword" to *Action in Waiting* by Christoph Blumhardt, 217–19. Farmington, PA: Plough, 1998.

———. *Against the Stream: Shorter Post-War Writings, 1946–52*. Edited by Ronald Gregor Smith. New York: Philosophical Library, 1954.

———. *Anselm: Fides Quarens Intellectum*. Translated by Ian W. Robertson. Cleveland, OH: Meridian, 1962.

———. *Die Auferstehung der Toten: Eine akademische Vorlesung über 1. Korinther 15*. Munich: Kaiser, 1924.

———. *Call for God: New Sermons from Basel Prison*. Translated by A. T. Mackay. New York: Evanston, 1967.

———. *The Christian Life: Church Dogmatics IV,4 Lecture Fragments*. Translated by Geoffrey W. Bromiley. Grand Rapids: Eerdmans, 1981.

———. *Church Dogmatics*. 13 vols. Edited by Geoffrey W. Bromiley and Thomas F. Torrance. Translated by Geoffrey W. Bromiley et al. Edinburgh: T. & T. Clark, 1956–69.

———. "Concluding Unscientific Postscript on Schleiermacher." Translated by George Hunsinger. *Studies in Religion* 7:2 (1978) 117–35.

———. *Credo: A Presentation of the Chief Problems of Dogmatics with Reference to the Apostles' Creed*. Translated by J. Strathearn McNab. New York: Scribner's Sons, 1936.

———. *Dogmatics in Outline*. Translated by G. T. Thompson. New York: Harper & Row, 1959.

———. *The Epistle to the Philippians*. Translated by James W. Leitch. Richmond, VA: John Knox, 1962.

———. *The Epistle to the Romans*. Translated from the sixth edition by Edwyn C. Hoskyns. Oxford: Oxford University Press, 1968.

———. *Ethics*. Edited by Dietrich Braun. Translated by Geoffrey W. Bromiley. New York: Seabury, 1981.

———. *Evangelical Theology: An Introduction*. Translated by Grover Foley. New York: Holt, Rinehart and Winston, 1962.

———. *The Faith of the Church: A Commentary on the Apostles' Creed*. Translated by Gabriel Vahanian. London: Fontana, 1960.

———. "Foreword" to *Predestination and Other Papers* by Pierre Maury. Translated by Edwin Hudson. London: SCM, 1960.

———. *The Heidelberg Catechism for Today*. Translated by Shirley C. Guthrie, Jr. Richmond, VA: John Knox, 1964.

————. *How I Changed My Mind*. Translated by John D. Godsey. Louisville: John Knox, 1966.

————. *The Humanity of God*. Translated by Thomas Wieser and John Newton Thomas. Richmond, VA: John Knox, 1960.

————. *Karl Barth Gesamtausgabe*. Zürich: Theologischer Verlag Zürich, 1971–.

————. *Letters, 1961–1968*. Edited by Jürgen Fangmeier et al. Translated by Geoffrey W. Bromiley. Grand Rapids: Eerdmans, 1980.

————. *On Religion: The Revelation of God as the Sublimation of Religion*. Edited and translated by Garrett Green. London: T. & T. Clark, 2006.

————. "Past and Future: Friedrich Naumann and Christoph Blumhardt." Translated by Keith R. Crim. In *The Beginnings of Dialectic Theology*, volume I, edited by James M. Robinson, 40–45. Richmond, VA: John Knox, 1968.

————. *Der Römerbrief* [Zweite Fassung, 1921]. Zollikon-Zurich: Evangelischer Verlag, 1940.

————. *The Theology of the Reformed Confessions*. Louisville: Westminster John Knox, 2002.

————. *The Theology of Schleiermacher: Lectures at Göttingen, Winter Semester, 1923/24*. Translated by Geoffrey W. Bromiley. Grand Rapids: Eerdmans, 1982.

Barth, Karl, and Rudolf Bultmann. *Letters 1922/1966*. Edited by Bernd Jaspert and Geoffrey W. Bromiley. Translated by Geoffrey W. Bromiley. Grand Rapids: Eerdmans, 1981.

Barth, Karl, and Eduard Thurneysen. *Revolutionary Theology in the Making*. Translated by James D. Smart. Richmond, VA: John Knox, 1964.

Bavinck, Herman. *Reformed Dogmatics, Vol. 3: Sin and Salvation in Christ*. Edited by John Bolt. Translated by John Vriend. Grand Rapids: Baker Academic, 2006.

Bayer, Oswald. *Martin Luther's Theology: A Contemporary Interpretation*. Translated by Thomas H. Trapp. Grand Rapids: Eerdmans, 2008.

Bender, Kimlyn J. *Karl Barth's Christological Ecclesiology*. Aldershot: Ashgate, 2005.

Berkhof, Louis. *Systematic Theology*, new edition. Grand Rapids: Eerdmans, 1996.

Berkouwer, G. C. *The Triumph of Grace in the Theology of Karl Barth*. London: Paternoster, 1956.

Bloesch, Donald G. *Jesus Is Victor!: Karl Barth's Doctrine of Salvation*. Nashville: Abingdon, 1976.

Blowers, Paul M., and Robert Louis Wilken, editors. *On the Cosmic Mystery of Jesus Christ: St. Maximus the Confessor*. Crestwood, NY: St. Vladimir's Seminary Press, 2003.

Bodamer, W. G. "The Life and Work of Johann Christoph Blumhardt." Th.D. diss., Princeton Theological Seminary, 1966

Boliek, Lynn. *The Resurrection of the Flesh: A Study of a Confessional Phrase*. Amsterdam: van Campen, 1962.

Bolt, John. "Exploring Karl Barth's Eschatology: A Salutary Exercise for Evangelicals." In *Karl Barth and Evangelical Theology: Convergences and Divergences*, edited by Sung Wook Chung, 209–35. Milton Keynes, UK: Paternoster, 2006.

Bowery, Anne-Marie. "Body." In *Augustine through the Ages: An Encyclopedia*, edited by Allan D. Fitzgerald, 105–8. Grand Rapids: Eerdmans, 1999.

Bradbury, Rosalene Clare. "Identifying the Classical *Theologia Crucis*, and in This Light, Karl Barth's Modern Theology of the Cross." PhD diss., University of Auckland, 2008.

Brazier, Paul. "Barth's First Commentary on Romans (1919) An Exercise in Apophatic Theology?" *International Journal of Systematic Theology* 6:4 (2004) 387–403.

Brown, Peter. *The Body and Society: Men, Women and Sexual Renunciation in Early Christianity*. New York: Columbia University Press, 1988.

Bultmann, Rudolf. *Faith and Understanding* I. Translated by Louise Pettibone Smith. London: SCM, 1969.

———. *Kerygma und Mythos*, vol. 1. Edited by H. W. Bartsch. Hamburg/Bergstedt: Herbert Reich-Evangelischer Verlag, 1960.

Burnett, Richard E. *Karl Barth's Theological Exegesis: The Hermeneutical Principles of the Römerbrief Period*. Tübingen: Mohr Siebeck, 2001.

Busch, Eberhard. "'Hochverehrter Herr Graf nicht so stürmisch!': Karl Barths Stellung zu Nikolaus von Zinzendorf." In *Neue Aspekte der Zinzendorf-Forschung*, edited by Martin Brecht and Paul Peucker, 239–54. Göttingen: Vandenhoeck & Ruprecht, 2006.

———. *Karl Barth: His Life from Letters and Autobiographical Texts*. Philadelphia: Fortress, 1976.

———. *Karl Barth & the Pietists: The Young Karl Barth's Critique of Pietism and Its Response*. Translated by Daniel W. Bloesch. Downer's Grove, IL: InterVarsity, 2004.

Bynum, Caroline Walker. "Faith Imagining the Self: Somatomorphic Soul and Resurrection Body in Dante's *Divine Comedy*." In *Faithful Imagining: Essays in Honor of Richard R. Niebuhr*, edited by Sang Hyun Lee et al., 83–106. Atlanta, GA: Scholar's, 1995.

———. *The Resurrection of the Body: in Western Christianity, 200–1336*. New York: Columbia University Press, 1995.

Carnley, Peter. *The Structure of Resurrection Belief*. Oxford: Clarendon, 1987.

Chung, Paul S. *Karl Barth: God's Word in Action*. Cambridge: James Clarke, 2008.

Clark, Elizabeth A. "New Perspectives on the Origenist Controversy: Human Embodiment and Ascetic Strategies." *Church History* 59:2 (1990) 145–62.

Collins, Randall. "The Classical Tradition in Sociology of Religion." In *The SAGE Handbook of the Sociology of Religion*, edited by James A. Beckford and N. J. Demerath III, 19–38. London: SAGE, 2007.

Collins Winn, Christian T. *"Jesus Is Victor!": The Significance of the Blumhardts for the Theology of Karl Barth*. Eugene, OR: Pickwick, 2009.

Cooper, Adam G. *The Body in St. Maximus the Confessor: Holy Flesh, Wholly Deified*. Oxford: Oxford University Press, 2005.

Cooper, John W. *Body, Soul, and Life Everlasting: Biblical Anthropology and the Monism-Dualism Debate*. Rev. ed. Grand Rapids: Eerdmans, 2000.

———. *Panentheism: The Other God of the Philosophers: From Plato to the Present*. Grand Rapids: Baker Academic, 2006.

Crisp, Oliver D. "On Barth's Denial of Universalism." *Themelios* 29:1 (2003) 18–29.

Crouzel, Henri. "La doctrine origenienne du corps réssuscité." *Gregorianum* 53 (1972) 679–716.

Croy, N. Clayton. "Hellenistic Philosophies and the Preaching of the Resurrection." *Novum Testamentum* 39:1 (1997) 21–39.

Cullmann, Oscar. *Christ and Time: The Primitive Christian Conception of Time and History*. Rev. ed. Translated by Floyd V. Filson. Philadelphia: Westminster, 1964.

———. *Salvation in History*. New York: Harper and Row, 1967.

Darragh, John T. *The Resurrection of the Flesh*. London: SPCK, 1921.

Bibliography

Dawson, R. Dale. *The Resurrection in Karl Barth*. Aldershot, UK: Ashgate, 2007.

Dechow, Jon F. *Dogma and Mysticism in Early Christianity: Epiphanius of Cyprus and the Legacy of Origen*. Macon, GA: Mercer University Press, 1988.

Dix, Gregory, and Henry Chadwick, editors. *The Treatise on the Apostolic Tradition of St. Hippolytus of Rome, Bishop and Martyr*. 3rd rev. ed. New York: Routledge, 1992.

Douie, Decima L. "John XXII and the Beatific Vision." *Dominican Studies* 3:2 (1950) 154–74.

Drury, John. "'From Crib and Cross to Resurrection and Ascension': The Resurrection of Christ as the Revelation of God Incarnate in Karl Barth's *Church Dogmatics* I/2, §§ 13–15." Unpublished paper. Online: http://www.drurywriting.com/john/Chris t'sResurrectioninBarthCD1.2.pdf (accessed June 2010).

Eitel, Adam. "The Resurrection of Jesus Christ: Karl Barth and the Historicization of God's Being." *International Journal of Systematic Theology* 10:1 (2008) 36–53.

Elert, Werner. *The Structure of Lutheranism*, volume I: *The Theology and Philosophy of Life of Lutheranism, Especially in the Sixteenth and Seventeenth Centuries*. Translated by Walter A. Hansen. St. Louis: Concordia, 1962.

Farrow, Douglas. *Ascension and Ecclesia: On the Significance of the Doctrine of the Ascension for Ecclesiology and Christian Cosmology*. Edinburgh: T. & T. Clark, 1999.

Fergusson, David. "Barth's *Resurrection of the Dead*: Further Reflections." *Scottish Journal of Theology* 56:1 (2003) 65–72.

Ford, David. *Barth and God's Story: Biblical Narrative and the Theological Method of Karl Barth in the* Church Dogmatics. Frankfurt am Main: Lang, 1985.

Forde, Gerhard O. *The Preached God: Proclamation in Word and Sacrament*. Grand Rapids: Eerdmans, 2007.

Forrest, David William. *The Christ of History and of Experience*. Edinburgh: T. & T. Clark, 1897.

Frei, Hans W. "The Doctrine of Revelation in the Thought of Karl Barth, 1909–1922: The Nature of Barth's Break with Liberalism." PhD dissertation, Yale University, 1956.

———. *The Identity of Jesus Christ: The Hermeneutical Bases of Dogmatic Theology*. 1975. Reprint. Eugene, OR: Wipf and Stock, 1997.

Freyer, Thomas. *Pneumatologie als Strukturprinzip der Dogmatik: überlegungen in Anschluß an die Lehre von der "Geisttaufe" bei Karl Barth*. Paderborn: Schöningh, 1982.

Fulbrook, Mary. *Piety and Politics: Religion and the Rise of Absolutism in England, Württemberg and Prussia*. Cambridge: Cambridge University Press, 1983.

Fuller, Daniel. "The Resurrection of Jesus and the Historical Method." *Journal of Bible and Religion* 34 (1966) 18–24.

Gager, John G. "Body Symbols and Social Reality." *Religion* 12:4 (1982) 345–64.

Gilby, Thomas. *St. Thomas Aquinas: Theological Texts*. Durham, NC: Labyrinth, 1982.

Gorringe, Timothy J. *Karl Barth: Against Hegemony*. Oxford: Oxford University Press, 1999.

Green, Clifford. "Karl Barth's Life and Theology." In *Karl Barth: Theologian of Freedom*, edited by Clifford Green, 11–44. Minneapolis: Augsburg Fortress, 1989.

Greggs, Tom. *Barth, Origin, and Universal Salvation: Restoring Particularity*. New York: Oxford University Press, 2009.

———. "'Jesus Is Victor': Passing the Impasse of Barth on Universalism," *Scottish Journal of Theology* 60:2 (2007) 196–212.

Grieb, A. Katherine. "Last Things First: Karl Barth's Theological Exegesis of 1 Corinthians in *The Resurrection of the Dead.*" *Scottish Journal of Theology* 56:1 (2003) 49–64.

Gritsch, Eric W., and Robert W. Jenson. *Lutheranism: The Theological Movement and Its Confessional Writings.* Philadelphia: Fortress, 1976.

Grube, Dirk-Martin. "Reconstructing the Dialectics in Karl Barth's *Epistle to the Romans*: The Role of Transcendental Arguments in Theological Theorizing." *Bijdragen* 69:2 (2008) 127–46.

Gunton, Colin. *Becoming and Being: The Doctrine of God in Charles Hartshorne and Karl Barth.* Rev. ed. London: SCM, 2001.

———. *Father, Son and Holy Spirit: Essays toward a Fully Trinitarian Theology.* London: T. & T. Clark, 2004.

———. "Salvation." In *The Cambridge Companion to Karl Barth*, edited by John Webster, 143–58. Cambridge: Cambridge University Press, 2000.

Guretzki, David. *Karl Barth on the Filioque.* Burlington, VT: Ashgate, 2009.

Habets, Myk. *Theosis in the Theology of Thomas Torrance: Not Yet in the Now.* Aldershot, UK: Ashgate, 2009.

Haga, Tsutomu. *Theodizee und Geschichtstheologie: Ein Versuch der Überwindung der Problematik des Deutschen Idealismus bei Karl Barth.* Göttingen: Vandenhoeck & Ruprecht, 1991.

Harnack, Adolf. *What Is Christianity?* Translated by Thomas Bailey Saunders. New York: Harper & Brothers, 1957.

Harris, Murray J. *From Grave to Glory: Resurrection in the New Testament.* Grand Rapids: Academie, 1990.

Hart, Trevor. "Revelation." In *The Cambridge Companion to Karl Barth*, edited by John Webster, 37–56. Cambridge: Cambridge University Press, 2000.

Hartwell, Herbert. *The Theology of Karl Barth: An Introduction.* Philadelphia: Westminster, 1964.

Hebblethwaite, Brian. *Philosophical Theology and Christian Doctrine.* Oxford: Blackwell, 2005.

Henning, Christian. "Wirklich ganz tot?: Neue Gedanken zur Unsterblichkeit der Seele vor dem Hintergrund der Ganztodtheorie." *Neue Zeitschrift für Systematische Theologie und Religionsphilosophie* 43 (2001) 236–52.

Heppe, Heinrich. *Reformed Dogmatics: Set Out and Illustrated from the Sources.* Revised and edited by Ernst Bizer. Translated by G. T. Thomson. Reprint. Grand Rapids: Baker, 1978.

Herrmann, Willibald [Wilhelm]. *The Communion of the Christian with God: A Discussion in Agreement with the View of Luther.* 2nd ed. Translated by J. Sandys Stanyon. London: Williams & Norgate, 1895.

———. *Systematic Theology.* Translated by Nathaniel Micklem and Kenneth A. Saunders. New York: Macmillan, 1927.

Hick, John. *Death and Eternal Life.* San Francisco: Harper & Row, 1976.

Howell, Martha C. *Women, Production and Patriarchy in Late Medieval Cities.* Chicago: University of Chicago, 1986.

Hunsinger, George. *Disruptive Grace: Studies in the Theology of Karl Barth.* Grand Rapids: Eerdmans, 2000.

———. *How to Read Karl Barth: The Shape of His Theology.* Oxford: Oxford University Press, 1991.

———. Review of *Barth's Moral Theology: Human Action in Barth's Thought,* by John Webster. Center for Barth Studies, http://libweb.ptsem.edu/collections/barth/reviews/MoralTheology.aspx, accessed 1 June 2012.

Jenson, Robert W. *Alpha and Omega: A Study in the Theology of Karl Barth.* New York: Thomas Nelson, 1963.

———. *God after God: The God of the Past and the God of the Future, Seen in the Work of Karl Barth.* Indianapolis: Bobbs-Merrill, 1969.

———. "The Great Transformation." In *The Last Things: Biblical and Theological Perspectives on Eschatology,* edited by Carl E. Braaten and Robert W. Jenson, 33–42. Grand Rapids: Eerdmans, 2002.

———. "You Wonder Where the Spirit Went." *Pro Ecclesia* 2:3 (1993) 296–304.

Johnson, Keith L. *Karl Barth and the Analogia Entis.* London: Continuum, 2010.

Johnson, William Stacy. *Karl Barth and the Postmodern Foundations of Theology.* Louisville: Westminster John Knox, 1997.

Jüngel, Eberhard. *Barth-Studien.* Köln/Gütersloh: Benziger Verlag und Götersloher Verlagshaus Gerd Mohn, 1982.

———. *Death: The Riddle and the Mystery.* Translated by Iain and Ute Nicol. Philadelphia: Westminster, 1974.

———. *Karl Barth: A Theological Legacy.* Translated by Garrett E. Paul. Philadelphia: Westminster, 1986.

Kattenbusch, D. Ferdinand. *Das apostolische Symbol,* Band II. Leipzig: Hinrichs'sche, 1894.

Kelley, J. N. D. *Early Christian Creeds.* 3rd ed. London: Continuum, 2006.

Kharlamov, Vladimir L. "'The Beauty of the Unity and the Harmony of the Whole': Concept of *Theosis* in the Theology of Pseudo-Dionysius the Areopagite." PhD Diss., Drew University, 2006.

Knight, Douglas. "Time and Persons in the Economy of God." In *The Providence of God: Deus Habet Consilium,* edited by Francesca Aran Murphy and Philip G. Ziegler, 131–43. London: T. & T. Clark, 2009.

Koehler, Edward W. A. *A Summary of Christian Doctrine: A Popular Presentation of the Teachings of the Bible.* Rev. ed. Reprint. St. Louis: Concordia, 1971.

Langdon, Adrian. "Our Contemporary from Now until Eternity: Christological Recapitulation of Time in Barth." *Princeton Theological Review* 17:1 (2011) 7–21.

Lash, Nicholas. "Eternal Life: Life 'after' Death?" *The Heythrop Journal* 19:3 (1978) 271–84.

Lauber, David. *Barth on the Descent into Hell: God, Atonement, and the Christian Life.* Burlington, VT: Ashgate, 2004.

Lejeune, R. *Christoph Blumhardt and His Message.* Translated by Hela Ehrlich and Nicoline Maas. Rifton, NY: Plough, 1963.

Lewis, Alan E. *Between Cross and Resurrection: A Theology of Holy Saturday.* Grand Rapids: Eerdmans, 2003.

Lessing, G. E. *Lessing's Theological Writings.* Edited and translated by Henry Chadwick. Stanford University Press, 1956.

Levenson, Jon D. *Resurrection and the Restoration of Israel: The Ultimate Victory of the God of Life.* New Haven, CT: Yale University Press, 2006.

Lona, Horacio E. *Über die Auferstehung des Fleisches: Studien zur frühchristlichen Eschatologie*. Berlin: de Gruyter, 1993.

Lorenzen, Thorwald. *Resurrection and Discipleship: Interpretive Models, Biblical Reflections, Theological Consequences*. Reprint. Eugene, OR: Wipf and Stock, 1995.

Louth, Andrew. *Maximus the Confessor*. London: Routledge, 1996.

———. *The Origins of the Christian Mystical Tradition: From Plato to Denys*. Rev. ed. Oxford: Oxford University Press, 2007.

Lowe, Walter. "Barth as the Critic of Dualism: Re-Reading the *Römerbrief*." *Scottish Journal of Theology* 41:3 (1988) 377–95.

———. *Theology and Difference: The Wound of Reason*. Bloomington, IN: Indiana University Press, 1993.

Lyden, John. "The Influence of Hermann Cohen on Karl Barth's Dialectical Theology." *Modern Judaism* 12:2 (1992) 167–83.

Lyman, J. Rebecca. *Christology and Cosmology: Models of Divine Activity in Origen, Eusebius and Athanasius*. Oxford: Clarendon, 1993.

MacKinnon, D. M. "Further Reflections." In *The Resurrection: A Dialogue by G. W. H. Lampe and D. M. MacKinnon*, edited by William Purcell, 107–12. Philadelphia: Westminster, 1966.

———. "The Resurrection: A Meditation." In *The Resurrection: A Dialogue by G. W. H. Lampe and D. M. MacKinnon*, edited by William Purcell, 63–70. Philadelphia: Westminster, 1966.

Malysz, Piotr J. "Storming Heaven with Karl Barth? Barth's Unwitting Appropriation of the *Genus Maiestaticum* and What Lutherans Can Learn from It." *International Journal of Systematic Theology* 9:1 (2007) 73–92.

Mangina, Joseph L. *Karl Barth: Theologian of Christian Witness*. Louisville: Westminster John Knox, 2004.

Marga, Amy Ellen. "Jesus Christ and the Modern Sinner: Karl Barth's Retrieval of Luther's Substantive Christology." *Currents in Theology and Mission* 34:4 (2007) 260–70.

McCormack, Bruce L. *Karl Barth's Critically Realistic Dialectical Theology: Its Genesis and Development 1909–1936*. Oxford: Clarendon, 1995.

———. *Orthodox and Modern: Studies in the Theology of Karl Barth*. Grand Rapids: Baker Academic, 2008.

McDowell, John C. "Barth's Having No-Thing to Hope For." *Journal for Christian Theological Research* 11 (2006) 1–49.

———. *Hope in Barth's Eschatology: Interrogations and Transformations beyond Tragedy*. Aldershot, UK: Ashgate, 2000.

Migliore, Daniel L. "Karl Barth's First Lectures in Dogmatics: *Instruction in the Christian Religion*." In *The Göttingen Dogmatics: Instruction in the Christian Religion*, volume I, by Karl Barth, edited by Hannelotte Reiffen, xv–lxii. Translated by Geoffrey W. Bromiley. Grand Rapids: Eerdmans, 1991.

———. *Faith Seeking Understanding: An Introduction to Christian Theology*. 2nd ed. Grand Rapids: Eerdmans, 2004.

———. "*Participatio Christi*: The Central Theme of Barth's Doctrine of Sanctification." *Zeitschrift fur Dialektische Theologie* 18:3 (2002) 287–307.

———. "*Vinculum Pacis*: Karl Barths Theologie des Heiligen Geistes." *Evangelische Theologie* 60:2 (2000) 131–51.

Moltmann, Jürgen. *Son of Righteousness, Arise!: God's Future for Humanity and the Earth*. Translated by Margaret Kohl. Minneapolis: Fortress, 2010.

———. *Theology of Hope: On the Ground and the Implications of a Christian Eschatology*. Translated by James W. Leitch. Minneapolis: Fortress, 1993.

Moore, Edward. "Origen of Alexandria and Apokatastasis: Some Notes on the Development of a Noble Notion." *Quodlibet Journal* 5:1 (2003). Online: http://www.quodlibet.net/articles/moore-origen.shtml (accessed June 2010).

Mueller, David L. *Foundation of Karl Barth's Doctrine of Reconciliation: Jesus Christ Crucified and Risen*. Lewiston, NY: Mellen, 1990.

Murphy, F. X. "Evagrius Ponticus and Origenism." In *Origeniana Tertia: The Third International Colloquium for Origen Studies*, edited by Richard Patrick Crosland Hanson and Henri Crouzel, 253–69. Rome: Edizioni dell' Ateneo, 1985.

Neder, Adam. *Participation in Christ: An Entry into Karl Barth's Church Dogmatics*. Louisville: Westminster John Knox, 2009.

Nielson, Bent Flemming. "Karl Barth—A Brief Introduction: Time and Eternity." Unpublished paper, personal collection.

Obitts, Stanley R. "Historical Explanation and Barth on Christ's Resurrection." In *Current Issues in Biblical and Patristic Interpretation*, edited by Gerald F. Hawthorne, 365–77. Grand Rapids: Eerdmans, 1975.

Oh, Peter S. "Complementary Dialectics of Kierkegaard and Barth: Barth's Use of Kierkegaardian Diastasis Reassessed." *Neue Zeitschrift für Systematische Theologie und Religionsphilosophie* 48:4 (2007) 497–512.

Olson, Roger E. "Deification in Contemporary Theology." *Theology Today* 64 (2007) 186–200.

O'Regan, Cyril. *The Heterodox Hegel*. Albany, NY: State University of New York Press, 1994.

Osaki, Setsuro. *Die Prädestinationslehre Karl Barths*, PhD diss., Göttingen University, 1966.

Pannenberg, Wolfhart. "Constructive and Critical Functions of Christian Eschatology." *The Harvard Theological Review* 77:2 (1984) 119–39.

———. *Jesus: God and Man*. 2nd ed. Translated by Lewis L. Wilkins and Duane A. Priebe. Philadelphia: Westminister, 1977.

———. *Systematic Theology*, volume 3. Grand Rapids: Eerdmans, 1997.

Pelikan, Jaroslav. *The Emergence of the Catholic Tradition (100–600)*. Chicago: The University of Chicago Press, 1971.

———. *The Shape of Death: Life, Death and Immortality in the Early Fathers*. Nashville: Abingdon, 1961.

Peters, Ted. *God as Trinity: Relationality and Temporality in Divine Life*. Louisville: Westminster/John Knox, 1993.

Prenter, Regin. "Karl Barths Umbildung der traditionellen Zweinaturlehre in lutherischer Beleuchtung." *Studia Theologia* 11:1 (1957) 1–88.

———. *Luther's Theology of the Cross: Martin Luther's Theological Breakthrough*. Philadelphia: Fortress, 1971.

Rahner, Karl. *On the Theology of Death* Rev. ed. Translated by C. H. Henkey and W. J. O'Hara. New York: Herder and Herder, 1965.

Richardson, Kurt Anders. "*Christus Praesens*: Barth's Radically Realist Christology and Its Necessity for Theological Method." In *Karl Barth and Evangelical Theology:*

Convergences and Divergences, edited by Sung Wook Chung, 136–48. Milton Keynes, UK: Paternoster, 2006.

Roberts, Richard H. *A Theology on Its Way?: Essays on Karl Barth*. Edinburgh: T. & T. Clark, 1991.

Rosato, Philip J. *The Spirit as Lord: The Pneumatology of Karl Barth*. Edinburgh: T. & T. Clark, 1981.

Russell, Norman. *The Doctrine of Deification in the Greek Patristic Tradition*. Oxford: Oxford University Press, 2004.

Sauter, Gerhard. *What Dare We Hope?: Reconsidering Eschatology*. Harrisburg, PA: Trinity Press International, 1999.

———. "Why Is Karl Barth's *Church Dogmatics* Not a 'Theology of Hope'? Some Observations on Barth's Understanding of Eschatology." *Scottish Journal of Theology* 52:4 (1999) 407–29.

Schleiermacher, Friedrich. *The Christian Faith*, second German edition in two volumes. Translated by H. R. Mackintosh and J. S. Stewart. New York: Harper Torchbooks, 1963.

Schmemann, Alexander. *The Historical Road of Eastern Orthodoxy*. Crestwood, NY: St. Vladimir's Seminary Press, 1977.

Schmid, Heinrich. *The Doctrinal Theology of the Evangelical Lutheran Church*. 3rd ed. Translated by Charles A. Hay and Henry E. Jacobs. Minneapolis: Augsburg, 1899.

Schneemelcher, Wilhelm. *New Testament Apocrypha: Vol. 1: Gospels and Related Writings*, revised edition. Translated by R. McL. Wilson. Cambridge: James Clarke, 1991.

Schwöbel, Christoph, editor. *Karl Barth—Martin Rade: Ein Briefwechsel*. Gütersloh: Gütersloher Verlagshaus Gerd Mohn, 1981.

Setzer, Claudia. "Resurrection of the Dead as Symbol and Strategy." *Journal of the American Academy of Religion* 69:1 (2001) 65–101.

Shults, F. LeRon. "A Dubious Christological Formula: From Leontius of Byzantium to Karl Barth." *Theological Studies* 57:3 (1996) 431–46.

Sonderegger, Katherine. "The Doctrine of Providence." In *The Providence of God: Deus Habet Consilium*, edited by Francesca Aran Murphy and Philip G. Ziegler, 144–57. London: T. & T. Clark, 2009.

———. "Et Resurrexit Tertia Die: Jenson and Barth on Christ's Resurrection." In *Conversing with Barth*, edited by John C. McDowell and Mike Higton, 191–213. Aldershot, UK: Ashgate, 2004.

Stoeffler, F. Ernest. *The Rise of Evangelical Pietism*. Leiden: Brill, 1965.

Tanner, Kathryn. *Jesus, Humanity and the Trinity: A Brief Systematic Theology*. Minneapolis: Fortress, 2001.

Thiselton, Anthony C. *The First Epistle to the Corinthians: A Commentary on the Greek Text*. Grand Rapids: Eerdmans, 2000.

Thompson, John. *Christ in Perspective: Christological Perspectives in the Theology of Karl Barth*. Edinburgh: St. Andrews, 1978

———. *The Holy Spirit in the Theology of Karl Barth*. Allison Park, PA: Pickwick, 1991.

Torrance, Alan. *Persons in Communion: An Essay on Trinitarian Description and Human Participation*. London: T. & T. Clark, 1996.

Torrance, Thomas F. *The Apocalypse Today*. Grand Rapids: Eerdmans, 1959.

———. *Karl Barth: An Introduction to His Early Theology, 1910–1931*. London: SCM, 1962.

———. *Karl Barth, Biblical and Evangelical Theologian*. Edinburgh: T. & T. Clark, 1990.

———. "My Interaction with Karl Barth." In *How Karl Barth Changed My Mind*, edited by Donald K. McKim, 52–64. Grand Rapids: Eerdmans, 1986.

———. *Space, Time and Resurrection*. 2nd ed. Edinburgh: T. & T. Clark, 1998.

Trigg, Joseph W. *Origen*. New York: Routledge, 1998.

Upson-Saia, Kristi. "Scars, Marks, and Deformities in Augustine's Resurrected Bodies." Paper presented at the American Academy of Religion Annual Meeting, Chicago, IL, 2 November 2008.

van der Kooi, Cornelius. *As in a Mirror: John Calvin and Karl Barth on Knowing God: A Diptych*. Translated by Donald Mader. Leiden: Brill, 2005.

van Driel, Edwin Chr. *Incarnation Anyway: Arguments for Supralapsarian Christology*. Oxford: Oxford University Press, 2008.

Van Til, Cornelius. *Christianity and Barthianism*. Philadelphia: Presbyterian and Reformed, 1962.

Waldrop, Charles T. *Karl Barth's Christology: Its Basic Alexandrian Character*. Berlin: Mouton, 1984.

———. "Karl Barth's Concept of the Divinity of Jesus Christ." *The Harvard Theological Review* 74:3 (1981) 241–63.

Ward, Graham. "Barth, Hegel and the Possibility for Christian Apologetics." In *Conversing with Barth*, edited by John C. McDowell and Mike Higton, 53–67. Aldershot, UK: Ashgate, 2004.

Webster, John. *Barth's Earlier Theology*. London: T. & T. Clark, 2005.

———. *Barth's Moral Theology: Human Action in Barth's Thought*. Edinburgh: T. & T. Clark, 1998.

———. *Karl Barth*. London: Continuum, 2000.

Wood, Donald. "'Ich sah mit Staunen': Reflections on the Theological Substance of Barth's Early Hermeneutics." *Scottish Journal of Theology* 58:2 (2005) 184–98.

Wright, N. T. *The Resurrection of the Son of God*. London: SPCK, 2003.

Zaleski, Carol. *Otherworldly Journeys: Accounts of Near-Death Experience in Medieval and Modern Times*. Oxford: Oxford University Press, 1987.

Index

Plato, by making the forms
exist on their own, paradoxically
gives matter more life than Aristotle.

My whole life is forever present to God
but am I forever present to myself?

I learned B. from a
prof + master / colleague who
didn't believe in, indeed...
+ when pressed, claimed he
learned this from B.

good news + bad news:
B. has an esch.
It's not all that good